Reg Harris

The Rise and Fall of
BRITAIN'S GREATEST CYCLIST

ROBERT DINEEN

EBURY
PRESS

1 3 5 7 9 10 8 6 4 2

This edition published 2013
First published in 2012 by Ebury Press, an imprint of Ebury Publishing
A Random House Group company

The Random House Group Limited Reg. No. 954009

Addresses for companies within the Random House Group can be found at
www.randomhouse.co.uk

A CIP catalogue record for this book is available from the British Library

The Random House Group Limited supports the Forest Stewardship
Council® (FSC®), the leading international forest-certification organisation.
Our books carrying the FSC label are printed on FSC®-certified paper. FSC is the
only forest-certification scheme supported by the leading environmental
organisations, including Greenpeace. Our paper procurement policy can be
found at www.randomhouse.co.uk/environment

Designed and set by seagulls.net

Printed and bound by CPI Group (UK) Ltd, Croydon, CR0 4YY

ISBN 9780091945398

To buy books by your favourite authors and register for offers visit
www.randomhouse.co.uk

For Mum and Dad

CONTENTS

# PROLOGUE

On the back straight of the Manchester Velodrome, Sir Chris Hoy and Jason Kenny are stalking each other like jungle cats, slowly edging forward, eyes locked on the other's cranks, waiting for the opportunity to pounce. Much rests on the outcome of their contest. The two men are battling for the one spot on the British team for an individual sprinter at the London Olympics. Hoy is by far the more decorated of the two, a knight of the realm and a triple champion at the previous Games; so popular he can sell Bran Flakes. But momentum is with Kenny. He beat Hoy to win the last World Championships. He has claimed a national title from Hoy. He is 12 years younger, too.

At first Kenny's lead is only a couple of bike lengths. Then it stretches to four. When Hoy slips back another yard, Kenny is suddenly gone, hurtling across the wooden boards, his black skin suit giving him the appearance of a tiny bullet train.

As Hoy tries desperately to close the gap, a roar rises from the 3,500 fans, electrifying the arena. The spectacle is typical of these 'Revolution' meetings. It has been almost since British cycling's modern revolution began. More often than not Hoy has prevailed but on this mild Saturday in January his apprentice is too good. 'It's down to the gap,' Kenny says. 'It's all about the first 20 metres, just getting as far ahead as possible.' The spectators are quick to applaud both competitors, knowing that their rivalry will run for months yet. Standing up with the crowd, I wonder how Reg Harris, the man who inspired the bronze statue to my left, would have fared against these men.

To judge by his closely contoured muscles, with thighs like frozen turkeys and quadriceps ripped, he would not have given up much to them in physique. Consider the inscription listing his achievements – five world sprint titles – and you know his talent was at the very least comparable to theirs. Note how relaxed Harris appears even in mid-sprint, with his mouth only slightly ajar, and you can imagine him coming off the banking on that final bend with all the technical skill that Kenny and Hoy just displayed. Read the old reports of his races and you can guarantee, too, that he would have thrived on the tactical battle just witnessed. As one writer who knew Harris told me: 'Track sprinting in Reg's day was all about being a ruthless, evil bastard. That's why it was so good.' He was also the consummate showman, who readily courted the crowd's adoration. Little wonder that veteran cycling fans across Britain donated the £60,000 needed to pay for the statue. They wanted to repay him for all the good times he had given them.

Yet spend 18 months researching his life, as I have done, and you discover that the man behind that legend is far more complicated than those fans could ever have known. You learn, for example, that he found the circumstances of his childhood so shameful that he kept them secret all his life. You find that the most powerful people in the sport conspired against him, yet still he prevailed. You are told also that he was as ruthless away from the track as he was on it, and made more enemies than he did friends. Gradually you learn that he was defined as much by his pursuit of women as that of success. In short, pick away at the surface of his life, and you discover that much about it was not quite as it seemed.

CHAPTER 1
1935

Standing up in the saddle, spinning out a few quick revolutions, Reginald Hargreaves Harris looked good even for his age. His narrow shoulders made him streamlined across the frame. His thighs were strong, his hips still. Once seated, his body barely moved above the waist: the most efficient method. Even after only a few moments of his studied preparation, the customers who had gathered around the rollers to watch him were impressed. 'We have the new Dennis Horn, it seems,' Charlie Auty said, resetting the silver chronograph with which he would time Harris's stationary sprint. 'Nobody else needed a warm-up, Harris. This better be good.'

Harris did not acknowledge the remark. He was focused instead on trying to record the fastest time on the Hercules Viper, the racing bike that Auty had put up on a set of rollers on his shop floor. It was a clever contraption, with two huge metal rolling pins beneath the bike's back wheel and one under the front. Each pin turned in the opposite direction to the wheels to ensure the Viper did not travel. Other than that, nothing attached the bike to the floor, making it supremely difficult to stay upright when cycling at speed. To do so, you needed unusual balance, concentration and for each movable part to be in its right place.

Harris dismounted and called for a spanner. He carefully lowered the saddle height and drew back the handlebar stem, ignoring the restless murmurs of his small audience. Returning to the saddle, he adjusted the pedal straps, pulling them tight, just enough to pinch his toes. If he was going to win this competition, he wanted as much purchase on the cranks as possible.

For the past fortnight Harris had watched one customer after the next fail to improve on the time set by the Hercules salesman, Bill Bailey Jnr, the minimum requirement for them to win the competition and take the bike home. Some had not lasted the quarter-mile distance and instead allowed the bike to topple to the floor. Others had grabbed on to the adjacent wall, rendering their effort void. A few more had succumbed to poor technique, standing up for too long in the saddle, so that their energy was soon spent. Others had started too conservatively, leaving them with too much time to make up. The majority were simply not fit nor fast enough, just as Bailey had expected. He organised roller competitions across the north-west of England and was rarely beaten.

Harris had watched Bailey carefully and was determined to do everything just as he had done. He would sit as soon as he had broken the gear resistance. He would dip his chin into his neck, helping to keep his head still. Most importantly, he would pull on the pedals as hard as he pushed. 'Aim for smooth cadence, son,' Bailey had told him. 'Every good cyclist does.'

Harris slowed to his starting position, stopping his right pedal just after the halfway point in its turn, ready for him to press hard. 'Can I begin?' Auty said. 'On your marks, set…' He dropped his arm with a flourish, hamming up his timekeeper role.

Harris had never cycled competitively before. He sprinted over cobbled streets that ran through Bury town centre on his short commute home. Occasionally, he wound up the pace towards the end of his Sunday countryside tours with the other young men of the Cyclists' Touring Club, but never had he entered a race. Only through the rollers competition had he found the confidence to compete. Somehow he knew that he would fare better than the others who had taken part.

For Harris had not been intimidated by Bailey's performance. He was fast and controlled but, Harris felt, no quicker than him when accelerating along The Rock – that wide, gravel-strewn thoroughfare through Bury where Auty & Lees was based.

'Halfway, Harris,' Auty said, eyebrows furrowed, pausing as if in disbelief. 'You're level with Bailey.' To beat Bailey had a cachet that you would not associate with defeating your typical salesman. For he was the son of Bill Bailey, by far Britain's greatest cyclist, the track sprinter who had won the world amateur sprint championship four times just before the Great War. His legend hung heavy over the sport even two decades on. Harris could scarcely believe it that his son had chosen their shop for his promotion when there was about half a dozen bike franchises in the town. 'Bailey was a splendid sight riding unsupported on the Viper,' he recalled.

Harris looked impressive at full pelt, too. His neck was still when others would allow theirs to dip. His shoulders were strong, pointing straight ahead. Instinctively, he arched his back like a veteran sprinter would. His speed was steady, despite the pain surging through his quads. He had willpower as well as talent, it seemed.

'Stop!' Auty cried, pausing to look up, first at Harris then the customers, all silent now.

Harris had not excelled in anything before. He had left school a year earlier at 14, the minimum age, with no qualifications and nothing on his record to suggest academic potential. Years later, he would even admit that he had been 'a bit of a duffer' in the classroom. He had not fared much better at sport either, showing little aptitude for the team games that dominated the curriculum. Only in the summer did he stand out, when he found he could run faster than his classmates in athletic events.

With so little to commend him, he had been lucky that Auty had offered him work as an apprentice car mechanic in his garage on the opposite side of The Rock. For with Lancashire still suffering the fallout from the Great Depression, any job was hard to find, let alone one with prospects. Yet Harris had failed at that, too, and was quickly removed from the role. He claimed that he disliked the dirt as he 'grovelled underneath the engine', though that seemed an unlikely excuse when he was forced instead to take up a position as a mere errand boy in a business with the strangest USP: Auty provided wheeled transport for 'each of the seven ages of man', from the perambulator to the pushchair, through to the tricycle, the bike, the motorcycle and the car. He even sold bathchairs for the elderly and infirm.

Wheezing now like a sickly child, shoulders sunken as the adrenalin flooded away from him, Harris lifted his head to his boss, desperate to discover if his performance had put him in contention to claim the bike for good. 'You've beaten him by two-fifths of a second,' he said, placing a gentle hand on Harris's back, waiting for him to suck up a few more breaths. 'But don't think you're taking the bike home. People will assume that I fixed the competition. Nobody would believe you've got that kind of talent.'

*

Harris bent down to try to read the chalk marking on the road, his bike laid against the monument to Robert Peel, Bury's most famous son. The message had been written about only half an hour earlier, but drops of rain had made the letters run. 'Serves us right for being late,' the cyclist next to him said.

'I prefer it this way,' Harris replied. 'Gives me something to chase.'

Kneeling beside one another, wet knees resting against the concrete, they considered what might be the Cyclists' Touring Club rapidly blurring destination. Sheffield, perhaps? No, too far. The others would never cross the Peak District by lunchtime. St Helens, then? Too close. Skelmersdale? Possibly, though they had not known the CTC to stop there before. It was a grey miners' town, not the kind of place that a troop of adventurous young men might wish to investigate.

'Southport,' Harris said, eventually. 'The seaside.'

'We'll be on their tails by noon,' the stranger said, extending a hand. 'Jimmy Battersby.'

Harris struggled to hide his surprise. He had heard much about Battersby but never encountered him before. Other cyclists talked about him in whispers, marvelling at his feats in local time trials and hill climbs, wondering how he found the discipline for a training regime far tougher than anybody else's. Younger cyclists who did not know him wondered even if he existed or at least if the stories about him were true. Occasionally they would spot a lone cyclist climbing a Lancashire hill and wonder if he was Battersby, fuelled by a determination that nobody else in the district had.

'You're the lad from Charlie Auty's shop,' Battersby said. 'The sprinter.'

Harris blushed. Even though Auty had kept quiet about Harris's performance, word had passed quickly from the customers to the local cycling community. In the several weeks since, Harris had fielded near-countless compliments from both customers and other men on the road. Shy even for his age, and unused to praise, he was still embarrassed when the subject was brought up.

Still, given his company, he thought it best to act tough. 'You might say that.'

Battersby smiled, then nodded towards Harris's bike. 'Still sit up and beg, then?' he said, pricking Harris's bravado.

About a year earlier, Harris had described to a neighbour called Donald Stage the thrill that he felt watching cyclists accelerate past him on The Rock, kicking up a shower of small, black stones behind them as they went. Somehow they evoked a freedom that had Harris enthralled. He had never ridden a bike and could not afford one, but watching them made him desperate to try it. Stage had passed word around the town and eventually found a bike that a teenager had taken apart and failed to reassemble. To his delight, Harris had salvaged it with the help of Auty's mechanic. Until now he had not minded its crude geometry, with flat handlebars and wide frame angles that forced him to perch almost vertical in the saddle, like the destitute would when seeking alms. 'It'll do to begin with,' Battersby said, breaking the silence. 'We'll get you a better one in time. That's assuming you want to train with me?'

Harris felt his stomach leap. He knew of nobody who trained with Battersby. He was too much of an individualist. The demands of his regime were too great. You could see its evidence simply in his weather-beaten face, with its cracked lips and skin pulled taut across his cheeks. Tall and wiry, he was about a decade older than Harris but could pass for being several years more. He was a serious man, too, known among other cyclists for reproaching himself when he did not perform as he expected. At a time when the Lancashire cycling scene was split between the 'traditionalists' and the 'pioneers', he was among the most prominent members of the latter group, men who had little time for the old Victorian traditions of the CTC: the dress code – plus fours, no shorts – the sightseeing and the picnics and the 'tour captain' who invariably set a gentle pace and blew a whistle before relaying instructions. Instead, pioneers wanted to expend their competitive instincts, which was anathema to the traditionalists who still regarded cycling solely as a leisure pursuit. Years later, Harris would describe his decision to accept Battersby's invitation as 'possibly the greatest cycling happening of my life'.

Battersby forced Harris to comply with his usual regime almost from the start. While before Harris had ridden for about 60 miles once at the weekend, now he covered twice that distance, usually on both Saturday and Sunday, and often over more demanding terrain. Together they crossed the toughest climbs in the Peak District. They headed to the hills of the Welsh border. Sometimes they journeyed to the opposite coast and stayed overnight at Scarborough, making their way home shortly after daybreak. When they could, they also covered rides of 50 to 60 miles during the week.

The training only increased when Harris took time off work and was told that they would spend it scaling the peaks of the Lake District. Harris hated climbing but soon learnt not to beg clemency when Battersby forced the pace uphill. 'I was met with the most terrific earbashing,' he said. 'He was the hardest of taskmasters.'

The benefits soon told, though. Now, on those occasions when he still hooked up with his friends in the CTC, Harris found that he would have scarcely broken sweat when more experienced riders were struggling for breath. Towards the conclusion of even his longest rides, he noted how much easier it was for him to unleash his finishing sprint; he beat almost everybody with it now. Physically, he had begun to change, too, with his leg muscles beginning to take on a definition that previously they had lacked.

Impressed by his young charge's commitment, Auty offered to sell him a shop-soiled Armstrong Moth on credit. Though an everyday bike, it was a marked improvement on Harris's hand-me-down, not least because it was targeted at the new generation of cyclist who – as its advert said – wished to generate a 'little extra speed'. To that end, it had drop handlebars, a frame more aerodynamic than a typical touring bike and some of the best mass-market parts that you could buy: new Reynolds 531 tubing made from a strengthened steel alloy, an elegant leather Brooks saddle, three-speed Sturmey-Archer gearing and slick Dunlop tyres. By the following spring, Battersby felt Harris was ready to compete in his first competition. This was a covert time trial.

Harris well knew the history behind such events. Several decades earlier the National Cycling Union had banned all road racing in Britain because they feared that the practice would cause accidents and prompt the authorities to outlaw bicycles from the roads altogether. Already finding it difficult to persuade the state to allow cyclists the right to use busy public highways, they had wanted to avoid giving the establishment more ammunition to use against them. Committed cyclists, however, studiously ignored that rule, regardless that breaking it could lead them to being banned from all of the union's official competitions. Instead, in a routine that now took place almost every weekend across rural Britain, they convened at dawn to compete in time trials, the staggered start chosen because it was more difficult to police. A dawn start-time, a 'secret location', and black clothing were used for the same reason. Hence their name: private and confidentials. 'We're putting you in the Withington Wheelers 25k,' Battersby said confidently. This was the principal novices' time trial in England's north-west. Battersby had arranged for Harris to represent the Lancashire Road Club, quite the privilege.

Alf Nottingham and Fred Green joined him in the team, arranging to share a tiny room in a guesthouse the night before. No allowance was made for latecomers and Harris was the first to start, rising wearily when it was still dark. For the first time he wished he had been introduced to religion just so he could have slept through the Sunday morning. He knew plenty of seasoned cyclists who obeyed the Sabbath. 'If you're late, we'll all be disqualified,' Nottingham said, smirking, eyes still closed. Grappling for his clothes – shorts, tights, alpaca shorts – Harris resembled a burglar in the shadows. For insulation, he stuffed scrunched pages from the *Bury Times* inside his top layer, then folded a post-race sandwich inside his breast pocket and cracked open breakfast: Egg Flip, the ubiquitous cyclists' cocktail. 'Yolk lines the stomach, alcohol keeps you warm,' Battersby had said.

Finally, he slung two inner tubes over his shoulder, wheeled his bike from the porch and out into the chill dawn. Two officials were awaiting him at the starting point.

Dressed in overcoats and heavy boots, they reminded Harris of policemen, with patronising tone to match. 'I assume you know the route,' one said, looking up briefly from his file, puffs of breath blowing around him. 'Through Lower Withington, north-east to Knutsford, then loop back home through North-wich. I see you're a debutant. Be careful not to blow up.'

Time trials required patience. Even the strongest rider risked expiring if he went too hard too early. But the timekeeper assumed correctly. Harris had scoped the route several times with Battersby and knew just how to pace himself. As long as he was focused and kept a steady cadence, he could travel comfortably at about 20mph for about the first 20 kilometres, and wind up to about 25mph for the final stretch. That would give him a time of about one hour ten minutes, a strong return for a debutant. Go faster and he might challenge for victory.

As it turned out, he had enough left to sprint at full pelt by the time he crossed the officials again, pulling so hard on the handlebars you feared he might prise them away from the frame. He said that was to 'satisfy my ego'. He shocked the timekeeper into showing him some respect. 'One hour, nine minutes, 17 seconds,' the official said, with an approving nod.

About another 30 riders fired through the Cheshire country-side that morning, embarking at one-minute intervals to produce the classical 90-minute competition. Only one, J. Wood, beat Harris but he still enjoyed success, taking home the team trophy because Green was only a second behind him and Nottingham a mere further two back. The cup itself is lost but the result is recorded in the club's history. The writer notes that 'not a single member would have realised' the significance of it.

One evening the following spring, Battersby took Harris to a road between Bury and Bolton and chose three landmarks beside it, two lamp-posts and a gate. The first was their start line, the second the point at which they would start sprinting and the third – about 200 metres further on – was the finish. This would be their course for the evening. Battersby wished to replicate conditions of a sprint race on a track. Though it usually lasted two laps, competitors usually began sprinting about 200 metres from the end. For that reason this was the only section of the race that was timed. 'We'll do four sets, 20 minutes' rest in between,' he said.

Racing until long after dark, Battersby initially allowed Harris a head start but soon realised the folly in that. As they persisted with this primitive form of interval training – the most efficient way to build quickly explosive fitness – so Harris's sprinting power increased exponentially. He would follow the regime for the rest of his career. 'I developed breathing, power and explosive energy,' he said, years later, marvelling at his mentor's instinctive appreciation for the sport's physiology.

Harris's working life was changing, too. He quit Auty & Lees for a position in a bakery because it meant his working day finished by mid-morning and allowed him more daylight hours through the winter during which to train. When that work dried up, he found a temporary job delivering coal and again took a pragmatic approach to its benefits, noting how hauling 10-pound sacks of the fuel around Bury provided him with a workout 'more strenuous than any to be had in a gymnasium'. He worked in a slipper factory, then a paper mill. Both were tough but Harris justified them to himself by saving money for cycling equipment, often volunteering for split eight-hour shifts in one day regardless that it broke youth labour laws. By the spring of 1937, he had enough to pay a bike-maker in Stockport to recondition the second-hand Selbach bike that Battersby had given to him. Once a tough road cyclist from Paris, Maurice Selbach fashioned some of the most coveted road bikes from his workshop in London, but Harris wanted it adapted slightly ahead of the new track season that was shortly to begin. He had the BSA chainset replaced by a Charter-Lea version because it was more easily changed. He wanted slightly shorter cranks to transfer his power more efficiently, even though the increase was only fractional, and possibly psychological. Like all serious bike men, Harris talked about needing to feel *part* of his prized possession.

Like most bikes then – and like all modern track bikes – the Selbach had one gear, a fixed wheel and no brakes. Gearing was about to be introduced to the Tour de France but all serious cyclists still trained on such a bike then. It improved fitness and pedalling style. By being unable to free-wheel downhill and unable to benefit from gearing on an incline, you developed the smooth pedalling style about which Bill Bailey Jnr had talked. In France, they called it *souplesse*, suppleness, because when properly executed a cyclist's leg muscles appeared supple. Harris knew his style had improved but was unsure to what extent when he entered his first track race at Bury Police Sports Day.

Harris had been attending these workers' union events for years. With so little alternative family entertainment available then, almost everybody did. Comprising not only cycling but also athletics and light-hearted events such as a tug of war, say, or an egg and spoon race, they helped to stitch the community together. On this particular Sunday at the town's football stadium, events included a mounted police horse display and a competition in which attendees were invited to climb a greasy pole. At the same time, and before a crowd of about 10,000, Harris would compete in a preliminary round of the one-mile handicap sprint.

With no pedigree as a track cyclist, he was given the full handicap of 100 yards. The other riders were staggered behind him. His mother, Elsie, and stepfather, Joe, were in the crowd. There was a crackly PA system, with one speaker erected by the start line. 'Four laps of the track, ladies and gentlemen, only the first two men shall progress,' the announcer said.

Harris started at three-quarters pace, slow enough to lure the back-markers into chasing him down quickly, but sufficiently fast to draw the energy from their legs – Battersby had told Harris to allow the others to catch him. He was confident Harris would still have the finishing kick – or the jump – to leave them behind at the end. He knew such a tactic would appeal to the showman in Harris, too.

At the bell Harris felt comfortable, coasting in second place. When he slipped back a place emerging from the penultimate turn, he was untroubled. Physically, he knew that he had plenty left. He did not realise that he had made a critical mistake.

In most sprints, the moments before the final 200 metres were the most important. For it was about then that a smart competitor launched his attack. If not that man, you had to be in position at least to respond. But Harris had allowed himself to become trapped just as the front two men streaked away and was unable to make up the gap. As he sloped away from the finish with the other also-rans who hoped to catch a lucky break in such races, he glowed red with fury. Already he hated to lose.

'The track requires an apprenticeship, too,' Battersby said, insisting that Harris cared less about results in his first races and more about the lessons learnt. 'There is a meeting at Fallowfield in July. *Manchester Evening News* is sponsoring it. By then you'll be ready.' Owned by Manchester Athletic and Cycling Club, the second biggest club in the city, Fallowfield was the most important track in the north. The most successful club in the region, Manchester Wheelers, were based there too. They often filled its 14,000 capacity and attracted Britain's best riders to their marquee events. For Harris, the *Evening News* meeting would serve as the perfect stage on which to impress.

He endured a tough few months. Beginning with a handful of handicap races, including one at a small event at Fallowfield where he was beaten by a strong regional rider called George Wood. Graduating to scratch races, he rode the cinder tracks in Sheffield and Leigh, the Manchester satellite town, and Staveley in Derbyshire. He returned to Gigg Lane and debuted on the red-ash track in Doncaster. He never did enough to win but was slowly learning how to negotiate riding in a bunch. He soon knew, for example, never to lead for more than 100 metres because that spent too much energy. If a cyclist launched a breakaway, Harris identified the strongest rider in the bunch and persuaded him to help him shut down the gap. On the slowest tracks – usually grass – he stayed further forward, clear of trouble.

He was prepared to take responsibility for breaking the wind resistance then because speeds were reduced.

More importantly, he learnt to handle himself physically, too. For track racing then was far more combative than its modern incarnation and rural meetings were the most aggressive of all. Judges could hardly be expected to police them properly when much chicanery took place up to 200 metres from where they stood.

To survive, competitors had to know how to negotiate the sly anarchy that reigned. Thus, if an opponent leant into Harris now, he barged him back twice as hard. If a rival used his head to try to push Harris aside, he returned a more forceful butt, knowing the leather straps on his helmet would cushion the blow. He angled his elbows in a bunch to ensure a little extra space too. Soon he was no longer treated as a boy among men. By July, he was confident enough to enter two events at the event organised to celebrate *Manchester Evening News*' diamond anniversary: the half-mile handicap and one-lap sprint.

Fallowfield was sold out by early on the Saturday afternoon, with spectators standing tight in the stand beside the home straight and about 20 deep along the grass banks. Many had arrived on their bikes, leaving them unlocked outside the venue. Later, thousands of them would race each other on their way home, splintering in different directions through the suburbs:

north along Wilsmow Road and into the city, south into the countryside, and even north-east towards Salford and beyond. 'You would have about 20 different races when you came out,' Joe Pilling, a former Manchester Wheeler, said. 'There were quite a lot of accidents. In that area there were a lot of tramlines around and quite a few would crash on them.'

Harris was determined to inspire a few such races. Not only had his race skills sharpened but his knowledge of Fallowfield's idiosyncrasies had improved, too. Given the light drops of rain, he had put on tyres with a slight tread to grip the softening red-shale surface. He stayed clear of the six-inch kerb on the inside of the track. It could catch on a pedal. He lost in the one-lap sprint but soon made up for that in the handicap. *The Bicycle* magazine said that he showed 'good awareness to stay clear of trouble' and 'a great turn of pace' to avenge his defeat by Wood, the pre-race favourite, and claim first place.

His prize for winning was a gold Albert watchchain; handsome jewellery but no good to Harris. He could barely afford a watch, let alone one of matching antique gold. Battersby smiled at him confusedly examining the precious metal. 'Sell it,' he said. 'Cuttler's will take it. You won't be the only one there.' Thomas Cuttler's was a pawn shop in Manchester that did a brisk trade with cyclists every Monday morning through the summer. Other pawn shops across the country did likewise, exchanging for cash the myriad inappropriate prizes that the young men of the sport won: grandfather clocks, say, cruet sets, or silver cutlery. The cyclists could not be given money directly because that would breach the amateur code. The NCU turned a blind eye.

To his disbelief, Harris was given eight guineas for the watch-chain, about two-thirds of its sale price. After a few months' training, fitted in around work, he had earned the equivalent of several weeks of his factory wage. How much more, he wondered, could he earn next summer if he gave up his job alto-gether? Given how difficult it was to find work, this was a bold plan, but he could not see much of a future otherwise, other than more demoralising, poorly paid employment. By the following summer, he was likely to have benefited from an extra year's growth, too, and a winter spent further increasing his stamina. As his future wife Jennifer said: 'He had seen a way out.'

CHAPTER 2
1938

In the late 1920s, Harris walked with his mother towards the front door of an imposing house belonging to the family of Ezbon Holding, the man whom Harris had regarded as his father before his recent death. The reason for their visit was uncertain but it seemed that Elsie Hargreaves was looking for help that she did not receive. Instead in what would become her only child's earliest childhood memory, the door was slammed shut in her face, leaving her to try to grind out a living however she could.

When not able to find work in the local mills, Elsie hawked wares from door to door, among them encyclopaedias that she would tie together and haul through the streets of Bury in the hope some might wish to improve on their sparse education. Short and stout, and afflicted with a weak heart, in photographs she wore tattered old floral print dresses and smiled stoically, regardless that the picture might reveal she was blind in one eye.

Struggling always to pay the rent, she was rarely able to set up home for long, with rent books showing that she moved from the hamlet of Birtle outside Bury to Garden Street in the east of the town, on to Horne Street near the football stadium on Gigg Lane then north to Rake Street. Each road was lined with narrow terraced houses, with more than one family living in most of them, and their exterior walls darkened by the black smoke that emerged from the dozens of factories in the town and often cast a pall above it.

Life had not been much easier for Elsie when Holding, her husband, was alive. For he had never fully recovered his health after returning from the war and struggled to find work in his two trades, shoemaker and musician, even though he had performed as a violinist in Bury's Theatre Royal. Their penury was also down to him not being given access to his family's wealth. Strict Methodists, the Holdings had made their money through a shop in the nearby town of Tottington where, initially, they worked as drapers before Ezbon Snr turned it into a business that sold musical instruments and performed portrait photography. There are no surviving pictures of him though there does exist an oil painting of his cousin, Sir Edward Holden, once a prominent Liberal politician for nearby Heywood and the former chairman of the Midland Bank who turned it into the largest bank in the world.

The widowed Hargreaves eventually remarried to Joe Harris but still life was difficult. His only employable skill was the ability to press hats into shape, a technique learnt from his father, a Jewish tailor. 'People have no conception of how hard things were then,' Frank Jefferson, who worked in the Co-operative grocers and often served Elsie, said. 'I was a bit younger than Reg and it was difficult for us. In his era, it was that bit more desperate. They were in the doldrums.' Little wonder Hargreaves gave Harris her backing when he approached her with his plan to quit work the following summer. She knew it just might improve their lot. 'Elsie saw that he had talent,' Bill Brown, Harris's teenage friend, said: 'I don't think she needed much persuasion.'

She was right to take the risk. Competing at Lincoln and Derby and Bootle and Scarborough and elsewhere, Harris won seven races, claimed second twice and finished third three times, claiming a prize each time. Mostly he competed at the community sports days, but also he returned to the Lake District and travelled to the hills of north Wales, in both cases to compete in 'flapper' meetings where you entered under a pseudonym to compete for a cash prize. It was another practice that the NCU tacitly accepted.

By the end of the summer, he had established a steady income, both through pawnbrokers and through neighbours and friends wanting to purchase a bargain from him. 'It was almost like being a mini-wholesaler,' he told the BBC. 'One had to be commercially minded. It was a question of selecting those occasions where the prize values were good and where one could challenge for two or three prizes in an afternoon. That might earn you 25 or 30 pounds when a fairly comfortable salesman earned five pounds a week.'

Word of his potential began to reach the press. The *Liverpool Echo* noted how frequently Harris 'ran rings around the locals' at Bootle's track. Bill Bailey devoted a few paragraphs to him in his weekly column for *The Bicycle*, unaware that his son had inadvertently set Harris on the path to this success. The former champion not only marked Harris down as a talent to watch but also complimented him on giving up long-distance competitions to concentrate on track sprinting. A similar approach had helped Bailey to develop more quickly early in his career. By contrast, he wrote, 'most cyclists will do any race available to them'.

The only blemish to Harris's progress was his refusal to tackle the best riders in a scratch race. Because he was competing for financial reward, he did not see much benefit in racing when his chances of success were slim. With the memory of his first track race still fresh, he did not want to risk convincing defeat either. Only when another rider insisted on a duel did Harris change his mind.

In the spring of 1938, Eddy Gorton was Manchester's fastest man. A Manchester Wheeler, he had been around the scene for years and had some success on the domestic scene but was not quite among the country's best. He had heard much about Harris and been told repeatedly that he might have the potential to usurp him. Gorton wanted to put such suspicions to rest.

Battersby relayed the challenge while between sprint sessions on the road.

'I'm not ready,' Harris said. 'Better to race for a prize.'

'You're afraid to lose,' Battersby replied.

This cut through Harris's self-deceit. He fell quiet. They were sitting beside the road, recovering their breath, the April wind picking up Harris's light auburn hair.

'What race is it?'

'The Wells Bequest Trophy, an important race, staged at Fallowfield.'

Harris nodded. 'We need to do another sprint,' he said.

The race took place a few weeks later. Harris complained he was feeling unwell before it. He showed no signs of illness during it. In a photograph taken as he approached the finish line, he looks in the pink of health, sitting up, shoulders relaxed, fringe slicked back. Two lengths behind him, the blond Gorton is pedalling hard, head bowed, arm muscles clenched, the rest of the field nowhere.

Quite what is racing through the two men's minds is unclear but you assume it was related to their respective physical horizons.

Harris's were rapidly broadening; Gorton's suddenly shrunken. 'It was a very significant moment in my career,' Harris said. 'I had learnt how to face up to one of the country's best on level terms and come out on top.'

Manchester Wheelers had been closely tied to the city's professional class almost since the day 55 years earlier on which two brothers Harry and Jack Feay teamed up with a friend called Jack Sherlock to create a club that would bring together the gentlemen of the city who could afford an 'ordinary', or penny farthing as they were later called. As with most nascent cycling clubs, they drew up strict rules about appearance and conduct, insisting that all members wear blazers and caps emblazoned with the club badge. They also instituted relatively high subscription fees to ensure they did not attract the wrong sort of cyclist. They wanted riders of a certain calibre, too, and demanded that any aspiring member had completed a 12-hour time trial. As the membership broadened, so they became associated with a certain lifestyle. They took out the lease on a subterranean gentlemen's club on King Street in the city centre where they played billiards, dined, cut business deals or simply talked through the journals and newspapers supplied. In time, one of their richest members, Jimmy Taylor, donated a house on the fringes of the city that members could use as a changing facility for their rural rides. I could not find a record of any other club in the country with such luxuries. With the club subscriptions, they acquired the two most valuable trophies in Britain, the Vitonica and Muratti cups. Both were gold and worth 250 guineas. For decades the Wheelers were seen as both successful sports club and a masonry-like social institution. You could join only by invitation.

By the late 1930s, however, it had begun to suffer a decline that only those closely involved in the club fully realised. For while previously cyclists aspired to join them, now they were repelled by the exclusivity the club represented. The young, working-class bike rider saw no attraction to joining a set-up with men much older than him and outside his social milieu, whose business connections were of no use to him. Like a true pioneer, to him their traditions seemed antiquated. In his history of the club, former Wheeler Jack Fletcher wrote: 'The Wheelers' pattern of plus-four suits, of collars, ties and bought meals held no attraction for the new generation, the butty-carrying, alpaca-wearing rider of the '30s. They wanted a more down-to-earth and democratic outlook.' As a result, new subscriptions had begun to slow and the trickle of fresh talent that had ensured the Wheelers' success had dried up. In the last eight years, Gorton had been the only Manchester rider to win the Vitonica and Syd Cozens had been the only Wheeler to win the Muratti. That was back in 1931.

In the summer of 1938, the club took action to redress the situation. Jack Fletcher, then in his twenties, was elected to the board in the hope that he would give their executive a more youthful appearance. His principal role was to serve as press secretary to ensure the club was properly covered in the two weekly cycling magazines and in the *Manchester Evening News*. His second new position was as captain of the new Sunday rides. Previously the old men of the Wheelers had refused to darken the Sabbath.

His friend Charlie Hawksworth was appointed to the new position of chief recruitment officer. His task was to find the best young talent across the north-west. The Wheelers had seen the Manchester football clubs, City and United, institute scouting networks and felt they could do similar. As the former track cyclist and cycling journalist John Dennis said, soon they were 'signing up anybody who was any good'. The first was a flame-haired teenage sprinter called Johnny Gandy, who was lured from Manchester Clarion, one of the many clubs that was associated with the socialist *Clarion* newspaper. Asked to justify the switch, Gandy's motives hardly appeared altruistic when he said the Wheelers had 'better facilities, a better standard of rider, and *other* advantages'.

On suggesting that they next target Harris, Fletcher was told that he should undertake the dirty work involved. By now Harris was closely involved with the Bury Road Club, which effectively doubled as the local branch of the CTC and tied him to the community, providing him with most of his friends. Given that Fallowfield was seven miles from his home, and that he would need to commute regularly, he needed good reason to switch allegiance. However, as Fletcher understood, Harris would not make any such decision without the approval of his mother. 'She was the power behind his potential,' he wrote, applying a diplomatic description for Elsie's overbearing personality, as anybody who visited Fallowfield understood.

For on the days when Harris competed there, she arrived several hours early to secure a seat by the finish line. With no interest in the other races, she would chat enthusiastically with her neighbour until her son was involved, at which point she would cheer louder than anybody. But she would also protest vehemently when a decision was ruled against him or when an opponent dared, say, to cut him up. In time, Harris would find the courage to insist that she kept her counsel but for the moment she remained the embarrassing mother.

Fletcher planned his approach carefully, recruiting three fellow young Wheelers to join him in his task: his brother Len, Jim Mallins and Harry Crowley, who was picked because his father had agreed to lend them his handsome Standard 10 saloon. Dressed in smart shirts and trousers, they turned up to

Harris's front door looking like bank clerks on the first day in the job.

Fletcher cut the most distinctive figure. Tall and slim, with small, round glasses and a pointed chin, he looked more intellectual than athlete. Harris vaguely recalled leaving him behind in a recent 1,000-yard sprint.

He asked Fletcher his business. 'It will become clear soon enough,' he said.

Elsie soon took over and ushered the men into the tiny front room. Fletcher picked an armchair. Two of the others settled on an armrest taking turns to speak. Fluent and rehearsed, they did not stop for almost an hour.

They told her about the club's history and the cut of its members. They talked about its facilities and the quality of the races they staged. Pointing to the car, adjusting a few cuffs, they explained some of the *other* advantages. They recalled, for example, how Dennis Horn had kept the Vitonica Cup when he won it for the third time in 1935. They had to buy it back off him, which almost made him rich. There was no reason why her son could not do the same. He just needed the Wheelers to help him progress.

Elsie listened and probed. She had no education but she was street-smart. She knew that her suitors had an ulterior motive. She could sense the desperation in their attention to detail.

When they produced a form for her to sign, she had not got to the truth of the Wheelers' predicament but she knew to raise her price. 'If you want him to join, you'll waive this fee,' she said, issuing a demand that required them to break a founding principle of the club.

Fletcher smiled. 'You're formidable, Elsie,' he said.

By this time, Harris had outgrown Battersby. On their training runs on the road, his superior stamina left his mentor struggling to keep up, while Harris's greatly improved acceleration meant that their sprint sessions now served little advantage to either man, such was the disparity between them. So, when Harris broke the news about his defection to the Wheelers, Battersby was not so much surprised as disappointed. 'This might be our last ride,' Harris said, watching as Battersby silently wound up his speed, as if trying to reverse physically the decision to leave him behind.

Harris did not mind that he had upset his friend. Battersby himself had taught Harris not to allow emotion to undermine his application and, besides, Harris had since found another potential teacher, who was far more learned in elite cycling than Battersby but similarly willing to serve as a father figure.

John Sibbit – Jack to his friends – was among the most celebrated figures in the Wheelers' history. He had first emerged on the competitive scene as a sprinter before the war, finishing second and third in the individual sprint as an amateur at the World Championships. Tall and strong, square-jawed with raven hair, he had enjoyed even more success on the tandem, winning 11 national titles and a silver medal at the 1928 Olympics. At the same time, he had run a successful bike-building business, progressing from his first premises in a railway arch beneath Piccadilly Station to a shop on nearby Great Ancoats Street, where he produced some of the most coveted frames in the north-west. Known almost as much for his temper as his talent, Sibbit was a man of unusual commitment. Duncan Hamman served as his apprentice. 'I almost quit on my first day,' he said. 'He shouted and swore at me from the start. I was terrified of him. Several times, I thought I was going to be sacked when I did something wrong. Over time, however, I began realise that was just his way. He was a perfectionist.'

This was a quality he shared with Harris. Perhaps for that reason they quickly bonded when Harris visited his premises en route home from morning rides. It may also have been that Harris somehow compensated for the frustration that Sibbit felt with his son, also called Jack, for his lack of interest in the sport. Whatever the reason, the sharp edges of his demeanour softened in Harris's company. 'It took a lot to stop Jack working but when

Reg paid a visit, they spent a long time chatting,' Hamman said, recalling proudly how he brewed Harris tea.

Often Harris simply solicited Sibbit for memories from his career, asking about the great stadiums abroad that he graced and the opponents against whom he raced. He discussed tactics with him too and checked with him that his training regime was correct (mostly, it was). At other times, he simply sat in silence as Sibbit closed his shutters of an evening and went to work on fashioning racing bikes from the apparently disparate collection of metal tubes on the workstation in the converted kitchen behind his shop.

Hamman remembered them as magical nights. First Sibbit scrubbed the tubes clean – dirt corrupted this alchemy – then he cut and smoothed the tube ends, before pinning them inside a Sibbit-inscribed lug. Then he layered the join with flux, the acid that helped the brass run. Finally he fired up a blow torch, heated a brass rod and, working swiftly, skilfully, applied it inside the lug to merge the metal in elegant union. 'If you did not do it quickly, you were in trouble,' Hamman said.

Called mitring, the process was age-old but Harris had not seen it before. It taught him to respect the bike. He refused ever again to ride a welded frame, with tubes that effectively were jammed together, creating the mess found at the joins of most production-line bikes. Harris thought that ugly and not nearly as strong.

After one such evening, a few months into the new outdoor season, Harris and his new mentor took to discussing Harris's recent progress. He had started full of hope at the Good Friday Meeting at Herne Hill, traditionally the first event of the season. The journey alone had been an adventure. Travelling with others from the Wheelers, Harris took the train to Euston then rode through London for the first time, passing St Paul's and coasting across Waterloo Bridge in a ritual that countless riders from the north did then.

He had been impressed by the venue, too. Its concrete surface was the fastest he had seen. Its slightly banked bends were the closest thing to the foreign tracks about which he had heard so much. With a 9,000-strong capacity it was not as big as Fallow-field but still it hummed with excitement when sold out. People streamed through the suburban roads to squeeze through its gates. They happily stood on the banks for hours until their backs were sore. They cheered the foreign sprinters who had turned up to top the bill.

A few of these were professionals, men such as Arie van Vliet of Holland, and the brilliant Belgian Jef Scherens. Not allowed to race against amateurs, they competed in a separate contest. They spent most of the afternoon reclining on the deckchairs in the track centre, keeping warm in their silk robes – though British fans reckoned them dressing gowns – while looking implacably confident. Beside them sat the leading foreign amateurs, including Jan Derksen, the prodigiously talented Dutch teenager, and the Italian Ferruccio Astolfi. Given their pedigree, they did not enter the sprint until its latter stages. Harris had hoped to prick their reputations by qualifying to race against them through the preliminary rounds. Instead he got caught in a bunch in his first contest and left the track early to travel home alone.

'You should have stayed,' Sibbit said.

'I couldn't bear to look at them.'

'You would have learnt something. You'll be racing them soon enough.'

Harris's form did improve in the less prestigious domestic races that followed. At the Butts track in Coventry, he convincingly beat Gorton again in a quarter-mile scratch race before a sell-out 10,000-strong crowd. Returning to Herne Hill, he entered a 'points' competition wherein the winner was chosen by points accumulated over a series of races and finished third behind Wilf Maxfield and Dave Ricketts, earning praise from *Cycling* magazine for providing 'the Londoners with their only opposition'. This was no mean compliment. The same age as Harris, Ricketts was reckoned the best young sprinter in the south; Maxfield was possibly the fastest man in the country. He had spent the winter in a track school in Paris learning how to ride the steeply banked indoor venues that were found abroad. A versatile cyclist, he had won the 10-mile race at the previous year's Empire Games. He was a blond, blue-eyed, tee-total ambassador for the sport.

In June, Harris was pitched for the first time against a very different figure in Dennis Horn, the Suffolk farmer with a mono-brow and crooked teeth, who had been at the summit of the sport for the best part of a decade. A keen showman, he claimed his training regime involved tilling fields and speed-skating across the Fens, though such bucolic charm masked a ruthless streak: he demanded discreet payments from promoters for the privilege of having him and his brother, Cyril, on their bills. He also appeared on the cards that were given away with Senior Service cigarettes. 'The Horns may well have earned as much as some professionals,' the cycling historian Peter Underwood wrote. Horn was upset by reports that described him as a veteran after Harris beat him at Herne Hill by three lengths. He said he was determined to avenge the defeat at their next scheduled meeting, the Vitonica Cup, in two weeks' time.

Sibbit was unconvinced. 'He's past it.'

'Think I can win it?' Harris said.

'If you do, you'll go to Milan.'

By that he meant the World Championships in August. Britain was due to send a three-man sprint team.

The rain hardly let up over the weekend of the Vitonica Cup. It started on Friday night and drowned the city until it returned to work, yet still Fallowfield was almost sold out. On its grass banks spectators sheltered beneath a canopy of umbrellas. Photographs show others stoic in the stand, collars turned up, faces clenched to the wind. Below them cyclists are caked in mud. One gave up trying to drive his bike through the wet shale and instead carried it over the finish line, a one-man protest against the elements.

By the start of the marquee event, Maxfield's fringe was lank against his forehead. Horn had never looked more menacing. Harris was most afraid of the fourth finalist, Hendrik Ooms, the Dutchman who had won the race for the past two years. Most continental cyclists struggled at Fallowfield because its shale was much slower than the tracks to which they were accustomed. Ooms, however, had grown up on grass venues and relished a slow run. It put more emphasis on his electric finishing speed.

Sibbit took Harris aside moments before the gun. 'I was terribly nervous,' Harris recalled. 'He was well aware of my tactical limits and encouraged me to accept his advice on the slippery track and go flat out from the crack of the pistol. A moment's hesitation on the part of the other three finalists, he felt, would give me far too good a lead to be caught at the end.'

Like a general preparing to fall out his men, an official inspected the quartet on the start line, each accompanied by a volunteer preparing to push him off. Once happy all was correct, the official fired the gun, triggering Harris's surge. The others could not believe he had chosen to break the wind. Within seconds he had a five-length lead, mud flying from his back wheel into the others' line of vision. Exchanging second place swiftly, seamlessly, they needed a lap to close him down, creating a train as they tucked in behind until the final bend.

Ooms attacked first, attempting to dart through the inside, only for Harris to eliminate the gap, forcing the champion to check his speed, skid and crash. Lying prostrate on the earth, cradling his head, Ooms was in no position to protest.

With Horn fading, Maxfield jumped next, taking an unorthodox outside line, not least because the inside lane now ran with water like an open drain. Harris spotted him too and closed the gap so incisively that *Cycling* said 'he ran the Londoner into the rails'. That was not quite true. A photograph of the scene shows how Maxfield remained in the saddle, but Harris was within touching distance. On Maxfield's opposite shoulder the crowd were almost as close. They look transfixed, several mouths agape.

The men ran parallel until the finish line, forcing the judges to consult a photo finish to declare the winner. Nobody was surprised Harris got the vote. The judges were Mancunian. This was a sport riven with regional rivalries.

Maxfield was furious. He lodged a protest against Harris's tactics but was swiftly dismissed. Ooms' delayed appeal suffered a similar fate, leaving him to go to hospital with a bleeding head wound. He was quickly bandaged and discharged.

By dusk, somebody had leaked to Maxfield a copy of the judges' photo finish – the culprit was never found – showing that he was half a wheel ahead as they crossed the line. This time he chose to appeal to the NCU.

An independent panel of officials heard the case but, if Maxfield was more confident of success, he did not reckon on the Wheelers' financial clout. They hired a lawyer who questioned the reliability of the camera's shutter speed and took issue with the angle of the shot. He cast enough doubt on its accuracy for the decision to stand. Decades later Harris said that 'I had always regarded this race with a measure of regret' – a rare expression of guilt – but he showed no such contrition at the time.

A few weeks later, in his column for *Cycling*, Bill Bailey wrote that 'Harris has put himself in contention for Milan, but to pick a sprinter with such limited experience would represent a gamble'. Bailey had in mind Harris's capitulation at the National

Championships two weeks after his breakthrough win. There he lost in a preliminary round to a Brighton rider called Les Glover who rarely troubled the country's best. Almost as bad for Harris was that his rivals for the national squad each performed to their potential, with Maxfield beating Ricketts in the final. With Horn's form now apparently in terminal decline, that pretty much ensured those two a place in the squad and left Harris and a cyclist called Freddie Tickler as the outstanding contenders for the third spot.

Tickler ranked just below the very best on the domestic scene. He had reached the semi-finals of the National Championships and represented Britain at the previous year's World Championships in Amsterdam, but that was partly because he had offered to pay his travelling expenses. To strengthen his case this year, he was willing to stump up the cash again, leaving the NCU to choose between a rider with experience and limited talent and one with unpredictable potential who came at a greater cost. Given that they were a notoriously conservative body, most expected them to reselect Tickler. Harris was surprised, then, when an envelope landed on his doorstep in the second week of August with 'Doughty Street, City of London' marked on the back. That was the NCU's address.

CHAPTER 3
1939

Harris was overwhelmed by the Vigorelli Velodrome as soon as he caught sight of it from the British team's tram that had travelled from Milan Central Station. At a distance, the huge, white-washed oval structure resembled a pristine spaceship that had landed among the unkempt apartment blocks and factories of this poor suburb to the north-east of the city. Given a tour of the facility by the Italian riders Astolfi and Bruno Loatti, he then discovered a wooden surface that glinted bronze beneath the floodlights, with historic timber boards that his hosts proudly explained had been salvaged from a demolished velodrome in Rome. Watching the foreign riders swoop up and down banking steeped at a 45-degree angle, with all the speed and elegance of birds in flight, Harris wondered what his chances were of mastering the track before the World Championships began at the weekend. 'It was like nothing else I had seen,' he said.

Climbing up to the terraces, the Italians showed him its concrete banking that flanked the full perimeter of the track, warning him to expect that its 30,000 capacity would be full for each day of the event. Turning to five-foot long cushions laid on the ground, they laughed as they explained that they were required to be of such length to prevent the crowd from using them as missiles. Not that it made much difference. Fans were still likely to hurl whatever they could lay their hands on – rotten fruit and coffee cups most likely – over the wire fence and towards foreign cyclists who dared to beat their compatriots, or officials who ruled against them.

Moving below ground, Harris discovered rider facilities more advanced than any that he had ever seen, with vast changing rooms, medical facilities and a workshop in which grease-stained mechanics tinkered with frames and components as sculptors would their art. He found banks of massage tables where soigneurs worked on cyclists' sore muscles. Harris had heard about British riders who tried self-massage as none of them could afford to employ somebody to do it for them. But then this was the fastest track in the world, the site for multiple world-record attempts in the four years since its construction, and a venue that had been built at the behest of a Fascist government – who had assigned their minister Enzo Vigorelli to oversee the task.

Harris wasted little time in getting on to the track. He began with slow laps on the inside lane, easing through the gradient at modest speed. Within a few days, he had found the confidence to increase his speed, so that he was almost sprinting around its quarter-mile circumference, no longer the typically crude English track cyclist abroad. Halfway through the week, he was even entertaining the possibility that he would be able to do himself justice once the competition began.

Then Harry Ryan, the team manager, took him aside.

'Stop training on the track,' he said. 'You're showing yourself up. The team, too.'

'Have you not seen our rivals?' Harris said. 'They've been cycling these tracks all their lives.'

'You're making us look like amateurs.'

'You don't need help with that.'

Harris had begun to lose faith in the NCU about a week earlier when it considered altering its initial team selection because Harris was unable to afford a new passport (or so he claimed). Harris's place in the squad alongside Maxfield and Ricketts was confirmed only when Dick Taylor, an NCU official from Bury, persuaded selectors that his family friend was worth the investment. Harris's frustration had worsened when he arrived at Victoria Station to catch their train to the coast and found that Ryan and his assistant, Harry Crowe, had brought their families along. Tensions had worsened on their arrival in Milan, once Harris saw the attention that officials from abroad paid his potential opponents, timing their laps, constantly correcting their bikes, soothing them when frustrated and admonishing them when their application dipped, with the two Harrys holed up in their hotel all the while.

These foreign teams were products of professional set-ups backed by much wealthier national federations who could afford to invest in their amateur talents and wished to satisfy, say, the French, Belgian or Italian public's thirst for success. Such an outlook sorely contrasted with the NCU's approach. Referred to pejoratively as the 'blazer brigade', they lacked money but clung to the old Victorian ideal about the Corinthian spirit of the gentleman amateur. Almost perversely, they feared that by developing an elite class of cyclist they would cut off the sport's recently developed working-class roots. They even had a rule that said no professional could ever return to the amateur ranks and compete in their competitions.

Harris was especially disappointed with Ryan because he had once succeeded against the foreign elite, winning silver in the amateur sprint at the 1913 World Championships and the same medal on the tandem at the 1920 Olympic Games. But, though Ryan knew about the shortcomings that Britons had to overcome abroad, he was also part of a generation that felt the modern cyclist – to quote Bill Bailey's word – was 'mollycoddled' and was privileged even to have been given an escort to Milan.

'Go back to your holiday,' Harris said. 'I'm staying till they turn down the lights.'

'This will not be forgotten,' Ryan said. 'The NCU have long memories. You don't want to be making enemies.'

Harris picked up his bike. 'You selected me for what I am, Harry, not what you want me to be.'

Back in England, the country was trying to comprehend the news that Germany's foreign minister had signed a pact with his Soviet counterpart by the terms of which the countries would support one another in the event of war – an announcement that most assumed effectively gave Hitler licence to continue with his expansion across Europe and to invade Poland, with his troops already gathered on its German border. With Britain and France having both agreed to defend Poland, the Nazi-Soviet agreement – reached after secret talks – seemed certain to embroil Europe's most powerful nations in conflict, regardless that Prime Minister Neville Chamberlain's government was trying desperately to reprise its recent negotiations with the Soviets.

In an office on Doughty Street, Edward Southcott, the president of the NCU, was struggling to decide how best to respond to the situation. If war broke out, the British team would suddenly be placed deep into enemy territory, given the Pact of

Steel that Hitler and Mussolini had signed three months earlier. Yet Ryan had not contacted Southcott since leaving London four days earlier, even though Southcott had tried to call his hotel and wired him telegrams.

As a last resort, he rang the British Embassy in Rome to inquire about the situation in Italy.

'I thought you'd given them permission to stay on,' the civil servant said.

Southcott was incredulous. He explained he had not even spoken to the squad.

'That's what the Associated Press bureau here is reporting. Same with the French team.'

Southcott had spoken to his counterparts in Paris and knew this was also untrue.

'Perhaps your messages are being intercepted. The Italians are very keen for this event to go ahead.'

The Italian press was not treating the diplomatic development as seriously as their British counterparts. On the streets people seemed hardly concerned with it, apparently satisfied that their financially crippled military was in no position to fight. Southcott asked the diplomat his advice. He could offer none. He was awaiting official instruction from Whitehall. Better to call the consulate in Milan, who might at least know the situation on the ground.

'Call the team home immediately,' the new civil servant said. If war was declared, he explained, the squad was liable to be interned, hence the train that had been arranged to transport non-nationals out of Milan on Friday. He suggested they took it. He even offered to speak to them.

By now the British squad had grown. The road team had arrived for their competition, which began on Monday. They were exhausted and bewildered. It had taken them hours to get through successive borders. Officials struggled to believe any Briton would be foolhardy enough to enter Italy at this time. Meanwhile, the track squad had been joined by the two British professionals, Harry Hill and Syd Cozens. Their competition began on Sunday. Hill had travelled with his mother and seen mobilised French troops when changing trains in Paris. Cozens had arrived from the Grand Prix of Copenhagen. He hitched a lift with a group of Dutch cyclists and had almost been stranded in Germany when they had run out of petrol with all spare supplies of the fuel commandeered by the military. A bright spark among them suggested they head to a pharmacy and buy dozens of a benzene-based medicine that could serve as synthetic fuel. They were fortunate to escape.

Gathered now in a hotel room, Cozens told Ryan he had no intention of returning home. As a professional, he did not fall within the NCU's authority anyway. Hill felt likewise. His mum must have been brave. They might have been inspired by the French team, who that morning had rejected a similar edict from their federation.

Harris followed suit. 'Give me my return ticket.'

Ryan's thoughts spiralled back two decades. As a young cyclist he had once fallen prey to similar ambition in similar circumstances, defying the union's advice by travelling alone to the World Championships in Copenhagen with Europe on the brink of conflict. Then hostilities were declared before the event, forcing it to be abandoned and leaving Ryan stranded in the Danish port of Esjberg, with ship workers unwilling to cross the sea because they felt it unsafe. Only after a week of frenzied negotiations and the offer of a huge bribe did they sail. Ryan could not be certain that Harris would have such luck should similar happen again.

'Not this time,' Ryan said. 'You're my responsibility.' He explained that the bikes had been placed on their crates. His family's bags were packed. Harris eventually agreed to do likewise, but once Ryan was out of sight, he returned to the velodrome, demanding to be entered as a one-man team. This broke the rules: no cyclist could enter without permission from his federation, but the Italian officials were willing to indulge him. They did not expect Harris to pose a threat to their best cyclists, and even agreed to lend him equipment. They were amused by the spectacle shortly afterwards when Ryan turned up, having taken a detour en route to the station. 'I was given the soundest possible reprimand,' Harris said. His bag had been packed for him.

The journey home was long and dry. There was not a drop of fluid nor a morsel of food on board. Already tense, the mood darkened when they passed into France and conductors marched through the carriages, pulling down window shutters and replacing ordinary light bulbs with blue-tinted versions. They did not want any Luftwaffe to mistake them for a train carrying military personnel. At Boulogne, the sprinters split with the party to refuel at a café. They devoured a buffet so eagerly that they missed their ship, leaving them to wait hours for the next route home. They eventually arrived at Victoria Station, 36 hours after Harris had been strong-armed on to a Milanese tram. A small group of men were waiting to meet them at the platform: Southcott, tall, bespectacled, his nerves frayed; Bill Mills, editor of *The Bicycle*, who got the scoop on their adventure; and the photographer Bill Jones who captured the team disembarking for posterity.

Standing in the centre of his photograph, Maxfield looks remarkably smart; hair neat, blazer on and tie still knotted. To his right, Ricketts is casually dressed, a little tired but still handsome, similar to the young Sean Penn. Harris, with his round cheeks and mouth slightly ajar, looks baby-faced, perhaps even innocent. Staring brightly at the camera, he certainly does not cut the figure of a teenager who had tried to take on the world single-handedly just as it was falling apart.

The cutback in Harris's cycling began with the blackout. He could not sprint at dusk because the streetlamps were turned off. Back lights for bikes were compulsory by then but he did not believe they would make him safe when car lights were turned down too. He was among the thousands of cyclists who believed that motorists would be less vigilant for them when they had only to look out for their flashing red bulbs at night.

Competition soon dried to a trickle. Even though military action had not begun, people had more pressing concerns now that the country was officially at war and had to prepare for the worst. In Bury they sandbagged the fire station and repainted the lines on the road to compensate for the worsened light. They recommissioned buses and set them up as mobile ambulances on The Rock. Young men aged over 20 and not in 'essential' employment were conscripted. Harris's riding partners soon reduced.

He took to cycling alone, both out into the countryside and through the city to its docks, where he would quiz workers whom he knew from their union sports days about life at sea. He had always fancied a life full of travel and adventure. Their stories stoked these daydreams. In March he told the military enrolment officer that he wished to join the navy. He was turned down.

The clerk took one look at his limited CV and decided the few skills Harris had acquired at Auty & Lees made him better suited to a tank regiment called the 10th Royal Hussars. Thus he was dispatched to a training camp at nearby Catterick, in Yorkshire, to join thousands of other naifs being prepared for war. He was told this would comprise a tactical and technical education but the latter was limited mostly to driving trucks up and down a patch of land behind the camp called Tea Pot Hill, pretending they were inside tanks. There was only one tank on the base.

The tactical lessons were non-existent. Countless hours were instead devoted to marching on the square to the barked instructions of the drill sergeant. Many were spent larking about. Private L.A. Passfield, interned at the facility at the same time as Harris, wrote in his memoirs that 'Catterick was no more a breeding ground for military professionals than it was a holiday camp without the organised entertainment'. The men were drunk in the mess hall one evening when news broke that the impasse known as the 'Phoney War' had finally been broken by Germany bombing Dunkirk. Some time afterwards Harris was told that his future lay in north Africa, defending the Suez Canal, close to where Italian forces had declared war after landing in Libya.

Harris recalled the journey as 'terrible'. It was almost unbearably long and conditions were cramped. Unable to travel through Franco's Spain, they sailed around the tip of Africa and north through the Indian Ocean and the Suez until eventually they arrived in Alexandria and headed west to thwart the enemy's progress. He soon found that life on land was even worse.

Temperatures in the Libyan Desert, where they spent most of their time, soared in the day and plummeted at night. Harris built pebbled walls around his tiny bivouac tent to break the wind. They were banned from drinking the local water supply. They soaked indigenous fruit in diluted potassium permanganate, an antiseptic acid more commonly used to treat weeping ulcers. With little to stimulate them, they suffered terrible boredom when not in conflict. As Private Ian Cowburn, another 10th Hussar, said: 'There was nothing but miles and miles of desert.' Occasionally a mirage broke the horizon, only soon to crush the hope it had inspired.

As Harris said, their equipment was 'hopelessly inadequate for the task'. Previously a cavalry regiment, the 10th Hussars had begun mechanisation only four years earlier but had not completed the task by the time they were called to action. As a result, their Crusader tanks had to be supplemented with Honey tanks borrowed from the American military. Compared to the German Panzers, both were sorely inefficient. They could fire over only half the range of the Panzer's 75mm cannon and their armour was not nearly as strong. Their only advantage was their superior speed and agility, leaving frontline Allied regiments such as Harris's to suffer casualties on a scale similar to that of the first World War.

In lands that were scarcely mapped, their intelligence units also frequently let them down. 'Often reconnaissance would tell us that a certain place was quite safe to spend the night in and that the enemy tanks on the horizon were decoys,' Harris said. 'We would try to snatch some sleep only to be rudely awakened by the thunder of German tanks passing almost through our midst.'

That they had success at all was impressive. In the first 18 months of Harris's deployment, the 10th Hussars put up a valiant defence when outnumbered near the Libyan town of Tobruk to ensure the Allied Forces under siege there were relieved. They contributed to a victory at Alam el Halfa, a tactically important ridge of Egyptian land. They were involved in a massacre of Italian troops at Beda Fomm. The poet Keith Douglass was there too. He recalled the 'vegetation of iron dead tanks, gun barrels split like celery and dead clinging to the ground'. Harris and his companions celebrated by looting Chianti from the abandoned camp.

By the autumn of 1942, however, momentum was with General Rommel's enemy forces after a succession of victories had put them one victory from marching on Alexandria. The last battle, just to the east of the Egyptian town of El Alamein, had ended in stalemate but if the Germans attacked again, the Allied Forces would be vulnerable to a defeat that could cost them control of the Suez and rob them easy access to the Middle East.

Prime Minister Winston Churchill took decisive action, replacing Claude Auchinleck with Bernard Montgomery as commander of the Allied troops in Africa – the Eighth Army. Montgomery instituted reinforcements of personnel and equipment, with new Sherman tanks arriving to earn them parity with the Panzer gunnery. Harris was still in his Crusader, patched up in a desert workshop, but this at least gave him hope. Famously bold in his approach, Montgomery then began preparations to launch an attack, claiming his ambition was not just to reverse recent losses but to 'knock the enemy for six out of Africa altogether'.

He ordered the construction of the dummy pipeline from deep inland that would run to the coast, hopefully tricking the enemy into thinking that he was intent only on reinforcing his defensive position. He arranged for all maneouvres to take place at night, with tank troops such as Harris's guided by the gas lamps that hung from the back of military trucks. As Harris's tank took up an offensive position, he was told to cover it with a thin aluminium veil in the hope that reconnaissance Luftwaffe would mistake it for a truck.

Though his privates did not know it, Montgomery was acting on intelligence from the code-breakers at Bletchley Park, who had recently cracked German communications in the region and discovered that their victories masked troubles among Rommel's army. For with the Allied Forces having retained control of the key Mediterranean ports of Tobruk and Benghazi, the enemy was running short on resources, both hardware and food supplies. Bletchley Park had also learnt that Rommel had taken ill, forcing him to leave for Italy. In short, his men were vulnerable. Now was the perfect time to attack.

On the night of 22 October 1942, Harris gathered with his troop around their wireless to listen to Montgomery's eve-of-battle address. 'The battle which is about to begin will be one of the most decisive in history,' he said, in his distinctive nasal tone. 'Every officer and man should enter it with the determination to see it through, to fight and kill, and finally to win. If we do this, there can be only one result. The Lord mighty in battle will give us the victory.' Montgomery believed victory was won first 'in the minds' of his men.

Harris cracked open another dinner of bully beef and biscuits. The troop had tried most variations. They had fried the corned beef, stewed it, even combined it with the biscuits, pretending the latter was Yorkshire pudding. Tonight they lacked the energy for such invention and ate it straight from the tin. They called that bully au naturel.

At 9.40 p.m. the New Zealand artillery regiment stationed to their east sent searchlights criss-crossing the black sky. Cowburn said their shells rang around their targets through the night 'like endless thunder'. Before dawn the 10th Hussars were given amphetamine pills to keep them awake and told to take up position. Harris was neither driver nor gunner, which meant he operated the radio or navigated, or both. Their remit was to pick off the Panzers that the artillery regiment had split up and possibly driven back, a relatively straightforward task if it did not require them to cross a huge patchwork of German minefields known as the Devil's Garden.

Given by their intelligence a supposedly safe route, the 10th Hussars found that the first few hours passed without incident. Given past experiences, this surprised them. With the frontline Panzer divisions in retreat, Anthony Wingfield, commander of Harris's squadron, recalled in his memoirs that he even felt 'the gods were on our side'. Divinity abandoned them at about dusk, however, when they fell under attack and were forced to give up their formation. With the tanks already positioned about 200 yards apart, now several were isolated, Harris's included. Others were hit.

Wingfield had chosen to issue commands over an open radio frequency to ensure everybody could easily listen. That also meant others could interrupt their superiors. Now, as tanks splintered across the explosive-strewn plains, nothing could be deciphered over the airwaves other than panicked shouting. 'The chaos that reigned was almost unbelievable,' Harris said.

His vehicle fell within range of an enemy Tiger tank, the type only recently arrived in Africa that was used mostly as a back-up to the Panzer and was even more powerful. When its shell connected with the Crusader's armour – failing to pierce it – Harris compared the sensation to what you might feel should somebody strike a hammer against a metal bucket placed over your head.

His companions evacuated, terrified that the petrol tank might catch light and the tank would 'brew up'. Already it was like a furnace inside, yet somehow Harris found a split second of clarity amid the pressure. Perhaps sprint cycling taught him this; maybe it was an instinctive skill. He considered his alternatives. If he followed the others out of the turret, he would be stranded in no man's land and within sight of the enemy. Given 'the different degrees of gentlemanly fighting' he had witnessed, he could not be certain of his fate then. Conversely, if he stayed put, and the tank did brew up, he would still have a few seconds to escape.

Quite how long he remained is uncertain but when the tank took a second hit, he sensed that it would not survive, so he risked disembarking into the battlefield. Dazed, slightly burnt, he was eventually picked up by a group of Allied soldiers. They arranged for him to be sent first to a field hospital, then to a more advanced medical facility, before finally he was dispatched to the base camp in Cairo, where he was told that he would serve out the remainder of his service in Britain. As the Eighth Army continued with their critically successful march west, he was told that all the men in his tank had been shot dead shortly after leaving him behind.

By comparison, his new life was paradise. Stationed at a barracks in Manchester, Harris's principal responsibility now was to transport goods and personnel around the site in a military truck. He was able occasionally to return home and soon started cycling again. 'The work was very much that of a civilian lorry driver,' he said. 'Altogether I found it very pleasant.'

Profiles of Harris will tell you that he was discharged from the military because of the burns he suffered but that was not true. They were only superficial – he suffered no scarring. Friends wondered if his hairline had been singed but it had begun to recede prematurely anyway. Besides, even Harris claimed that he did not understand why he was declared unfit for service after a routine medical check-up. Bill Brown, however, understood that Elsie had used her powers of persuasion to convince somebody that Harris deserved to be released. 'I don't know exactly how, but his mother got him out,' he said.

CHAPTER 4
1945

Like many war veterans, Harris was feted as a local hero on his discharge from the military, with the story of the burning tank adding lustre to his reputation. To his credit, he never showed off about his experiences. He hardly talked about them at all, but he did not disabuse people of their misconception about his injuries either. Perhaps he felt he had endured enough to earn sympathy anyway.

Soon after his discharge, Charlie Auty had offered him another job, this time with increased responsibilities that allowed Harris to use his nascent charm and cycling celebrity to sell the product on which he excelled. Slowly he began to return to competition, too. There were nothing like the prizes available before the war, but he still had enough money to build a young man's modest social life.

One night shortly after his re-employment, he visited The Stanley Arms pub that was also on The Rock. It was a huge, cavernous place, a focal point for the town, with one room that was devoted to live music, a parlour to where the older customers retreated for some relative quiet, and a main bar where he found his old teenage playmate, Florence Stage, serving drinks.

'Hello, Sweety,' he said, employing his favourite pet name for potential conquests.

'I was wondering when you would privilege us with a visit,' she replied.

'You've blossomed, Flo.'

'Still the same then, Reg?'

Before the war their families had lived beside one another on Horne Street. Florence's uncle, Donald, had found Harris his first bike. Her father, Billy, had captained Bury football team when they were in the first division of English football and when they won the Lancashire Cup. With his savings Billy Stage had bought The Stanley Arms on retiring from the game.

Florence agreed to a date. Before long they were courting. She knew about Harris's reputation as a ladies' man but she could not help but fall for him. Though still reserved, he was more confident now than as an adolescent and had developed into a good-looking young man, with a smile that lit up his face and a physique that was already beginning to look athletic again. He knew also how to compliment a girl, paying special attention to Florence's pretty eyes, good skin and carefully presented blond hair. With slightly protruding front teeth and a thin upper lip, she was not classically good-looking, but she was gregarious, smart and had an easy way with people. Within a year of that first meeting, she had agreed to marry him and set a date for Sunday, 7 April 1945 at Bury Parish Church.

The photographs from it made the front page of the *Bury Times*. Posing in front of the church's red-brick wall, Harris looks proud in his three-piece suit, chest puffed out, arms folded behind his back. Perhaps he was thinking about the slap-up meal that awaited them nearby in The Old Boar's Head or the short honeymoon booked at the Lancashire seaside resort of Lytham St Anne's.

While linking his arm, however, Florence seems less comfortable. Wearing an Elizabethan-style satin dress, and a camellia-adorned head-dress, she looks serious, perhaps even sullen. Her eyes are downcast. Perhaps her demeanour denotes shyness; unlike Harris, she was unused to appearing in the local press. But the conversation she had with her father before entering the church must also have affected her mood. For Billy, knowing that Harris's womanising was far worse even than Florence suspected, felt that the groom would never be tamed. 'I'd rather walk you to your grave than down the aisle to marry this man,' he had said.

*

By now, as the *Bury Times* noted, Harris was a 'triple national sprint champion', having claimed three titles at the first reprisal of the National Championships in the previous summer. In an event that was split between Manchester and the south, to allow for the limitations on travel while the hostilities continued, Harris won the 1,000-yard sprint and five-mile race against a field of mostly northern riders at Fallowfield before travelling to the grass track at Slough to take the quarter-mile crown. In so doing, he beat Lew Pond and Ken Marshall, two Londoners who had emerged as the quickest men in the country in his absence abroad, as well as a talented young Manchester Wheeler called Alan Bannister. With Maxfield having died in conflict, and Ricketts having failed to live up to his youthful potential, Harris had already established himself as the fastest sprinter in the country.

As a result, he had been selected as part of the four-man British team that travelled to Paris to take on the French in the countries' first international cycling match after the war. This was a chastening experience. Competing on the pretty Vincennes track in woodland outside the city on a balmy Monday in June, Harris found that he could not ride slowly on the track's steeped banking, regardless that at only 33 degrees it was shallower than many continental tracks – the most precipitous were 45 degrees. This allowed his French rivals to force him into the lead and to ride in his slipstream while he tried to attack crudely from the front. Eliminated in the semi-finals of the sprint competition, he decided afterwards that he would need to get better acquainted with riding on tracks abroad if he was to progress to international success.

With Auty happy to allow his famous employee extra time away from work, Harris spent much of the rest of that year, and of the following winter, travelling to amateur events overseas. Often taking Florence with him, he competed in Zurich and Copenhagen and Paris again among other tracks, often flying in the decommissioned warplanes – that was commonplace then – without thinking to complain about the lack of a pressurised cabin or the discomfort felt sitting beside his bikes on the long wooden benches that ran the length of the plane. He was happy simply to be able to afford the flight, helping to fund them by smuggling race tyres to France because they cost about five times as much as they did in England. 'It was not the most upright thing I have ever done,' Harris said. The cycling writer Tim Hilton said Harris also often returned from overseas with a selection of watches that he hoped to sell on, having strapped them to his arm beneath his jacket before he marched through customs.

He soon found that the style of racing was very different abroad. For while the British format of massed fields on flat tracks had changed little since Victorian times, in those countries where cycling was a mainstream sport – such as France, Belgium and Switzerland – sprinting was far more evolved. There fields rarely involved more than three to four competitors, while the most prestigious contests comprised only two. Called match sprinting, this was the sport's blue riband event.

Its first principle was the same as in any cycling race: try to avoid taking the lead because it allowed an opponent to benefit from you breaking the wind. In match sprinting this meant much of the race involved the front man trying to cede his position, by feinting to attack, say, and tricking his opponent to do likewise, or by accelerating then stopping suddenly, a difficult skill with no brakes. He might even stop moving altogether, instead shuffling back and forth to stay upright, daring his opponent not to do likewise.

Yet such tactics were complicated by the risk that the second man faced. For if he allowed too great a gap to his opponent – by reacting slowly to an attack, for example – the race could be lost because invariably he had little time to make up for his mistake. Similarly, if he jumped too early or too late, his advantage was ruined. With several such contingencies, two-lap races could take anything from a minute to more than half an hour. Through the endless baiting involved it had become known as cat and mouse cycling.

Most British fans disliked such racing, thinking it boring and slow. Conservatism probably informed their outlook too. Somehow, such subtlety was typical of the pretentious French – where it was most popular. There, fans appreciated the psychology at work and understood that track sprinting involved speed of thought as much as bodily endeavour. They called its best practitioners *les aristocrats du cyclisme*.

Harris inevitably needed time to adapt to it. In one of his first indoor races in Paris, he performed well enough to reach the semi-finals but lost convincingly to Lucien Gillen of Luxembourg because he was under-geared. Such a mistake pointed to over-confidence, suggesting that Harris believed he could compensate for less power in his transmission through his sheer physical prowess. In Geneva, he was soundly beaten by a Swiss rider called Oskar Plattner, then perhaps the most feted amateur cyclist and certainly the most skilful, able to control the bike beautifully on the steepest incline. Harris admitted: 'I never know what he is going to do next.' Roger St Pierre, the veteran cycling journalist, said. 'I loved Plattner. He was a crafty little shit.'

However, as Harris's technique improved, so did his results. He twice avenged the defeat by Plattner with victories over him in Geneva and Zurich and undermined the improving reputation of Andre Rivoal, the 21-year-old Frenchman, by defeating him in Paris and Herne Hill. He also successfully defended his national sprint title and, perhaps most impressively, beat Marshall in the final of the Grand Prix of Paris, then the most prestigious race outside of the World Championships. The only downside to these successes was the difficulty he had getting his prize money past customs officials. Shelagh Dennis was married to the track cyclist John Dennis, a contemporary of Harris. She said that Harris circumvented this problem by leaving cash with contacts abroad. 'You were only allowed to take £25 out of England,' she said. 'It was marked in your passport. So you couldn't come back with £25 because they wondered what you'd been up to ... Reg was quite adaptable and he had many friends.'

His reputation overseas soon began to grow. Louis Gérardin, the brilliant professional sprinter from France who had medalled in the World Championships three times before the war, identified Harris as the best young rider on the circuit. 'Harris has what only a few riders are born with and none can acquire: a jump that can win races on his own,' he told *L'Equipe*.

In south London, Claud Butler, then Britain's biggest independent bike-builder, decided that he was prepared to pay Harris to ride one of his products. He had done this previously with Maxfield before the war, circumventing the rules of amateurism by claiming that he worked for the company. Harris happily signed up to a similar arrangement, earning five pounds a week for work that he claimed required him to fulfil some responsibility for Butler every day. Aside from the occasional public appearance, what this comprised was difficult to fathom, given that his Clapham factory was 220 miles from Harris's home. 'It was a sham job as an export representative,' Alan Geldard, a training partner of Harris's, said.

According to Geldard, Harris did not trust Butler's bikes and instead rebranded the frames he had built elsewhere – including some from Jack Sibbit – with transfers showing the Londoner's name. 'A lot of that went on in cycling generally, through commercial necessity. I can't actually tell you if he did ride a Claud Butler bike but they were not recognised as the top racing bikes and Harris was definitely riding a specially built French bike then, and other bikes too.'

The 'job' was a huge development. It allowed Harris to return to cycling full-time, not just through the summer either, but year round. As a result, through trial and error, Harris had soon settled on a carefully calibrated regime that would alter little in the years ahead and was far more advanced than any other British amateur of the time. He spent winter building up his core stamina by riding several times over about 50 miles during the week and twice that distance at the weekend. At the start of spring, he halved the distance of the midweek sessions but increased his gear size from 69 to 84 inches, enough to plateau his stamina while also increasing his average speed to a steady 15mph.* This ensured he started the summer season familiar with the gear resistance used in a race.

Harris developed other habits beneficial to his performance, too. He began to take hot baths after each ride and massaged his legs, preventing his muscles from stiffening up. Though hardly scientific, his diet was healthy and chosen with some thought, comprising mostly fresh meat, fish, fruit and vegetables, albeit while also indulging his love of sweet pastries and trifles. He ate at least every four hours to keep his metabolism fuelled and, to avoid indigestion, never had a meal more than 90 minutes before a race.

He continued with his sprint sessions in the afternoon, too, occasionally at Fallowfield but more often on nearby Mauldeth Road where its tarmac gave way to concrete – he called it 'the patch' – which meant it more resembled a foreign track. It had a natural camber, allowing him to build up speed much as he would when swooping down from a banking.

---

* Based on a Victorian calculation, gear size was worked out by dividing the number of teeth on the chainwheel by those on the sprocket, and multiplying the result by the diameter of the wheel. Fausto Coppi, the great Italian road rider and contemporary of Harris's, rode the toughest climbs on a 48.6-inch gear. A track sprinter rode anything between an 86- and 110-inch gear.

He preferred to ride in a group, partly for company but also because it made road trips easier as the cyclists could take turns forcing the pace at the front – they called it 'riding bit and bit'. Initially, he found it difficult to attract companions during the working day but, as his celebrity increased, that problem declined. Soon there was no shortage of Wheelers willing to leave their business behind for the privilege of riding his tail. As Geldard said, 'You were basking in his glory when you were riding with him.'

Ken Pearson, then a young club rider, was among those who rode with Harris and recalled him as a polite and jovial personality whose general mood seemed to be improved by the vistas opening up before him. To illustrate his character, Pearson recalled how once a group of Wheelers emerged from their clubhouse to find Harris happily sitting alone beside the road and their bikes disappeared. His poker face hid perfectly that he had connected the frames with a rope and hoisted them up between two trees, leaving them hanging above their oblivious owners like clothes on a washing line. 'That was typical of him,' Pearson said.

Harris was then the typical champion British cyclist, mixing as easily with the grass-roots of the sport as he did with the elite. Duncan Hamman recalled a loosely organised (and illegal) race that took place most Sundays, running from a cyclists' café in Handforth to the Cheshire village of Cheadle. 'All the Manchester clubs used to meet at the café then have this great, massed sprint,' he said. 'I remember a bunch of us coming down Schools Hill, when I suddenly found myself sandwiched between Reg and Bannister. I was terrified, thinking: "If I fall off, and bring Reg Harris off, every cyclist in the country would hate me."'

By the late summer of 1946, Harris travelled to the first reprisal of the World Championships since the war as most experts' joint-favourite with Plattner to win gold in the amateur event. Had it not been staged at the Oerlikon track in Zurich, with its 44.8-degree bankings, Harris might even have been considered the most likely to triumph. However, located close to the centre of the city, its 333-metre distance made it smaller than most outdoor tracks, and perfectly suited to Plattner's greater technical skill. As a native of Zurich, with his own apartment there, he would also benefit from the support of the crowd and from familiarity with the idiosyncrasies of the track surface. Though concrete, it was badly laid, forcing the back wheel to bounce heavily and making the bike difficult to control. Henri Lemoine, the French cyclist, had recently raced there with a loin of beef sewn into his shorts to cushion his behind from the blows.

The championships retained their pre-war format, too, which meant that riders competed in one-off three-man races – 'three-up' was the technical term – until the quarter-finals where they became two-up and were decided in a best-of-three system (the professional version was two-up throughout). Anybody who lost in an early round was given a second chance to progress through a repêchage race that could involve three or four men. A seeding system ensured Harris and Plattner could not meet before the final. Instead by a quirk of the draw, in the round before the quarter-finals – the round of eighths – Harris was pitched against two Italian riders whom he had beaten only for them to re-emerge through the repêchage, Ferdinando Teruzzi and Fabio Innocenti.

Both were furious at their bad luck and insisted that the organisers had erred by putting them against the same man twice. When their protest was dismissed they refused to race, despite being petitioned by representatives from their own federation to accept their fate. For half an hour, frenzied negotiations ensued, until officials from the sport's ruling body, Union Cycliste Internationale, delivered an ultimatum that said both would be expunged from the competition if they did not take to the start line. Teruzzi agreed, only to suffer another beating, setting up a duel between Harris and the Dutchman Car Byster in the last eight. Possibly because the argument had left Harris with only 15 minutes' recovery time – compared to Byster's 45 – Byster dictated then won their first race, leaving them to contest a decider after Harris drew level in the next with a jump from about 300 yards out.

Before any sprint, the riders drew to decide who had to take the lead from the gun. Given that responsibility for their first race, Byster resumed it for the third, retaining a narrow lead until he attacked halfway down the back straight on the second lap. On such a short track, Harris needed to respond immediately, lest he gave up a critical lead. Instead, he dithered for a few crucial seconds, leaving him to have to try to overtake on the outside of the final turn, a supremely difficult task because the track geometry forced him there to travel a third further than his opponent. The effort cost Harris too much energy for him to get any closer than a length by the finish line.

In his post-race analysis, Harris blamed his defeat solely on the delay, claiming that he had not had sufficient time 'to recover his breathing' but nobody seriously believed that when he was able to win the second race. Harry England, the editor of *Cycling* and probably then Harris's staunchest supporter in the press, captured the general opinion when he suggested that Harris had cracked under the pressure of favouritism – which had suddenly increased once two leading opponents had declared him too good for them to bother even racing him. 'Harris had been told so often that he was a certainty that the truth then whelmed in upon him that he had to win,' England said. 'I don't think he was called upon to race too soon but I think he thought it too soon and, to an artistic temperament such as Harris's, that would be as real as if the facts supported it.'

Put simply, his fear of losing brought on defeat.

Harris was not the only Briton eliminated in a quarter-final at those championships. Tommy Godwin, a rider with the Birmingham Rover club, was defeated at the same stage of the four-kilometre individual pursuit. Their performances were the best from the British team but Godwin had been almost as disappointed as Harris because many had considered him a medal prospect.

Tall, muscular, and boasting formidable stamina, Godwin had emerged as Britain's best long-distance track cyclist during the war. In the past two years he had won three national titles over five and 25 miles, and beaten Harris in the Muratti Cup, even though the Manchester Wheelers had halved its distance to five miles to give their man a better chance of success. Within Britain, Godwin was cultivating a fame comparable to Harris's, with them often topping the same bills, turning up to find spectators shouting their name, and signing autographs when they emerged from dressing rooms. Consequently, he knew Harris as well as any cyclist then. 'I expect next to Reg, I was the biggest draw,' he said. 'I would be the gaffer in the distance races. He would have a good chance in the sprints.'

When I met Godwin in his immaculate house in suburban Solihull, his wife Eileen had been hospitalised after a bad fall (and sadly, would not fully recover, passing away a few months later) yet my host was in stoically welcoming mood.

He began by recalling the compelling circumstances of an expatriate childhood in Massachusetts where he first took up sport in a Connecticut boxing gym, schooled by an overbearing father who wanted his son to learn how to defend himself. At school he was introduced to coaching systems far more advanced than any in Britain, enabling him to train himself once the family returned home to Birmingham and Godwin discovered his talent on a bike. When not working as an electrician, he focused on his sport, devising an idiosyncratic but effective training regime that combined cycling with hours spent on working a punch bag, power walks, breathing exercises and ice skating; unlike running, ice skating builds muscles in a way that is helpful to cyclists. Inviting me upstairs – though aged 91, he was still perfectly mobile – he dug out the tangible rewards for making himself so strong, producing medals and trophies and certificates, all immaculately preserved. He opened up files of photographs, many of Godwin in his prime, others of his best opponents. He read the devotion on one of them. 'To Tommy, our number one five-miler, best regards, Reg Harris,' he said.

His pride here was surprising because Godwin disliked Harris intensely and had twice refused our interview. 'I do not want to be stirring up trouble,' he had said, changing his mind only when I agreed to talk him only about his career. Yet he could not help but bring up his old nemesis as the memories began to flow. 'We were not the best of friends,' he said, even though he attended Harris's wedding. 'We had our ups and downs. There were things that happened that I didn't appreciate or respect him for.'

Godwin and Harris clashed partly, you felt, because – as Shelagh Dennis said – 'they were two big egos' who solicited adulation at the same events. But they were also quite different men. Harris enjoyed the limelight yet in person was reserved and tried to keep much of his life private. He was slow to interject with his opinion when in a group and liked most the company of a small circle of friends. By contrast, Godwin was ebullient, outgoing and sociable. I spoke to several people who knew him and all spoke well of him.

Their familial circumstances were very different, too. Godwin went everywhere with his father and, as a young man, was firmly under his control. In an interview with *The Times*, his eyes welled when he recalled how hard Charles Godwin was on him. By contrast, since returning from the war, Harris had become an arch-individualist and made a virtue of the freedom granted him by Joe Harris's decision to take only a passive role in his life. 'Parents who are over-eager to help their children can do them a great disservice,' Harris said. 'Even those parents who make a point of being present when their offspring is racing are putting a big handicap in their way. The last person a boy needs around him at such times is his father. When he is out on the track in a competition he is on his own.'

Godwin believed that Harris suffered badly for this authority deficit, both on the track and away from it. He hated, for example, that Harris sold his trophies as well as his prizes. To Godwin, this was to disrespect the event. For his part, Harris could not see the reason to keep silverware that represented merely cycling success when it could be upgraded for material wealth. That suggested life success.

Godwin also had carnal temptations in mind. He recalled how his father dragged him from the girls who used to gather after a race to compete for their heroes' attention. 'We'd come out of the dressing room and all the "bobby socks" – the girls – would be there and the old man would be, "Come on, he's got a wife and kid at home, and we've got to catch that 7.20 train",' he said. Godwin claimed Harris felt no such compunction. 'Everybody knew about it,' he said. 'He never tried to cover it. He was just besotted by this idea of women. He loved them and he thought they loved him.'

Godwin knew of three mistresses that Harris kept in London alone. One worked for Swiss Air. 'After one victory at Herne Hill, he presented her with his winner's bouquet at the finish line, even though Flo was watching in the stands. He never seemed to be concerned that people would notice what he was doing.'

Godwin felt that Harris allowed his ethics to slip on the track, too, claiming that he would go to unacceptable lengths to win. This was possibly unfair; everybody broke the rules then.

Yet still he felt justified describing in fine detail some of Harris's unsavoury moves. He recalled how Harris flicked open a pedal strap and tried to claim a technical failure after Godwin had inflicted a rare defeat on him in a 550-yard sprint at Herne Hill. He recounted a Madison race at Fallowfield in which cyclists competed in pairs, accumulating points in interim sprints over a 40-lap event. Apparently Harris pulled on Godwin's saddle just when he was overtaking him, denying Godwin victory. In his fury afterwards, Godwin drew back his arm ready to punch Harris, only for Syd Cozens to hold him back. Had he followed through, the blow would probably not have damaged Harris as much as the insult that Godwin spat during another Madison, this time at Herne Hill. Moving up to Harris's shoulder with both men at full pelt, he said: 'You want a race? Come on then, you bastard.' Godwin used the obscenity for its original meaning. 'I was aware that he was an illegitimate child,' he said. 'Flo had told Eileen years before.'

Dated 1 March 1920, Harris's birth certificate supports this suggestion. For only Elsie has signed it, with the space for his father's name left blank, even though most profiles of Reginald Hargreaves Harris say that he took his first surname from his father. Instead Hargreaves was Elsie's maiden name and possibly her mother's, for the father's signature is missing from her birth certificate, too, with only Suzannah Hargreaves present to witness her daughter's arrival into the world, in Heywood on 30 March 1895. Suzannah listed her occupations as baker and laundress, suggesting that Harris was the poor illegitimate child of a poor illegitimate child.

Godwin and Harris had travelled together to the World Championships in 1946, taking the boat and several trains in a journey that lasted two exhausting days. For the 1947 championships, the NCU told the team that they would have to take similar transport, adding that they could afford to put them up no more than 24 hours before the event. Adamant that he required several days both to get used to a track and to acclimatise to a new city, Harris arranged instead to travel by plane, booking into a different and more expensive hotel to the British team because his was more convenient for Parc des Princes, the venue hosting the event.

Harris loved to compete there. He was no aesthete but he liked Paris and the implied history of its architecture. He thrived on the atmosphere created by the 44,000-strong crowd that the arena could hold, with spectators looking down from the top of the bankings, like the Romans did gladiators. He loved also to race in front of such well-informed fans, who ranked cycling perhaps second only to football among all sports. The track design suited his capabilities, too, with unusually long straights that placed more emphasis on speed than skill. Harris was still not as comfortable as the best foreign riders were on steeped banking, hence he wanted several days to sharpen his touch.

Harris's season had passed impressively. He had retained the national sprint title with a narrow victory over Marshall and followed that with a triumph at Parc des Princes over René Faye, the 23-year-old from Limoges whom the French press had thought to be a future world champion. As if to add to their disappointment, Harris then twice defeated Jacques Lanners, Henri Babinot and Henri Sensever, a trio of French amateurs who toured Britain early in the summer. However, he had struggled on his initial rematches with Byster, losing three times in succession before beating him twice. Afterwards Harry England suggested that the World Championships defeat had spooked Harris, while others claimed that he could not beat Byster if level with him on the home straight. Harris dismissed both complaints. Instead he was relieved to have travelled to Paris with less expected of him as a result. 'Going with less to lose was a tremendous advantage,' he said.

His progress through the competition suggested he was more ruthless than relaxed, though. He qualified for the final unbeaten, but only after having had to re-run two races because he had strayed outside the sprinter's line – the red line that runs 85 centimetres from the inside of the track and marks the area that no competitor can cross in the final 200 metres of a race without a clear lead over his opponent. Designed to improve safety (and extant today), the rule was introduced shortly before the championships, apparently without the NCU informing Harris. 'The officials once again very nearly caused me to lose my chance to win the title,' he said.

Byster qualified from the other side of the draw, though some were concerned whether he would turn up at all. An enigmatic figure, he had failed to appear at several scheduled races during the season and had suffered almost as many surprise defeats as he did wins. Yet always he seemed to produce his best at a major event, relying usually on his ability to sprint very quickly over a short distance. To beat him, Harris knew he had to attack early and exploit his greater reserves of stamina.

In their first race, he picked his moment about 300 metres out, darting down the banking and inside Byster just as he had edged upwards. Executed at the perfect moment, this forced Byster suddenly to change his direction and cost him a crucial second or two. Ahead initially by two lengths, Harris eventually won by three, prompting journalists to attribute to him a recent addition to their lexicon: 'the killer instinct', which Harris assumed was inspired by the war. Conflict had normalised his pitilessness.

Drawn as the lead-out man in the next race, Harris left nothing to chance and wound up almost to maximum speed at the bell. Byster stayed with him for three-quarters of the lap but was bereft of all acceleration by the finishing straight. In a venue that was once a park preserved for nobility, and later Parisian aristocracy, Harris had claimed the title that he long dreamed about in the hope that it would elevate him to a new class. 'As I stood watching the Union Jack climbing the flag-pole, listening to the strains of "God Save the King", I felt deeply moved,' he said. 'It would have been wonderful to have won in 1946, the thrill could never have been as special as it was now.'

On a crisp, clear evening the following January, a group of officials gathered at the Wheelers' smoke-clouded dining club to pay tribute to their new world champion. With Harris seated at the top table, and Florence beside him, the Wheelers board member Sidney Bowkett began the first speech by putting Harris's achievement in its historical perspective, reminding the audience that only twice before had Britain produced a world champion sprinter on the track: Bailey and Thomas 'Tiny' Johnson, the brilliant Fulham rider who triumphed in 1922. Frank Urry, representing the Midlands Cycling and Athletic Club, followed that by praising Harris's 'sartorial splendour'; as usual when now in public, Harris was clad in a three-piece suit – this one tweed. In a long night of devotions, Tom MacDonald, the Wheelers president and Harris's closest friend in the club, then turned to opinion of Harris abroad, quoting the celebrated French sports journalist Jacques Goddet. 'Harris was so good now to be unbeatable,' he had written. 'There should be an age limit for amateurs, after which a rider who wants to continue his sprinting activities must turn professional.' MacDonald thought this highly amusing. 'They have given up on even hoping that they might beat Reg,' he said. In what Harry England promised would be the final encomium, the *Cycling* editor said Harris had 'elevated the standing' of the forthcoming London Olympics. He hoped his friend would postpone turning professional so that he could compete in the Games, then open only to amateurs. 'They are the pinnacle for any athlete,' he said. 'And Reg would head to them as the country's best chance of gold.'

For Harris this decision was not straightforward. His ultimate ambition had always been to turn professional. Its competitors were regarded as the sport's kingpins. They were paid handsome appearance fees across Europe almost every week

RIGHT: A young Reg Harris with his mother, Elsie, in 1926.

BELOW: Harris with his mother and stepfather, Joe Harris, circa 1920s.

JIM LOVE ARCHIVE

MARILYN HUGHES

TOP LEFT: At Herne Hill riding for the Manchester Wheelers, 1939.

ABOVE: Harris in uniform. He served in Africa with the 10th Royal Hussars during the Second World War before being discharged as medically unfit in 1943.

LEFT: Reg and his first wife Florence on their wedding day, 7 April 1945.

MARILYN HUGHES

RIGHT: Already practising for fame – a studio portrait of Harris, taken in 1945.

BELOW AND BOTTOM RIGHT: Harris displays his physique as part of a study for Sir Adolphe Abrahams, the founder of modern sports medicine in Britain, who described Harris as being built like an engine. Harris's incredible thigh power and ripped quadriceps would rival even today's elite cyclists.

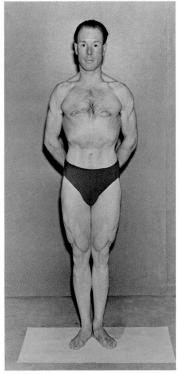

ABOVE: Harris was criticised by some as being cold towards his mother, Elsie. But in private he was an affectionate son, as this picture shows.

BELOW: Polishing his trophies with his young family.

TOP: Finally wearing the rainbow jersey after winning his first world title in the amateur sprint. Paris, 1947.

ABOVE: Back where it all started, giving a roller racing demonstration in the world champion's jersey – as a teenager, Harris discovered his talent for sprinting on a similar device.

RIGHT: Harris featuring on a souvenir copy of a Manchester track racing programme in 1948, now billed as the 'sprint champion of the world'.

ABOVE: Harris looking relaxed as he is greeted by fans on arriving for the 1948 Olympics.

OLYMPIC GAMES

29 JULY 1948 14 AUGUST
LONDON

ABOVE: Although he had high hopes of winning gold at the London Olympics, Harris was beaten by the 19-year-old Italian Mario Ghella in the individual sprint, with Harris taking silver.

RIGHT: On the podium with Ghella and Axel Schandorff who took bronze. Years later, Harris said of his silver medal, 'Wins are what you fight to achieve … anything less than gold is such a disappointment … and I had a token to mark the failure.'

BELOW: Harris and Alan Bannister racing in the tandem. They were beaten by Italians Renato Perona and Ferdinando Teruzzi, leaving Harris to claim his second silver medal.

BELOW: Harris and his great rival Arie van Vliet prepare to race in the semi-finals of the 1949 World Championships in Copenhagen in Harris's first year as a professional.

BELOW: Waving to the crowd after defeating Jan Derksen (2nd) and Van Vliet (3rd) to become professional world champion for the first time.

ABOVE: Again racing against Van Vliet who was now reigning world champion after winning the title in 1953.

RIGHT: Harris celebrates his fifth and final world title in Cologne in 1954, reclaiming the rainbow jersey from Van Vliet. British team manager Benny Foster is on Harris's right.

and enjoyed lucrative sponsorship deals. But it was not easy to break into their ranks. With room for only about two dozen track sprinters, an aspiring professional faced fierce competition simply to secure a place on the bill, let alone to win races. To establish himself on the scene, he had to travel constantly and betray significantly improved technical skill. One professional said: 'You must be prepared to fight tooth and nail, bite your lips to the point of pain. You learn in a school that gives no quarter in events. You learn five or six languages. On the track the tactics will chill your bones. There is no season and life is continuous training.'

To nail down the best contracts possible, the best time to graduate was after winning the world amateur title, yet Harris understood that 1948 might present his last chance to compete in an Olympics. He knew also that he could realistically hope to win three events there: the sprint, the kilometre time trial and the tandem. Perhaps most attractively, he would be competing on Herne Hill in front of his fans. After months in which the cycling press speculated about his decision, he had promised to reveal it at this evening's Wheelers event. 'I joined the club as a nobody,' he said. 'Throughout the war the Wheelers were the only cycling people to maintain contact with me. Last year when I was beaten you supported me. I am still the same Wheelers boy and you are my friends.' His audience applauded, knowing that this was as much barbed criticism of the NCU as it was tribute to them. 'I will look for your advice, then, when I represent the country this summer at Herne Hill.'

CHAPTER 5
1947

Florence was not so much upset as alarmed by the letter that Harris's discarded conquest had posted to their home. In a desperately sad missive, its heartbroken author was threatening to commit suicide if Harris would not accept her back. 'You need to contact this woman, Reg,' Florence insisted, unsuccessfully.

By now Florence was accustomed to Harris's infidelities. Sometimes she discovered them through gossips in the town. Almost as often Harris blithely relayed his latest success. 'Oh Flo, I think I have fallen in love again,' he would say on his return from another cycling trip that had taken in his other favourite physical pursuit. He seemed not to mind that he was casually breaking Florence's heart.

She had tried leaving him several times only to be persuaded back. He insisted that she meant everything to him and that the other women meant nothing. Despite his behaviour, Florence still loved him and you did not break up your marriage easily then.

However, in the winter of 1947, Harris's emotional commitment began to waver when he met Dorothy Hadfield on the platform at Macclesfield train station. She was heading to London. Harris was travelling to a race with Bill Brown. He did not need much encouragement once a pretty girl had fallen within his radar. 'He was a bit of a charmer,' Brown said, adding that Hadfield was a local beauty queen though I am not sure that is true. I heard several of Harris's girlfriends described as such but never found evidence for their success. Either there is an unwritten history of pageantry in England's north-west or his mistresses were so attractive that men assumed their looks had won reward.

Hadfield was certainly attractive, though, elegant and slim, with prominent cheekbones and pretty eyes. 'She reminded me of a famous model called Barbara Goalen,' Shelagh Dennis said, touching her cheek at the memory of Dorothy's skin. 'She was blond and smooth.' Her father, Harry, sold fruit and vegetables on a market stall and they lived in a modest terrace in Macclesfield, but she aspired to a much finer life. She liked expensive clothes and loved to eat out. The blunt edges of her Cheshire accent had begun to smooth.

Tommy Godwin recalled an incident that captured the difference between her and Harris's wife. 'Reg brought Florence a wonderful dress home on one occasion, and said, "I bought this to go to the Manchester Wheelers celebration dinner." She said,

"I'm not made for this sort of thing. I'm not that type of girl."
She was a bit too laid-back. Reg was a high flier. He wasn't satisfied with his life with Florence.'

Perhaps for that reason, Harris did not want to lure Florence
back when she left him again. Instead he changed the locks to
their home as if to ensure there could be no rapprochement.
Before long he was living with Hadfield instead. 'That was scan-
dalous in '47, if somebody left their wife and went to live with
somebody else, without marrying them,' Dennis said. But
Dorothy fitted more easily the template Harris had laid out for
his life. She was more inclined than Florence to travel abroad,
too. She even shared his passion for fast cars and proudly took
up position in the passenger seat of his handsome new silver
Wolseley as they prepared to leave for the 1948 Good Friday
Meeting at Herne Hill.

This was Harris's second car. The engine in his first, a Ford
V8 Pilot, had blown up shortly after purchase, prompting him
to upgrade to one of the most coveted marques then, a handsome machine, with body panels that it shared with the MG, the
classic Wolseley bonnet and grille – think mobster's car in 1930s
Chicago – and an interior that combined polished wood detailing
and pigskin seats. With 33 horse power, it was not the fastest in
the Wolseley range but Harris found it eased sweetly through to
90mph at a time when speed restrictions applied only on urban

roads. He was threatening that speed when he crashed on the A52 near Abingdon, shortly after leaving Hadfield's home, flipping the car over several times and leaving its passengers trapped and motionless.

By terrible coincidence, Harry Hadfield was first to the scene, driving past on his commute home. He found Dorothy unconscious, head lolled to the side, like a ragdoll. Harris was awake, panicked and unable to move his legs. 'What have you done, Reg?' Harry said.

Years later Harris would deny responsibility for what happened, claiming that one articulated lorry had tried to overtake another and forced him from the road. Geldard, a friend to the couple, remembered differently. 'When Reg drove a car, he drove fast,' he said. 'He would speed. Today he wouldn't last long before he got his 12 points. That crash was all his own fault. He was forced to go into a gateway or opening, turning off the road because there was a car coming towards him. There were no motorways then and roads in those days were two-lane roads. If you had somebody coming towards you when you were speeding, where else do you go?'

Other people who served as Harris's passenger recalled his approach to driving similarly. Neville Tong, a former Empire Games champion, said: 'He was very aggressive. He thought he was the only man allowed on the road. We went down to London one day. He clipped another car. I had a look and pointed it out, but he said, "Well, he shouldn't be in the way." And that was it. There was a bit of the back wing gone. He didn't stop.' Norman Sheil represented the British track team in this era. He described Harris as an 'absolute idiot driver', recalling an encounter Harris had with a policeman who had pulled him over for speeding. Having talked himself out of a punishment, Harris said to the officer: 'Do you want to go first or shall I give you a head start?' Geldard recalled how Harris would look for other car-owning cyclists to race en route to a meeting.

On this occasion, though, his recklessness had cost him dearly. The couple were swiftly taken to Derby Royal Infirmary to endure what must have been among the longest nights of their lives. Dorothy drifted in and out of consciousness, only coming round properly near dawn to discover she had facial injuries, a broken wrist and a sprained ankle. Harris had fractured two verte-brae. He was expected to recover but doctors ruled out him cycling competitively again for several months.

He demanded a second opinion, then a third. After several days in a hospital occupied mostly by local miners who had suffered subterranean injuries, he eventually found a surgeon, Ian Fletcher, who was at least prepared to encourage him to become slowly active again, giving Harris gentle tensing exercises that would strengthen the muscles supporting his damaged spine. Fletcher would not go so far as to rekindle Harris's dream but he at least wanted the patient protected if he was to persist with it.

Later Harris claimed he was interned about a month but he loved to dramatise the truth. Instead, he subverted medical advice and discharged himself after little more than a week in hospital, signing a document that waived staff of any responsibility should he suffer a setback. When he was photographed on a tentative training ride within another couple of weeks, people wondered if he had exaggerated his complaint. Though Geldard was not taken in by Harris's white lies, he understood otherwise. 'He had various crashes but within about a month he would be back winning again. It's not that he was faking it. It shows his utter determination to get to where he wanted to be. It was his life's goal to be the world's best sprinter.'

He was back competing but his performances were far from consistent. He lowered the lap record at the Butts track in Coventry to 34.8 seconds and beat Marshall to win the Victory Cup at Herne Hill. He claimed two easy wins on the grass on the Isle of Man yet also lost in Doncaster to an unknown club rider named Len Turner and was eliminated in the heats of an 880-yard handicap at Bourneville, later refusing to emerge for his second race. Harris put that down to a 'misunderstanding', though most assumed he was too concerned by his form to risk losing again. With the date approaching on which the NCU would announce their Olympic selection, there was talk that Harris had not allowed his back to heal, assigning added significance to his first major race at Fallowfield since the crash.

Even Harris was surprised by the interest in the Muratti Cup meeting on Saturday, 10 July 1948. A few miles away, England were battling Don Bradman's 'Invincibles' in the third Ashes Test, the most excitedly awaited sporting event of the Manchester summer. It attracted more than 133,000 spectators but still Fallowfield turned people away from its comparatively modest event, leaving fans to trudge back disconsolately along Moseley Road just as Harris was passing them in the other direction in the saddle. The roads were so busy that he had been unable to turn up in his new car, a silver MG (to the back of which he usually tethered his bike, precariously).

His principal events passed pleasingly. To the delight of the estimated 18,000 fans, he won the 1,000-yard sprint without great difficultly, beating the Dane Axel Schandorff in the semi-final and Alan Bannister in the deciding contest. That avenged the shock defeat that Bannister had inflicted on Harris in the final of the National Championship and, given Harris's greater pedigree, was almost certainly enough to propel him ahead of his clubmate in the race for the one sprinter's spot in the Olympic team. As if to confirm his good form, Harris then won the 550-yard sprint, too, leaving the Muratti race as his only remaining commitment.

'I'm pulling out,' he told MacDonald shortly before the race was due to begin.

The Wheelers chairman was upset. He had promised spectators an illustrious field and Harris held the most attraction of all those entered.

But he was insistent. 'It's five miles. I won't win it. It'll put me at risk. And, besides, you've paid off the Danes.'

This was true. Desperate for Godwin not to win what would be his third Muratti, the Wheelers had bribed the three Danes involved to team up against the reigning champion – as they later admitted to him.

'If Tommy finds out, he'll get the Brits on his side,' Harris said. 'It will be carnage.'

MacDonald drew a breath. He knew better than to get angry; Harris responded best to diplomacy. 'But your name is on the card, Reg,' he said. 'We've promised these people that you'll compete. You don't need to win. Coast it, avoid the trouble.' The tactic worked. Harris did nothing that might undermine his reputation with fans, but he had reason to regret the decision within the first few laps. Tucked in behind Geldard, his teammate's front tyre blew, forcing both men to crash, sending them sprawling to the ground. Harris responded furiously, spitting insults at Geldard for using what Harris felt was a tyre unsuited to the surface, even though that was hardly unusual then. Even the best riders used whatever equipment they could lay hands on. But every cyclist hated to crash, particularly one as proud as Harris. An accident reflected badly on your technique, suggesting that you had failed either to anticipate or to react to a situation properly. 'That's where his nasty side came out,' Geldard said, bristling at the memory. 'I did something purely accidental. You accept that you are going to get more punctures on red shale on a concrete or asphalt track. You couldn't help it, but that was Harris.'

His anger was soon submerged by pain. A photograph taken moments later shows Harris being led from the track. On his right is an official, one hand placed on Harris's back, providing emotional support. To his left, a St John's Ambulanceman – they were ever-present at the track – is cradling Harris's arm. It is bent. His helmet is lopsided. He looks ashen-faced, as if the implication of what has just happened is draining the life force from him. The medical staff rushed him to Manchester Infirmary.

At the time, Harris insisted his wrist was badly sprained. Later he claimed an X-ray had revealed a fracture at the tip of the radial bone. He even named the surgeon who examined him, Lloyd Griffiths, suggesting that Harris had played down his injury to ensure that he was selected for the Games. For he was not going to allow another damaged bone to quell that ambition just yet, regardless that the competition began in a fortnight. 'I've got to do all I can to be able to compete,' Harris told Griffiths.

The British public mostly disapproved when its government accepted the International Olympic Committee's offer to host the 1948 Games because it had been denied the privilege four years earlier. To be willing to stage an event that would cost £750,000 (about £20 million in 2010) seemed foolish when people were still having to survive on food and energy rations, when two million were unemployed, when a housing shortage had yet to be resolved and while Prime Minister Clement Attlee was investing millions in the creation of the welfare state that would include the institution of the National Health Service. As the *Evening Standard* wrote in September 1947: 'The average range of British enthusiasm for the Games stretches from lukewarm to dislike. It is not too late for invitations to be politely withdrawn.'

As the date approached for the competition, however, the public mood began to turn. Partly they were enthused by the trials that different sports held in the months leading up to the Games. Thousands turned up at White City Stadium to watch track and field athletes compete for a place in the British squad. Over a succession of Sundays through the summer of 1948 you could watch the best cyclists in the country do battle at Herne Hill for the same privilege. Crowds swelled at Henley Regatta knowing that its events would play the most prominent role in selectors' decision-making. Gradually people became enthused by the rare privilege of being able to watch the world's best sportsmen and women in competition. A public address from King George VI encouraging his subjects to support the Games helped, too. As Dorothy Tyler, a high-jump competitor from London, said: 'The Games felt like the light coming out after the dark days of war.'

As the athletes arrived from overseas in the weeks leading up to the Games, they helped to lend parts of the city a new cosmopolitan complexion. There were almost 4,000 in total, with the men put up in RAF digs in Uxbridge and Richmond, and the women staying in accommodation around the city centre. Tyler recalled how few hours were spent training, leaving time to socialise and go sightseeing. 'London's streets are made daily more picturesque by the groups of people from other lands,' the editorial in *The Bicycle* said. 'Many are cyclists, others are doing their best on hired machines. This is our opportunity to extend to the visitors the warm hand of comradeship.'

The men of the British track cycling team were spared the trip from west London to Herne Hill by Bill Mills, a cycling journalist, who offered to put them up in his house on Half Moon Lane, within walking distance from the track. There they slept on camp beds laid out on the floor while Godwin's mother joined them to provide meals, cooking spam fritters for breakfast and toad in the hole for tea. In photographs of the team larking about on Mills's lawn, dressed in short-sleeved shirts and smart shorts, they look relaxed, even carefree. As Godwin said, they did not know any better because they were used to austerity. They were not surprised, however, that such accommodation had not met with Harris's approval and that he had booked into his favourite hotel in St John's Wood instead. 'Harris saw himself on a pedestal and we were down there, the ordinary guys,' Godwin, the team captain, said. This was possibly harsh. Harris just liked his luxuries, insisting the hotel was a 'home from home for me'.

Managed by Bill Bailey, with Harry Ryan as his assistant, the track team was required to spend each day of the fortnight before the Games at Herne Hill for what was billed as training but was really last-minute trials. Bailey had not yet decided which of the six cyclists in the team pursuit should make the final quartet and wanted them to race against one another to help him decide. 'We should really have been working on tactics,' Geldard said.

Harris had also to undergo a trial for he had been picked in the individual sprint and the tandem on the condition that he proved his fitness during this period. To his disgust, he had been overlooked for the kilometre time trial because it was scheduled to take place immediately after the tandem event, leaving Godwin to fill the spot instead.

Harris did not arrive at Herne Hill until a week into their preparations, quietly slipping into a seat in the grandstand beside Harry England.

'The place looks good,' Harris said.

'It should. It cost them three grand,' his friend said.

The old Victorian venue had needed renovation even before the war and had rapidly deteriorated during it once the government demanded that it was given over to the storage of barrage balloons, damaging the track and leaving weeds to take root around the apron and through the cracks in the track surface. On being chosen as an Olympic venue, however, it had been given funds for a complete makeover. The track was relaid in bitumen. The existing stand was repaired and repainted. A temporary one was built along the back straight. Gates and turnstiles were replaced. Press facilities were improved, too, with telephone boxes erected behind the reporters' seats. For the finishing touch, flags from each of the countries represented were hoisted around the perimeter of the track.

Now the competitors from those nations were taking turns to prepare for the four events ahead.

'The Danes look good,' England said. The Danish team always looked good. The Danish federation ensured their team wanted for nothing. They had been following a training regime tailored for the Games since winter. They did gymnastics, hand-ball and cross-country skiing – as well as their own sport – improving dexterity, coordination and stamina respectively.

'What about the Italians?'

'Guerra, the reserve, just did a 12.5 split. Ghella, the young lad, went faster: 12 and 12.4. They keep asking about you.'

Harris's one appearance since his crash had brought mixed results. Competing at the Westoe Cricket Ground in South Shields, his first appearance on Tyneside, he won the one-lap sprint in a track record but was then humiliated by a local rider in his next event after failing to follow an early attack. He subsequently with-drew from an event in Bootle for reasons that were not made public. When he had failed to turn up to training at Herne Hill, speculation had grown that he was struggling to get fit.

By now the competitors and their entourages had begun to spot Harris in the stand. A few had pointed at him, talking in whispers. Others could not keep their eyes away from him. Harris got up, stepped over the white picket fence that fringed the grandstand, picked up his bike and waited for them to clear the track. Turning to England, he said: 'I'd better give them their answer then.'

His performance was perfect. Taking only a short break between his two sprints, he exactly matched Mario Ghella's times, then promptly departed the track, passing word to England that he was returning to Manchester. He asked him to tell Bailey.

Returning first to his hotel, Harris found the team manager had requested a phone call. 'Reg, I am demanding that you stay in London,' Bailey said. 'Nobody is exempt from team instructions.'

'I've proven my fitness. I'm going home for the week. That will be the best way for me to prepare.'

Harris gave a litany of reasons. A heatwave had broken and he would rather train in the cooler climate of the north-west, even though it was only a few degrees cooler than in the south. He insisted that he would rather practise on Mauldeth Road with his trusted partners, away from the busy Olympic venue. He said that he was an 'individualist who had achieved in the past by acting in isolation'. Turning to the tandem, he pointed out that Bannister felt there was no need for them to train (which was true).

He necessarily avoided the truth. Harris did not want to train at Herne Hill because he did not want opponents – or the British selectors – to realise that he was struggling for fitness and could not perform more than a few sprints in succession without suffering a sharp decline. 'I was temporarily but a shadow of myself,' he said, later, with typical formality. 'It seemed to me poor strategy to be carrying out my training routine on a track where the terraces were lined with all the other riders and officials from the competing nations. That's a great thing if you're going to destroy everybody in sight and demoralise the entire entry. But I wasn't really that good.'

He received another phone call when he arrived home shortly before midnight, this time from Mills, who also served as secretary of the Olympic Training Committee. 'You've broken training, Reg,' he said. 'I'm afraid I've been instructed to tell you that you must report back to the track by midday tomorrow.'

'Or what?'

'I'd rather not speculate.'

Harris was training in Manchester when the deadline passed. He received another call the following afternoon. The issue had been escalated to Adrian Chamberlin, the committee chairman. 'If you're not back by six this evening, Reg, you'll be slung out of the team,' he said. Months earlier, Chamberlin had promised that not one Olympic cycling title 'would leave these shores', yet now he was threatening to block Britain's most likely winner from competing at all.

'Well, if you do that, you'll have to satisfy this country that you've got somebody better to put into it,' Harris said.

By the following morning, there were reporters outside Harris's house. By the next day it had become the headline story of the Games regardless that other events had already begun, with the *Daily Express* and the *Daily Mirror*, the leading mass-market papers, covering the impasse on their front page. The *Mirror* used the headline: 'Harris: I'll train my way or not at all.' It quoted him: 'Unless I can train with my own lads here on the ground I've used for 16 years, I can't get Olympic form. If the worst comes, I'll sit in the stand.'

By now everybody knew of the NCU's threat but fierce opposition had delayed them going through with it. Most persuasively, the National Association of Cycle Traders had suddenly threatened to hold back half of the £850 they had promised to an Olympic training fund that had already been spent (on, among other rare privileges, sunbed sessions to increase the team's vitamin D levels). Christopher Woodard, the team doctor, had spoken out in support of Harris, insisting that he would benefit from a week at home (though their friendship possibly informed his stance). Published on the Wednesday of that week – the day of the NCU's second deadline – the cycling press had criticised the NCU for being overly bureaucratic. Lord Burghley, the chairman of the Olympics, had also expressed his disquiet. As Harris was Britain's only world champion in an Olympic event, everybody but cycling officialdom wanted him to compete.

The third phone call came from Tom MacDonald. By now nobody within the NCU was prepared to talk to Harris directly. 'They're offering a compromise,' he said. 'They want you to stage a race-off with Banny.'

'What? For the sprint?'

'Yes, at Herne Hill tomorrow evening, 6 p.m.'

The race was supposed to be secret but there were several hundred spectators at the track by the time Harris turned up in his MG, among them reporters from the national press. They were the first to approach him – he always gave great quotes. 'It's ridiculous to say my actions upset the rest of the team,' he declared. 'I'm not a member of a team. I'm an individual sprinter and I can't see that any grown man should be upset by what I've done.' They then approached his passenger for a response but made the mistake of referring to Dorothy as his wife. 'I'm not Mrs Harris,' she said before refusing further comment, leaving one article to describe her instead as the 'tall blond in black'.

Inside the apron Bannister had been waiting patiently with the other members of the team. Short, wiry and a pound under ten stone, Bannister cut a very different figure from Harris, both physically and temperamentally. He worked as an engineer and insisted he was motivated more by his job than cycling, saying before the Olympics that his greatest ambition in sport was to complete a 24-hour time trial. He preferred to detract attention away from himself. He was popular with teammates but modest to a fault.

Harris felt he could intimidate him. He rang him before their race-off, expressing his incredulity that Bannister should even think that he might defeat him, regardless that he had once that season. 'If I've got to come down and demonstrate my ability to beat you, it will do no good to either of us,' Harris had said. Probably for the same reason, he had brought with him to Herne Hill the new Raleigh that he planned to unveil at the Games – he was prepared to do anything to sow doubt in Bannister's mind. Thus, leading the first race, he produced every tactical trick he could summon. He stopped then started. He went snail slow, accelerated suddenly, then wound down again. He snaked up and down the bankings.

It was almost excruciating to watch. He was dictating Bannister's physical movements much as a cruel child would his carefully trained pet, trying not to force Bannister into the lead but attempting merely to unnerve him. Once he was finally confident that Bannister's confidence was shot, he attacked, exploiting his teammate's hesitation to win by several lengths. The second race followed much the same pattern as the first. 'At that critical time, Bannister was fitter and faster than Harris,' Geldard said. 'But Harris won that selection by sheer personality. Bannister was a completely different sort of person and Harris dominated him tactically.' Godwin confirmed Geldard's account. 'Bannister was a very edgy guy and a nervous wreck. He was nowhere near the lad we had been watching for the past couple of weeks.'

For the third time, then, Harris had resuscitated his Olympic dream just when it appeared to be dying, albeit this time at a cost.

For, less than 48 hours before the first race, Bailey resigned in protest at Harris's selection. Adamant that Harris should have been dropped, the team manager felt his authority had been irrevocably undermined. 'I believe that no matter how good a man is, no matter what titles he holds, he should be prepared to cast aside all claims to individual attention and become a team rider when occasion demands,' Bailey said. He was not prepared even to attend the competition. 'I have finished completely with cycle racing government and the NCU.'

He held to that promise, too, ensuring that the first great hero of British cycling had been forced to quit the sport by the incumbent.

CHAPTER 6
1948

By the end of the first week of the Olympics, Britain was still searching for its first champion. The athlete Alastair McCorquodale, their great hope in the sprint, had finished only fourth in the 100 metres final. Some thought Lloyd Johnson could emulate his brother Harold by winning the 50-kilometre walk, just as the latter had done in the 1936 Games. But Johnson, too, finished one place outside the medals. In a sold-out Wembley Stadium, the British women had won three silver medals, with Dorothy Manley finishing behind the great Fanny Blankers-Koen in the 100 metres, and Audrey Williams and Maureen Gardner claiming the runners-up spot in the 200 metres and 80-metre hurdles, respectively, fine achievements and not widely expected. Aside from a bronze in the swimming from the Scotswoman Catherine Gibson, however, that was the sum of the host nation's podium appearances to date. As a result, by the time Harris arrived at Herne Hill on the Monday of the second week, the hope that he might finally break the gold duck had amplified.

The velodrome looked handsome in the morning sun. Fans filled the two grandstands and lined the grass bankings. Thousands had turned up on bikes, depositing them on the grass beside the track, leaving them unlocked, confident that they would still be there on their return. A café had been set up for the event, brewing coffee and tea and serving hot sandwiches, lacing the air with enticing aromas. With a thermometer track-side touching 80 degrees, you could occasionally see the surface softening beneath the cyclists' tyres as Harris arrived at the start line for his race against the Australian Charlie Bazzano. The venue's construction crew had not anticipated such prolonged good weather when they laid their tarmac.

Despite his fears, Harris had progressed serenely through the preliminary rounds two days earlier. He began by defeating the long-limbed Indian cyclist R. Mullafiroze in two hopelessly one-sided races and dispatched Mario Masanés with similar ease. Thriving in the equatorial heat, the young Chilean had shocked seasoned observers by defeating the French champion Jacques Bellenger, but was sorely exposed by Harris's immaculate tactics. In the first race, he jumped on the railway banking – the line ran just behind it – to open up an unassailable lead on the back straight. In the second, he sold Masanés a feint at the bell then surged past him on the home straight like an intercity express. 'Yes, I think I'll win, but from now on I'm adopting a lips-sealed policy,' he told reporters afterwards. Finally he was tired of the attention that the row had focused on him.

On the other side of the draw, Ghella, aged only 19, had confirmed the promise he had displayed in practice, needing only four races to eliminate the Canadian Bob Lacourse and the dangerous American Jackie Heid, in each case with almost an identical tactic. While his opponents' attempts to unsettle Ghella consisted of weaving around the track, he simply rode steadily until 300 metres out, then unleashed a devastating sprint. Few cyclists could hold their top speed for that long but, clearly, he had an unusual strength.

In the semi-final, Ghella faced Axel Schandorff. In usual circumstances, the Dane's greater experience would have made him favourite, but he had suffered a traumatic build-up to the Games, undergoing several blood transfusions only weeks earlier in an unsuccessful attempt to save his elderly father's life. That he lost to Ghella by only a wheel in their first race was to his credit. That he was easily beaten by the Italian's near-explicable power in the next was not much worse than Schandorff could realistically have expected. Harris whitewashed Bazzano, too, producing the final that everybody in attendance had wanted.

Maurice Jefferies, then an emerging pursuit rider, was among them. He had volunteered to work as a steward and recalled showing the UCI president Achille Joinard to his seat, though he was interested only in the event ahead. 'The main thing was Harris was going to win,' he said. Brian Annable, who much later would mentor Sir Chris Hoy at the Edinburgh Cycling Club, recalled the build-up similarly. He had spent two days cycling from Leicester for the event, sleeping with friends in a farm barn because they could not find digs. 'I was on the railway banking, standing in the trees,' he said. 'There were thousands of us, umpteen deep, all standing. The atmosphere was unbelievable.'

Harris arrived first to the start line, right on time. Smiling, his back bolt straight, he looked relaxed. Dressed in black shorts and the heavy woollen top supplied by the NCU – it was designed for road riding, thus wholly unsuitable for the track – he even found time to exchange a few waves with the crowd. His countenance worsened, however, during the ten minutes that passed before Ghella was carried out from the dressing room beneath the stand, his arms flanked over the shoulders of the two burly minders either side of him while a third Italian wheeled his bike. Legs dangling in the air, his face sullen and drawn, Ghella looked like a house-fire victim being transported to safety.

John Dennis was reporting on the event. When I asked for his interpretation of the peculiar spectacle, he shot an imaginary syringe through his arm. Alan Geldard said: 'They didn't want it pumping through his system till he needed it. He was doped to the eyeballs.'

Slowly, they placed Ghella on the bike, then went through an overly elaborate examination of it. They claimed his back wheel needed inflating and that his pedal cleat had fallen loose. These were elementary oversights that the Italians would never usually commit, suggesting that they were trying to unnerve Harris. In response, he lifted his foot and theatrically asked a bystander to check his sole, too. 'Reg was no mug,' Annable said. 'Once Ghella was strapped in, he walked off and pretended he had something wrong with his bike. He wasn't going to be psyched out.'

A photograph of the incident shows Harris sitting beside the outside lane, arms around his knees, apparently no more troubled than a bored schoolboy at assembly. But he did not know about the lengths to which Ghella's coach Giovanni Proietti had prepared for this event.

Using contacts in England, Proietti had compiled a dossier detailing Harris's performances in each of his prestigious races over the previous 12 months, breaking down his strengths, weaknesses and the tactics that he most often applied. Clearly, he had found (correctly) that – despite his showboating – Harris was unnerved when any aspect of the build-up to a race did not run as he wished. Just as wisely, Proietti had sent Ghella to train apart from the national team at Piacenza because of all the velodromes in Italy it most closely resembled Herne Hill, with its concrete surface, flat straights and 33-degree bankings on its turns. After warm-weather training in northern Africa over the winter, the coach had scaled back his handsome rider's private life, too, to the point that he said it was 'practically non-existent'.

Such attention to detail might explain why a flicker of surprise swept across Harris's face when he felt at close proximity the force of Ghella's jump 300 metres from the end of their first race. Perhaps in trying to comprehend such speed, Harris momentarily hesitated and was trailing by five lengths by the turn. He eventually ceded defeat 50 yards from the finish line, sitting up in his saddle to the disbelief of the crowd. Later Harris would claim that his injuries were beginning to tell. He said his back was sore and stiff and that the anaesthetic on his wrist had failed to dull the pain. That might have been true but it was clear in the second race that he still had much energy in reserve.

Leading them out, Ghella tracked a slow course around the outside lane, occasionally slowing almost to a standstill in the hope that Harris would accept the silent invitation to swap positions. He refused, instead laying off Ghella by about five lengths for the first lap, then drawing a little closer as they entered the critical point in the race on the penultimate bend.

When Ghella jumped this time, Harris was prepared, staying within his slipstream for 50 yards, before dipping outside to launch a second attack, then a third. Julio César León, the Venezuelan cyclist who had been eliminated in the preliminary rounds, was among the crowd. 'It was like something out of a movie,' he said, through a translator. 'The two of them were of equal standard but Ghella was shorter than Harris and flatter across the frame, so he had a way of cutting more sharply through the wind in the last 100 metres.'

Some in the crowd were entranced. Others shouted encouragement as Harris passed, desperately trying to will him into the lead. They failed. 'I had read about Harris's legend back home and he did not disappoint. You could see the strength of his character,' León said, unaware that chemicals might have influenced the race. 'But Ghella was just a little too good.'

Proietti and his back-up staff swarmed the finish line. *Cycling* magazine noted with incredulity how they 'showered their man with kisses' before hoisting Ghella onto their shoulders in celebration. Harris marched straight to the sanctuary of the dressing room, desperate for privacy, but he had not reckoned with the persistence of the national press. Its reporters found him alone apart from a swarm of bees that had also infiltrated the facility. A policeman was called to disperse the insects but the brief proved beyond him. Much arm-flapping ensued. It seemed Harris could not even lose without some theatrical setback. 'I am certain no other English rider could have done better,' he said, finally. 'The accidents that I have had this season caused me to lose a lot of international racing. That is worth more than weeks of training. I think I shall beat Ghella in the World Championships in Amsterdam.' Before that competition, however, he had to contest the tandem alongside the man he had humiliated only a few days previously. It began in a few hours' time.

Tandem partners in modern track cycling are chosen carefully. Usually they are a similar weight and height to ensure an even distribution across the frame. Harris and Bannister had been pitched together simply because they were the fastest men in their club, yet somehow they gelled. Because of his size, Bannister rode 'stoker', putting his head down and pedalling furiously. He was light with fast feet and fitted snugly behind Harris. As front man, the more decisive Harris dictated tactics and provided most of the explosive power that fired their finishing sprint. Few words passed between them in their opening rounds but they performed sufficiently to reach a semi-final the following Wednesday against Gaston Dron and René Faye, the Frenchmen who were the pre-competition favourites for gold. In a two-kilometre event, the British pair surprised them by winning the first race and were preparing to attack in the second when their front tyre punctured, forcing them to career terrifyingly across over the track.

Through its increased weight, a crash on a tandem was potentially much more dangerous than on an ordinary bike. As Geoff Cooke, former manager of the national team, said, 'You're going a second quicker than solo and there are two of you so when you go down, you go down. It takes great courage to ride it.' With a damaged wrist, it took great courage from Harris to keep it upright, too. Pain surged through his arm but he knew their hopes rested on him retaining control. 'It was full on, they swerved a lot, Harris twisted his shoulder holding it up,' Annable said. As always with a puncture, the official called a re-run by which time Harris had recovered sufficiently to help them secure another victory.

The Italian pair Renato Perona and Ferdinando Teruzzi had dominated the other side of the draw. In their first race, they covered the final 200 metres in 11.2 seconds, still the quickest time of the event. In their semi-final they had completed a 2–0 win with a six-length thrashing of Jean Roth and Max Aeberli of Switzerland. Teruzzi, the sprint champion of Lombardy, had especially impressed. As pilot, he steered the bike through the track as smoothly as an eel travelled through reeds. In the Italians' first race of the final, however, he met his tactical match when Harris drew the sting from an Italian attack by drifting almost imperceptibly to their outside, forcing them to check their speed. He had cut down on them but with enough subtlety for the judges to grant him the benefit of the doubt. His subsequent burst of speed secured victory. In the next race, Teruzzi levelled his personal battle with Harris by capitalising on the Briton's brief lapse in concentration to attack on the back straight and win.

By now dusk had set in and you could not see clearly from one end of the track to the other. The press were demanding that the final was postponed until the following day. The cyclists were similarly troubled and insisted at the very least that the photo-facility was turned off because the flash bulb could blind them. As the judges convened to discuss the situation, the crowd emitted cat calls and jeers as word passed to them about what was being considered. They wanted a conclusion to the event. Eventually, the officials sated them, having been told there was not money left to run to an extra day.

In the deciding race, the two pairs exchanged the lead three times until, to the view of most spectators, they disappeared into the gloaming around the final turn. Then the grandstands fell almost silent, desperate to know what was afoot. One wag shouted: 'Are you there, Reg?'

Suddenly Harris emerged into view, his shoulder level with Teruzzi's, each man venting all of their energy. As they finished the judges – an international panel – were unable to separate them, but the English fans were certain who had crossed the line first. 'We couldn't afford the grandstand but I got myself as close as possible to the finish line,' Shelagh Dennis said. 'I was directly opposite and I still swear Harris and Bannister won. I was 18 years old and your eyesight's pretty good then. I was with a crowd of people who were equally keen spectators and they thought the same.' After what felt like an age, the officials decided otherwise, leaving reporters to dial up the 25 freshly installed telephones and file by match-light another story of how Britain's great hope had narrowly failed.

Britain's cyclists did not nearly deliver on Adrian Chamberlin's promise that they would win a full set of golds but they enjoyed a successful Olympics nonetheless. To add to Harris's achievements, the road team won silver and his track team-mates claimed two bronze medals, one from the pursuit team in which Geldard and Godwin featured, and another from Godwin in the equivalent individual event.

To celebrate the NCU organised a dinner in London a week later. Supposed to include a set of congratulatory speeches, it descended into a shouting match once Lew Pond – a reserve on the track team – criticised the officials' inadequate preparations. To illustrate his point, he recalled how the track team had acquired equipment from an opportunist local supplier who realised the inadequacy of their resources only days before the event, a farcical scene that forced one competitor to withdraw from a race because his shorts were too tight. Still smarting from the morale-sapping, last-minute trials that had been demanded of them, the riders spoke out in support of Pond. 'Our morale was low,' he said. 'We have something to learn from the Italians in that respect. They were far more efficient.'

All that was strange about this latest row with 'the blazer brigade' – the derogatory title by which nearly all cyclists referred to the NCU – was that Harris was not involved. Instead he had headed straight back to Manchester after the Games and refused to return, dropping off the certificates given to authenticate his silver medals to his friend Harry Hall, who ran a bike shop in the city.

Harris had produced the best individual British performance of the Games. The sailing team had won one gold and the rowers two but they were all in paired events. Nobody had medalled twice in solo events, yet Harris remained disconsolate about his achievement even into middle age, even though by then no

British cyclist had won metal in an Olympics (and would not do so until Chris Boardman's gold medal in 1992). 'Wins are remembered,' Harris said, decades later. 'Wins are what you fight to achieve. The most important events to me have got to be Olympic and world title events so anything less than gold is such a disappointment that I would feel I had done it very, very wrong and I had a token to mark the failure. A lot of people might feel that to achieve silver or bronze shows distinction. It's all a question of where one's sights have been.'

CHAPTER 7
1949

On Friday, 20 September 1949, Harris rang the NCU in a state of panic. Having submitted his application to turn professional a week earlier without properly thinking through the decision, he had realised on reflection that now was not the best time for him to give up his amateur status. He had endured a good season but one studded with disappointing results. He had failed to live up to his reputation at the Olympics. Perhaps more damagingly still, he had lost to Ghella again at the subsequent World Championships in Amsterdam, getting beaten in successive races shortly after midnight in front of 50,000 fans, following an exhausting schedule in which riders were required to complete all their races in one day. If he turned professional now, Harris would have to head abroad to establish himself quickly on the winter indoor circuit. However, having repeatedly pushed his body to the limit in recent weeks, he needed to rest.

He was worried about money, too. For in the weeks after the Olympics, Claud Butler had suddenly ended his contract with

Harris for reasons that nobody ever quite understood. Without a basic wage, Harris would be forced to live abroad on appearance fees and prize money alone, none of which was guaranteed. He wanted, then, to withdraw his application. Dick Taylor, the NCU secretary, answered the phone.

'Dick, have you had the board meeting?' Harris asked. They had not; it was scheduled for midday. Harris was top of the agenda.

'I want to stay with the union,' he said, assuming its members would be relieved. By remaining amateur, he would appear at more domestic meetings and be able still to represent the British team.

Taylor called him back in the afternoon. 'Sorry, Reg, once you apply for professional status, you are considered professional,' he said. Nobody outside the NCU board had previously heard about such a rule. Most assumed that the NCU wanted to punish Harris for consistently flouting their authority, most publicly at the Olympics. And very likely, they no longer wanted to work with him. 'They say you can reapply in 12 months.'

Ideally Harris needed to head abroad as quickly as possible, giving himself a few months to sharpen his technique and improve his physical condition before the European Winter Sprint Championships. This was necessary because the standard among professional riders was much higher than that to which he was used. With no other option, then, he sold his MG, bought a more practical Vauxhall saloon in which he could place his equipment when travelling to races and headed to an apartment on the outskirts of Brussels that he had arranged to rent with his friend, Emile Gosselin. A year into his paid career, and brought up among professionals as an amateur on the Belgian scene, Gosselin indoctrinated Harris into a lifestyle that was even more Spartan than the one to which he was accustomed, yet at the time was followed by most young professionals.

They slept early and long and rarely socialised; Harris could not afford to, anyway. They rose shortly after dawn, ate a light breakfast and spent several hours on the road, before refuelling with a typically continental heavy lunch. They cycled to the Palais des Sports velodrome to spend each afternoon sharpening their speed and track craft, the most important aspect of the regime for Harris given that his technique on small, fast indoor circuits was still comparatively deficient. 'I lived a modest existence but I felt as though I had fallen on my feet,' he said, regardless that he had to survive on savings.

Like all indoor velodromes on the continent, the Palais des Sports was an egalitarian institution, where senior professionals were given few privileges and made to train and compete alongside club riders. On a Sunday, men such as Harris and Gosselin were not even allowed to compete at a venue hidden in woodland because that day was reserved for the best young amateurs from Belgium and France. Yet in a way, such anonymity suited Harris because it meant that he could quietly improve, making mistakes away from the public gaze. For all his disappointments the previous year, he knew that he still had much to live up to in the winter championships, not least because Ghella had decided to remain amateur for another six months. That meant Harris was billed as the brightest new talent on the professional scene.

The championships ran on a league format, with eight meetings staged at different indoor arenas across Europe. All the professionals entered, with the leading contenders being the world champion Arie van Vliet, Jan Derksen, Oskar Plattner, Louis Gérardin and Jef Scherens, who had dominated the sport before the war. Below them, there was a kind of 'second class' of rider, men such as Lucien Gillen and the Belgian Ray Pauwels, both excellent athletes but not quite as quick as the elite cabal. Harris's initial performances suggested that he, too, had some distance to make up – he finished last in Ghent, then spectacularly crashed after allowing the bike to slip from his grasp on the first bend at the Vel d'Hiver. A photograph of the incident shows Harris sliding down the banking like a collapsed puppet.

Not for the first time, he was quick to play up his condition. He insisted from his hospital bed that he had been told 'the consequences were grave', sparking speculation that he might have damaged his back again. Years later he claimed that he withdrew from competition for several weeks to allow the 'weakened parts' of his body to repair. Contemporary records show that he was actually competing again within a week. 'He was a bit of a hypochondriac,' Godwin said. 'Always on to the doctor. There was always something wrong. "Got to have this put right, that put right." Whenever Reg had a bad period, he had to have a reason for it.' Or perhaps he wished a good result to reflect even better on him, for his subsequent performances suggested there was little wrong with him. In the next meeting, he finished sixth on the supremely tight bends of the 250-metre track at the Sports Palace in Antwerp. A week later, having returned to Ghent, he was fifth, an especially encouraging result because he finished ahead of Scherens. Known as 'Puss' for his feline cunning, Scherens turned 40 in 1949 and was no longer as quick as in his youth, but still excelled on the short tracks through his tactical expertise.

Harris said that during this period he acquired a 'tenth-second consciousness', developing new techniques that saved him tiny fractions of time. When preparing to overtake, for example, he laid off by a further length to ensure he diverged less from a straight line when he passed his opponent. At the start of the race, he regulated his breathing so that he would exhale when the gun fired.

He adjusted slightly the critical angles of his frame, too, those between the horizontal plane and the head tube and seat tube respectively. By tightening the former to 74 degrees, his bike steered more responsively. By increasing the latter to the same angle, he edged slightly towards the handlebars, ensuring a more aerodynamic position. Neither measurement is unusual by modern standards but both were ambitious then: the first adjustment placed greater demands on his technique, the second on his strength.

He also increased the height of his bottom bracket by almost an inch to $10^{15}/_{16}$ inches, giving him more purchase on the pedals, and decided that from now on all new frames would be sized at $22^{5}/_{16}$ inches – the distance between the bottom bracket and the centre of the top tube – an inch shorter than he had previously commissioned. That, too, afforded him increased control.

So careful was he about his specifications that you could often spot him with a tape measure checking everything was correct on his bike before a race, it being easy for parts to shift a critical few millimetres out of position while being transported in the boot of his car. In that regard, he held a rare advantage over most of his foreign counterparts, who had emerged through systems in which they relied on mechanics and coaches to look after their machines. For, as a self-sufficient British bike man, Harris had learnt to do such dirty work himself. 'Ask a continental his frame angles and his response will be incomprehension,' he said. 'He would laugh at you worrying about such things. He believes position can be got right on any reasonable machine. Having come up the English way, I know more about my machine than probably any continental sprinter. I'm confident such an approach is right.'

By now he was more comfortable, and was happier in his personal life, too, having moved to an apartment on the outskirts of Paris where he was joined by Dorothy. He still trained hard, spending afternoons at Vel d'Hiver, but also found time to explore the city in the evenings and occasionally at the weekend. Such all-round improvement had its reward in the penultimate race of the championships in Zurich, where he capitalised on the relatively long straights to claim his first professional victory in the omnium, an event that combines the results from several different races. He completed the championships by finishing second to Scherens at the Vel d'Hiver, convincing the continental press that the winter had thrown up a new contender for the more coveted summer titles. 'The Englishman has no equal for producing two to three bursts in one sprint,' *L'Equipe* said. 'It appears that he is passed or being held and then suddenly he flashes past his rivals. He is seriously challenging the heavyweights for pure sprinting.'

By now Harris, too, had pinpointed this as his principal weapon, one to which most sprinters aspired but only a few could achieve. A double jump, as it was commonly known, involved producing an extra explosion of acceleration just when your opponent assumed you were travelling at top speed. As well as physical prowess, it required some physical deception to relay the impression you had nothing left to give. When executed successfully, it could earn an extra half-second by taking an opponent by surprise, often breaking their spirit. 'That was probably his winning quality,' Roger St Pierre said. 'As the other rider matched him, they'd get a false sense of security as they were coming round – off his wheel, or on his shoulder – then he'd give another kick.'

Shortly after that final race in Paris, Harris and Dorothy returned to Manchester uncertain about where their future lay. She was homesick. Harris sympathised. Though content in Paris, he missed the camaraderie of the Wheelers and the familiarity of the Cheshire and Lancashire country lanes. Ideally, he preferred the countryside to the bustle of a living in a city apartment. Returning home for good would suit him also because the outdoor season would involve almost as many races in Britain as it would abroad. Conversely, the facilities available to him on the continent were far superior to those in England. Much rested, then, on his opinion of an extensive redesign to Fallowfield.

That had happened over the winter. Inspired partly by Harris's success, and by continued excellent gate receipts, Manchester Wheelers had invested £8,000 in rebuilding the track so that it more closely mirrored the leading venues abroad. They widened the bends to 220 feet and built up the bankings so that now they had a 33-degree incline. They relaid the surface, too, in concrete, which would produce a much faster ride (though would also render the track unusable when wet). They hoped that the improved venue would help them to attract and to school properly emerging talents, many of whom would have been drawn to the sport by Harris's success. Their hopes would strengthen significantly if Harris was sufficiently satisfied with it to make it his training base, too.

On MacDonald's request, the Wheelers arranged for Harris to complete a test ride a month before its planned opening. They convened on a chill weekday evening in March, with a handful of Wheelers officials, a journalist and photographer. Harris listened as Bert Anderson, the Wheelers president who had recently been appointed chairman of the NCU, delivered his sales pitch. 'The architect based his design on the Parc des Princes, Reg, your favourite track,' he said. 'The top layer of concrete is the top grade, six centimetres thick. You won't see cracks in it any time soon.'

'What do the locals think?' Harris asked.

'The old-timers are furious but they don't understand cat and mouse,' Anderson said. He had suffered protests from those who were suspicious of the varied riding seen abroad. 'It's too foreign for them. But the rest of us are excited. It's fast.'

Dressed in plus-fours and a light jacket – even for a casual engagement, he did not let appearances drop – Harris accelerated into the first turn, then cut a perfect parabola out of the back straight and into the second bend, as if practising how he might grandstand for the supporters who would be standing on the new concrete terracing.

Picking up speed in a slight tailwind, he swooped into the home stretch with a skill that caught even his fiercest admirers by surprise. The reporter called him 'a changed man' from the forlorn, uncertain figure seen in competition at the end of the previous year. 'It has its faults,' Harris said. 'Both transitions are overstated. My back wheel kept jumping emerging from them.' Anderson took note, pencil in hand. 'It is quick, though, and smooth,' he continued. 'It will serve me better than Mauldeth Road.'

Everything, then, had fallen into place. His form had returned. His physical condition was much improved. Technically, he had sharpened up with preternatural speed. Most importantly, Raleigh had realised his potential over the winter and offered him a sponsorship deal of £1,000 a year, more than enough for him to live comfortably even without race winnings and appearance fees. He was returning home.

The happy confluence of circumstances told in his results as the outdoor season began. On his return to Herne Hill he thrashed Ghella by ten lengths in their first meeting since the World Championships, a result that would typify the disparity between them as professionals (and fuel the belief that Ghella had been heavily doped in his stand-out season). Harris then beat Plattner to become the first Briton to win the Grand Prix of Copenhagen since its inception in 1898. At the end of July, he became the first Briton to reach the final of the Grand Prix of Paris, losing to Van Vliet. In a breathtakingly intense fortnight before the reprisal of the World Championships in Copenhagen, Harris competed in an incredible 35 races at seven events across three countries. By the conclusion to them, he had suddenly established himself among many observers as the second favourite to Van Vliet to win the professional version of the world title, with Derksen third. In his preview of the event, Harris's biographer George Pearson wrote: 'Between Harris, Van Vliet and Derksen, Harris is probably the fastest. His record this season has been formidable, having reached the final of every open sprint race since March, but Van Vliet has come out on top in their recent meetings. His greater experience could count.'

*

You found surreptitious bookmakers at most velodromes in Britain then. With gambling banned, they would worm their way through the crowd, discreetly offering business before disappearing again quickly enough for officials to avoid catching sight of them. Gambling was outlawed at most other European venues, too. Only in Denmark was it allowed, producing profits that made its cycling federation the world's richest. The biggest wagers were laid at the Ordrup track in Copenhagen, the country's flagship venue, where thousands of pounds changed hands on a Tote betting system, and that made it probably the best-equipped velodrome of all, with expansive riders' facilities, four restaurants turning a brisk trade at each corner of its two stands, and a huge, state-of-the-art scoreboard that listed riders, winners, race times and the briskly updating odds. In a city where one in ten inhabitants owned a bicycle, and the venue sold out weeks in advance, it resembled a frenzied trading house as much as a sports venue when Harris arrived in the final week of August 1949. As MacDonald, his travelling partner, wrote, 'everyone was unusually keyed up: riders, officials, attendants, even press men seemed to be operating on a higher pitch than normal'.

Ergonomically, the track was not quite so advanced. Built in the nineteenth century, its bends were narrower than most and discouraged overtaking, while the finish line was drawn unusually early in the home straight, a frustration for fans who loved to see riders in battle on that final stretch. Tactically, these two shortcomings meant that whichever rider held the lead emerging out of the back straight was most likely to win. In other words, unless unusually brave or foolhardy, you had to attack early on the final lap to prevail.

By the weekend the temperature was 27 degrees Celsius, leaving the pungent sea air to hang heavy around the velodrome floor. Harris applied just the required tactics to reach the semi-finals alongside the two principal Dutchmen and Gérardin, then probably the fourth quickest on the circuit. While the draw for the previous rounds was decided before the event, the organisers went through that process again for the semi-finals, thus supposedly pitching the fastest man against the least fancied. Usually this process took minutes but as evening approached in the Ordrup, the UCI spent what felt like an age trying to settle on the rightful contests. When eventually they announced that Van Vliet would race Harris, hardly anybody outside the administrators' cabal agreed with the decision. Many suspected the French-dominated UCI had tried to help their man. 'They claimed it was because Harris was inexperienced, and because Gérardin had reached the final a year earlier,' Pearson wrote. 'You wondered if it was really to give Gérardin an easier route.'

Harris turned puce. Van Vliet was now the only rider that he feared. The Dutchman was incandescent. Then the strongest personality on the circuit, he remonstrated long and hard with officials, insisting he should not have to face Harris until the showpiece. He tried to get Harris to join his protestations, too, but the debutant lacked the confidence to stir up such trouble. Instead he was happy to draw confidence from seeing Van Vliet unnerved. For that rarely happened. Known as 'the Professor', Van Vliet usually exuded a calm, almost academic air, enhanced by his small, round glasses and a long pointed chin. He had barely blinked at the 1936 Olympics when refusing to shake Hitler's hand. Yet the prospect of racing Harris had him riled. Only when the UCI threatened him with suspension did he give up his challenge and agree to race.

Harris offered a wink to the press box as he made his way to the start line but that evidenced more bravado than peace of mind. For as he emerged from the final bend in the first race he hesitated momentarily and allowed Van Vliet to surge into a lead that his staying power ensured he did not relinquish along the back straight. In his desperation, Harris was forced to try to overtake on the next bend, a move that was both dangerous and unlikely to succeed, given that the surface geometry required him to travel a third further than his opponent. Van Vliet won by about three lengths.

Drawn as lead-out man in the second race, Harris eased up to the banking at the start and displayed his vastly improved technique by riding the straights with his head turned to face Van Vliet behind him, ensuring he could respond quickly to any sudden movement that the Dutchman made. This was a supremely difficult tactic and one that required Harris to judge his position on the track by the angle of the lengthening evening shadows and his position relative to the stadium surroundings. 'This was something Reg told me about,' St Pierre said. 'You have to learn to ride the length of the straight without ever looking ahead. That's artful.' When he hit the transition out of the penultimate turn this time, Harris showed none of his previous indecision, swooping down to create suddenly a lead that he held down the straight and around the bend. No opponent in the world would have been able to respond successfully to that.

As they took 20 minutes to recover before the deciding duel, the excited crackle from the stands that had soundtracked all previous races fell quiet. There was a great amount of money resting on the race but most knew that the world title was almost certainly at stake, with neither man likely to lose to either of their potential opponents in the final on this form.

The photographer George Moore described what happened when Van Vliet had the lead at the top of the banking just after the bell, his head turned to track Harris's movements. 'Harris was slowly dropping back,' he said. 'I sent out silent prayers, urging him to keep up when instead he looked over his right shoulder into the crowd!' This seemed inexplicable. 'The effect was astonishing. It seemed as he turned his head, he touched a switch that galvanised Van Vliet into an explosive jump.' By the turn Harris had closed the gap but he appeared to be spent, struggling for breath. 'I had to whip across the track and get pictures as they came off the banking.'

Then Harris produced his double jump. Moore said the move elicited 'a half gasp, half groan' of surprise from the crowd. 'Arie was shaken, momentarily, both physically and psychologically,' Harris said. 'By the time he recuperated there was not sufficient distance left for him to challenge.' Harris won by three lengths.

About an hour later, Harris posted the fastest time ever recorded in a world final, clearing the final 200 metres of his second successive victory over Derksen in 10.9 seconds. That was a suitable fashion in which to become the first man ever to claim the professional title in his debut season, but the victory over Van Vliet really earned Harris the hallowed rainbow jersey given to every cycling world champion. For, even though Harris could recall in unusual detail many of the thousands of races in which he competed, he described his performance in that deciding race against Van Vliet as 'possibly the best of my life'. Edward Southcott, still the NCU president and a veteran of several decades' attendance at the event, called it the 'greatest victory' he had ever seen.

Sharing a Carlsberg on the train home with MacDonald, Moore asked him about the apparently inopportune moment when Harris had chosen to look over his shoulder. 'Tom explained that Reg knew Van Vliet had only one real jump, so if he could lure him into making such a jump and was strong enough to catch him, he could then beat him to the line.'

Harris had fooled his friend twice in one race.

The rhythm of a professional cyclist's season was very different then. A competitor such as Harris might have timed his preparations to peak at the World Championships but he did not wind down after them. Far from it. Instead, he capitalised on the interest that it had generated for him to make as much money as he could. Within 48 hours, then, Harris was competing in Paris for the first of a series of what were billed as 'revenge races' against the three semi-finalists. Before the end of the week he had travelled to Aarhus and Amsterdam, where 55,000 spectators imagined themselves sharing in Van Vliet's catharsis as he comfortably beat Harris. By the following Monday, both men were in Herne Hill, exploiting the currency of their brand while it was at its most valuable. Along with Derksen, Gérardin and Plattner, they completed the whirlwind tour with a 'champion of champions' competition at Fallowfield.

The cash earned was significant, particularly Harris's. As world champion, he could increase his usual appearance fee by about 60 per cent, giving him between £80 and £100 an event, depending on the size of the venue. That is about £2,500 in modern currency, but almost a third of the national average wage then at a time when most professional sportsmen brought home little more than most in employment.

Exhausting travelling schedule aside, it was easy money, too, because most of the revenge races were fixed. Usually the elite riders arranged between them that they would win in front of their home crowds. Inevitably, they mixed up the results a little to avoid suspicion but generally the result list from that fortnight tells the story: in Paris, Gérardin prevailed; in Aarhus, Van Vliet, with Harris second; Amsterdam, Van Vliet, with Derksen behind him. You might guess who triumphed at Fallowfield.

Yet they also followed an unspoken rule that they should try to make these races as exciting as possible and that nobody should ever suffer a humiliating defeat. So, at Herne Hill, Van Vliet beat Harris by half a wheel in their first race only for Harris to edge him out by inches in the next. In the deciding contest, Harris gave up the lead and waited until what seemed a fraction too late to attack, yet somehow won by a length, manipulating the crowd's emotions much like a playwright in a crude three-act drama. 'They were professionals and professionals were paid to put on a show,' Maurice Jefferies said. I asked if you could see through the artifice. 'Sometimes it was obvious, sometimes it wasn't. Usually, if you're a track rider, you could see what was happening, but the crowd wouldn't see it. They loved it. They were fantastic races, after all.' Jim Love, a pursuit rider who served as a reserve on Britain's 1948 Olympic team, said: 'You had to be really on the button to realise it. It was very convincing. These guys were no fools. They needed the appearance money.'

Quite how many other races were fixed through the season is uncertain. Some will tell you that any result outside of a World Championship or grand prix could not be trusted. Others insist grands prix were open to negotiation, too. A few wonder about the legitimacy of the blue riband event. Whatever the truth, the majority were certainly orchestrated. At a time when money was scarce the professionals saw this as the only means by which they could ensure that their arm of the sport would continue to thrive, regardless that it required them to deceive press and fans week after week.

As a result of the general suspicion about their contests, and the peripatetic nature of their trade, the elite riders were given a nickname within the cycling community that stuck. They were known as 'the circus'. 'Harris and Van Vliet came to Derby once, a big, saucer-shaped track,' Geoff Cooke said. 'They put on 86-inch gears and were pedalling like mad, neck and neck up the finishing straight. But they were actually a second slower than the amateurs. That put it in perspective. It was a show.'

CHAPTER 8
1950

For many cycling fans, provincial races in Britain were their only opportunity to watch Harris in action, for few of them could travel abroad and footage of his victories was restricted to short clips that played at the end of Pathé newsreels and ran in local cinemas – only nine per cent of Britons owned a television then. Yet even those who travelled to those meetings rarely got to hear him speak: he did not deliver victory speeches and was interviewed only very occasionally on the radio. Even in the press dialogue from him rarely appeared. Sports journalists interviewed only occasionally then and had nothing like the modern rapacity for quotes.

As a result, Harris became a kind of blank canvas upon which fans could project any personality they wished. Inevitably, inspired by his heroic achievements, implacably confident demeanour and the careful way he dressed away from the track, they imagined him as the classic English gentleman who had conquered all before him without ever losing his cool. That image was enhanced at the start of 1950 when he gave his first widely covered speech on receiving the *Daily Record* Sportsman of the Year award.

The precursor to the BBC Sports Personality of the Year, this had been conceived only two years earlier but was already highly coveted. Much as with its successor, the *Record*'s winner was decided by a public (postal) vote and was regarded as the finest British sportsman. Harris had finished second behind Denis Compton the previous year, polling half as many votes of the 88,291 cast. In 1950, he triumphed ahead of the cricketer again and Tommy Lawton, recently the subject of a record £20,000 transfer from Chelsea to Notts County. For a cyclist to trump heroes from by far the country's two most popular sports was praise indeed.

Most of Britain's leading sportsmen and women were present at the Savoy Hotel in London that evening, among them McDonald Bailey, the sprinter who would set the 100-metre world record, the snooker world champion Fred Davis and the footballer Raich Carter. The sprinter Maureen Gardner, the Olympic silver medallist, was there too, along with the figure skaters John and Jennifer Nicks, soon also to become world champions. Aneurin Bevan introduced Harris to the raised platform with a joke about it being time Britain produced a champion cyclist when the country produced so many darned bikes. Harris thanked the minister for health, politely acknowledged the crowd and delivered the following address: 'We have in this country a lot of very fine athletes, cricketers, footballers and what have you,' he said. 'Yet, somehow or other, when it comes to international competition, generally speaking we seem to fall just a little too short of the mark. I can't help thinking that if people here in this country of ours were given anything like just 50 per cent of the facility that is given to our opponents from the continent, that the prestige of this nation would be upheld in a very much better manner.'

What might first have struck those unfamiliar with hearing Harris was his accent and pronunciation. The cycling historian Les Woodland said Harris once spoke with an accent that could have 'drawn pigeons from the sky' yet nearly all trace of his Lancashire accent was gone, with its vowels flattened out and distinctive pronouns now conventionally pronounced. Though he never admitted to it, most assumed he had taken elocution lessons because he now spoke like no other young cyclist from his region.

Much more striking than that, though, was the content of his speech. At the time, athletes were not given to being outspoken on the rare occasion that they were given a public platform. A year earlier, Compton had accepted the award by thanking everybody to whom he owed an emotional debt and promising 'to keep pleasing the public'. Yet, without hesitation, Harris had criticised State support for elite sportspeople even with a senior government figure present. It did not bother him that his argument suggested that many of those present had failed to fulfil their athletic potential. He knew that his words would be broadcast in cinemas throughout the country and he did not wish to let the opportunity pass. 'In those days, you've got to bear in mind that the rules were the rules,' St Pierre said. 'You said, "yes sir, no sir". You wore a dark suit; you wore a tie. You stood up for ladies on a bus. There were no exceptions for anybody. But somebody like Reg, he's not going to like all that. He was a rebel, maybe with a cause.'

Partly this was because Harris often applied the formidably high standards that he set for himself to other people, a trait that emerged in another speech given at about that time, at the Wheelers annual dinner. Here again much of the night was given over to tributes to their most illustrious member but special mention was reserved, too, for a teammate of his, Cyril Cartwright. A 21-year-old coal miner, Cartwright had a year earlier been struck down with pneumonia and told by doctors that he should give up hope of riding in the forthcoming season. Inspired by Harris's refusal ever to trust cautious medical opinion, however, he had fought back from the illness and was competitive again with a month of the World Championships, earning selection in the amateur version of the individual pursuit. Though few had given him much chance of success, he had returned with a silver medal to complete probably the Wheelers' finest ever season. Standing up to address admirers sated on cigars and wine, Harris began by congratulating his colleague but then took on a demanding tone. The NCU, he said, should have been ashamed that it sent Cartwright to Copenhagen only 48 hours before the event. Had Cartwright been given more time to prepare, Harris was confident he could have won gold. Lest such praise might inspire complacency, Cartwright was then reminded that he had not nearly fulfilled his potential. 'I am certain that much greater success lies ahead for Cyril,' Harris said. 'He could succeed as a professional but I am certain he will realise that the hard work has only begun.' A quiet, modest man, Cartwright avoided such provocation in his response, instead merely thanking the Wheelers and Harris for their continued support, which in retrospect seemed strange because before long he would often refuse even to train with his illustrious teammate.

There was one other channel through which the public formed its impression of Harris: his relationship with Raleigh. Often that was through public appearances promoting their brand but mostly it was through the posters of him that the company arranged to have put up in the thousands of bike shops in Britain.

Generally, these portrayed him in one of three poses: mid-sprint, celebrating victory in the saddle or standing beside his red Raleigh frame. In at least one design, he was dressed in tweeds on a country lane. Here he was the classical country gent, perfectly composed, pipe in hand (probably his own: he had outgrown cigarette smoking by then). Around dawn in the golden age of advertising, he cut the marketing man's perfect archetype: the self-made hero who, in having realised all his aspirations, could inspire countless more in everyman.

Beneath each portrait was the slogan 'Reg rides a Raleigh', with which he would become synonymous, regardless that he did not always ride the brand that paid him. 'Lots of people bought them because of Reg Harris's name but, if the truth be known, at first he rode bikes made by some other hand-built firm and Raleigh put their transfers on them,' Duncan Hamman said. Only later did Raleigh employ frame-builders sufficiently expert for Harris to trust them.

After his professional World Championship victory, Raleigh ran off 7,000 of these posters, and commissioned hundreds of pounds' worth of advertising in the press, strengthening a brand association that was almost certainly unprecedented in British sport. By the spring of 1950, however, having so heavily exploited Harris's victory in Copenhagen, Raleigh decided that they needed a new achievement from him with which to promote their new lines. George Wilson, the Raleigh managing director, approached Harris at the start of the weekend-long Cycle and Motorcycle Show in Earls Court. Staged in March, this was the industry's most important such event. 'Reg, we could do with a world record,' he said. 'You're going to Milan this weekend. If you could pull if off there while the show is still on, all our dealers would be overjoyed.'

Wilson suggested he try for the kilometre landmark, making his cheeky request only more unlikely. For it was the holy grail of world sprint records, a challenge that through its singular demand on speed and stamina is considered probably the most formidable of all track landmarks. The existing record had stood since 1939 when the Italian Fabio Battesini covered two and a half laps of the Milanese venue in 1 minute 10.2 seconds. Most assumed you would struggle to get close to that time on any other track. Even there only the wildly ambitious would attempt to break it without tailored preparation. Yet, reluctantly, Harris agreed, even booking a second flight from London on Saturday evening when his morning plane from Manchester was cancelled owing to heavy storms.

Across Europe the elements were similarly inclement. The flight was turbulent and unpleasant. Harris slept little, having arrived in his hotel in the early hours. He rarely did anyway in Milan, so noisy were its weekend streets. When eventually he went down to the track, he found its surface damp and howling winds trapped inside its walls. His record attempt was scheduled for midday, shortly before a full programme of racing, which itself preceded the conclusion to the Tour of Lombardy. He could not postpone his attempt to later in the day. A UCI official suggested that he withdrew: 'Dupont has already pulled out. There is enough racing to keep the fans satisfied.' Jacques Dupont, a Frenchman, won gold in the kilometre time trial at the 1948 Olympics. He had arranged weeks ago to attempt the record.

Harris took a few moments to consider his situation. Raleigh would be furious if he returned home without attempting the record simply because of rain. His other recently acquired sponsors, Brooks and Dunlop – both of whom paid him £500 annually – would be unimpressed, too. Besides, he reckoned the surface was just about safe enough. It would just be difficult to generate speed when riding into the headwind along the back straight. He turned to MacDonald, again his lone companion.*
'Tell them to change up to a 92,' Harris said.

The crowd had swelled almost to capacity now with thousands of men dressed in heavily worn suits that they pressed fresh

---

* I asked Bill Brown why Harris brought only MacDonald with him to these events. 'He knew all about money,' he said. 'He did the negotiating.'

for the Sabbath. Many had gone straight from Mass to worship their heroes of the track.

His massage complete – he always had one now before a race, even if self-administered – he went to the start to find that the wind had dropped and was blowing much less forcefully into his face. Having completed several kilometre time trials in training over the past two years – and privately claimed that at Fallowfield he had once lowered Battesini's mark – he knew the psychology that the challenge demanded. For the first 100 metres, he sprinted hard to get his cadence up. For the next 400, he concentrated on riding smoothly, while for the final lap and a half, he focused merely on trying to compartmentalise the pain. By the final straight, he was lost in the anaesthetic of the crowd's roar. The record fell by two-fifths of a second. 'It was the toughest race of my life,' he admitted. 'I had never felt so exhausted. I could hardly stand up. It was worth it, though.'

Raleigh were delighted. They had already the fastest cyclist of his era: now they had the quickest of all time, too. Within a week they had adverts running in the cycling press announcing that fact and found such an upturn in sales that they decided such record-breaking attempts should become a feature of Harris's career, for not only did they make for good copy but they provided a simple way to refresh their campaigns. They also provided Harris with a new revenue stream; now it mattered less that the absence of any other professional track cyclists in Britain provided him with limited opposition at race meetings. He could just expand his repertoire by riding on his own.

The crowd did not mind because record attempts made for curiously compelling spectacles, in which a wall of sound followed Harris around a track, much like an aural Mexican wave. Across Britain crowds cheered and banged on hoardings as he pursued some new landmark. By June of 1950, he had broken every short-course British record, from the 100-yard dash to the kilometre time trial completed from a flying start (his world record was from a standing start, the more prestigious version). More often than not, he bettered a landmark that Bill Bailey had set several decades earlier, ensuring that Harris obliterated his old nemesis from the record books much as he had driven him from the sport. 'Reg had an ability to put up with more than others,' Trevor Fenwick, formerly a professional road cyclist and a training partner of Harris, said. 'Often, after I had given up at Fallowfield, I would be sat on the side of the track, watching him, struggling, his breath heavy and forced, but he would not give up. He had this tremendous willpower.'

In competition meanwhile, Harris was perhaps even more successful than he had been over the previous summer, winning two of the four major grands prix in Amsterdam and Brussels, reaching the final of the other two in Copenhagen and Paris.

Reporting on Harris's appearance on the Preston Park track in Brighton before 8,000 spectators, John Dennis said his friend looked in the 'pink of condition' despite the sweltering heat. Clearly he had benefited from the first of several close seasons that had not been disrupted by injury.

Harris concluded his responsibilities that day with a four-man sprint competition that pitched him against Jackie Heid in the semi-finals. The only American sprinter on the circuit, Heid had only recently taken unofficial membership of the circus, having spent several years having to supplement his earnings from the sport by smuggling bike parts and kit around the continent. Capable of explosive short sprints and most dangerous over the final 150 metres, he had won bronze in the previous year's amateur World Championships, but nobody should have been surprised that the Englishman went through to the seaside show-piece against Van Vliet.

For, in knowing that the spectacle of any sport is improved by a standout rivalry, Harris and Van Vliet had been careful to cultivate theirs that summer. They had ensured that they contested the majority of finals among orchestrated meetings, while also encouraging promoters to play up the inevitable duel that would unfold between them. They had shared victories sufficiently to retain a sense of jeopardy to their contests – though Harris, as world champion, had won more than he lost

– and benefited greatly from the differences between them, a necessity to any compelling opposition. About four inches taller than Harris, and less robust, Van Vliet sat back in the saddle, back almost straight, pressing the pedals with the balls of his feet. Harris edged forward, pedalled with his toes and arched his spine as deeply as any sprinter did. An insouciant type, Van Vliet was happy to remind people that he had not wanted to become a sportsman and planned instead an easy life in the family business, selling Audis to Holland's middle class, until his brother dissuaded him. Harris took pride in being self-made or, as Harry England put it, 'not the product of Fallowfield, or competition, or the revival in track sport, but an accident of our time'.

Thousands turned up to watch them compete. In Britain alone in 1950, they graced Halesowen and the grass venue in Staines, the Bockworth Colliery Sports Ground on Tyneside as well as Paddington, Herne Hill and Fallowfield, prompting Harris to claim that their 'rivalry kept alive British interest in the sport'. Possibly that overstated the truth, but ask any fan of the sport then and they turn rheumy-eyed at the memory of their contests. 'Harris and Van Vliet knew that they needed each other,' St Pierre said. 'Their rivalry was money through the gate.'

Through circumstance and mutual respect the men grew close. Along with the others within the circus, they often travelled together to events, socialised in cities abroad and even hosted one another at their homes, though Harris admitted the latter gesture was laced with ulterior motive. 'This was how I got to know my rivals,' he said. 'Van Vliet says he never trains and that would be the impression he leaves after brief contact, but after a longish stay at home the truth is revealed: he chafes to be out on the bike.'

By August of 1950, Harris knew that Van Vliet was determined to wrest back the world title in Liège.

The stadium in the Liège suburb of Rocourt was a mess when the competitors arrived. The Belgian federation had planned to unveil its renovation in time for the event but had failed to resolve an industrial dispute with construction workers, leaving them to strike in the months leading up to the event. The venue was only half completed.

When Harris turned up a fortnight before the event, he was horrified to discover scaffolding inside the track and prefabricated huts around its perimeter, with changing facilities and terracing unfinished, and electric cables exposed on the ground. 'It was among the worst organised championships I'd ever seen,' he said. Nothing, it seemed, worked: not the floodlights, the result boards, nor the signals that lit up during the pursuit competition to illustrate which team had crossed the line first.

Located in an industrial area of the city, the surroundings were forbidding, too. Harry England recalled that even the 'hotel accommodation was insufficient'.

All this was anathema to Harris. He needed everything about his preparations to be perfect. If something was substandard or faulty or likely to malfunction, he was left prey to contingencies over which he had no control. Some felt the same personality streak informed the hypochondria about which Godwin talked. 'Harris was never at his best when presented with something he did not like,' Woodard said.

To worsen his frame of mind, the pressure of favouritism had returned. While in 1947 and 1949, he had not been outright favourite for the tournament, now everybody felt he should win and such expectation made him uneasy. In a sport that can be decided on a split-second mistake, such pressure always did, regardless of the implacable front that he presented in competition. 'The continentals saw Harris as the typically phlegmatic Briton,' Alan Peters, a *Daily Mail* sports writer, said. 'In truth, he was always tense at championships. His only thought was to race, race, race and get the business done.'

He tuned out those anxieties to progress through his opening two rounds without defeat, against first the young Swiss cyclist Armin von Buren, then Gosselin, who had been left behind by his old training partner in the sport's hierarchy. That put Harris through to a semi-final against Derksen – Van Vliet and Gérardin would contest the other – on the following Monday after the preliminary races because heavy storms had lashed eastern Belgium and washed out the deciding rounds over the weekend. Officials had tried to dry out the surface by using petrol to set it alight, but that did little more than provide the press with a photo opportunity to compensate for the lack of result.

Harris had grown to like Derksen immensely. He had visited him at home in Amsterdam and got to know his wife and son, who told me that his father reciprocated Harris's fondness. Derksen took Harris coarse fishing at dawn on the city's canals, insisting that they dressed in oilskins and 'silly hats'. Their personalities, it seemed, dovetailed. In public Harris liked attention, while in person he shunned it. Derksen was the reverse. Harris described him as 'the animator-in-chief of any meal with the boys', but nerves struck him terribly in competition. Often he would spend the entire night before an important race sleepless in his hotel room. During a race, he shrank from aggressive riding and placed more value on sportsmanship than most of his rivals. 'Possibly no big-timer has lost more races through his distaste for the rough stuff,' Harris said. 'He accepts defeat as he accepts victory: quietly.'

Yet such timidity left him vulnerable to intimidation. Often Van Vliet would visit him a few days before the Dutch National Championship, purporting to want his company but really to let Derksen witness his confidence. 'Arie was a great friend but he could be a pain in the arse,' Derksen wrote. 'He did this to get at me. He would talk non-stop, knowing I just wanted to be on my own, pacing the room.'

In Rocourt, Harris did not need to attempt to unnerve him because Raleigh performed the task for him in the small hours of Sunday evening by pinning up posters in Harris's dressing room congratulating him on successfully defending his world title. The men behind the stunt were Harry Traynor, editor of the in-house journal *The Raleighram*, and Sidney Woods, their advertising manager. 'They were plastered all over the walls,' Harris said. 'They had thousands of them printed.' It was the ultimate mark of disrespect. Perhaps for that reason Derksen was beaten in successive races, first despite summoning an unusually powerful sprint finish that left him trailing Harris by only half a wheel, then by ten lengths after Harris ruthlessly attacked on the bell, knowing such a surprise move would exploit any apprehension sown in Derksen. For once, the Dutchman left the arena without shaking hands with the man who had beaten him, and without watching the final with Van Vliet.

Belgian cycling fans much preferred the road version of the sport to the track. With no compatriot to cheer on, only a handful of spectators had turned up for Harris's victory over Derksen and only a few hundred had arrived in time for the final. The place, then, was ghostly, depressing, when the two finalists rolled away from the start line. From the press box you could hear the sweet tinkle of their inch-pitch chains. Chains with links half that length – the standard size today – were sold then but men such as Harris and Van Vliet preferred the old type because they considered them better able to withstand the almighty force that only elite sprinters could apply to them.

Van Vliet knew the limited tactical possibilities that were available to him. He could not beat Harris for acceleration and he could not keep up with the champion over any distance below 200 metres – or a furlong, as track aficionados called it. His only hope was to catch Harris unawares early on and open up a lead that would be sufficient to compensate for the power-gap between them. As John Dennis said, 'Harris was beatable, just not very often. You had to be smart.' Tactically, though, few were smarter than him, hence Harris seemed already to know that Van Vliet would attack with 250 metres left in their first race and attacked almost simultaneously, grabbing the lead.

Van Vliet stayed with Harris and put everything into a courageous second jump on the final turn. By then, though, he was too late. As if resigned to the impossibility of legitimate success, Van Vliet snaked in the next race, forcing Harris to check his speed suddenly on the penultimate turn as the Dutchman pulled sharply back up the banking despite having just attacked. That was dangerous and probably breached the rules. Had Harris raised his hand to signal a protest, it almost certainly would have been upheld.

But he did not feel the need to resort to that and instead showed impeccable patience to smoothly close the gap to Van Vliet to six, five, then four lengths heading out into the turn. By the home straight, he was level with the Dutchman. By the finish line, the naked eye struggled to tell them apart. A photograph shows the tightly packed spectators craning in unison behind the finish line for a better view.

Harris won by half a wheel. 'Last year Harris hoped to win, this year he had everything to lose: status, earning power and self-confidence,' the acclaimed cycling journalist Jock Wadley wrote. Fifty-five years since the first championships, he was inspired to consider Harris's place in the pantheon. 'When racing on his terms, no one in history would touch him; not Piet Moeskops, the four-time champion from Holland with a great jump and brilliant head for manoeuvre; not Lucien Michard, another man with four titles and the master tactician; not even Jef Scherens, the seven-time winner, with his devastating short sprint when coming off a wheel on the home straight.'

CHAPTER 9
1951

A world champion has a duty to cycling. An unwritten code says he should give back to the sport. He must, for example, attend the most significant races in the following season, allowing promoters and federations to profit from having him on their bill. Expected always to wear the rainbow jersey – and, in 1950, obliged to buy several such garments from the UCI – he had also to comply with a certain standard of conduct. He had to show sportsmanship and always give his best. In 2011, Mark Cavendish was asked about this tradition when he won the World Road Championship. 'I want to do the jersey proud,' he said. 'I feel the support and honour that comes with it.'

Little wonder the sport's establishment was furious when Harris announced that he would not compete at any track meeting over the winter of that year. He had decided instead to accept an offer from the impresario Eric Morley to tour the country with his recently created Mecca brand, performing on rollers as part of an evening's light entertainment that often also included bingo, ice skating and ballroom dancing (a year earlier Morley had popularised the latter by devising the BBC's *Come Dancing* television show). Harris had given the leading track promoters the opportunity to match Morley's offer but they refused, allowing him to enjoy a winter less strenuous than any he had endured since returning from the war. 'The money was far more than the continental track promoters had offered,' Harris said, 'and very much easier than struggling to reach far-flung parts of the continent in appalling weather conditions.'

The purists were appalled because Harris had snubbed tradition for an event that was more theatre than sport. Prevented by the NCU rules from competing against the amateurs who also attended the rollers tour, he simply turned up to the venue and pedalled as fast as he could two to three times a week in an attempt to lower successive world records for the device. His quickest time was 96mph.

Harris could afford to take this decision because he had become all-powerful within the sport. The sprinting elite had always been a kind of law unto itself, in which its members decided which races to attend and who would win them, but now they had one member who was clearly superior to the rest. As a result, if any of Harris's rivals wished to taste victory they required him to acquiesce.

Through the force of his personality he cultivated that status away from the track, leading negotiations with promoters and manipulating relationships within the circus to ensure nobody threatened his power. In short, he was the ringleader. 'Somehow the group hinged around Reg,' St Pierre said. 'You might compare it to the effect Fausto Coppi had as a road rider. If you saw a group of riders and Coppi was among them, whether he was leading, at the back or in the middle, the bunch seemed to revolve around him. It was the same with Reg. If they were sitting on a bench inside the track, he was in the centre. If the riders were wearing their gowns, his was bigger and fluffier than anyone else's. He just had this aura about him. He was in charge, part of the group yet somehow above it.'

You might compare him to the head of a mafioso family complete with captains. Certainly they enjoyed the rewards of their success much as wise guys would. Abroad they ate in the best restaurants. Harris now had acquired a taste for steak tartare and expensive red wine – he was even building a vintage collection for his home and indulged most nights. While on a tour that winter he turned his palate to brandy and fine cigars. Smoking was frowned upon in the athletic world but Harris insisted that in moderation it helped him to relax.

Nearly all of the elite shared a passion for fast cars. Harris now owned a Jaguar and an MG that he had ordered straight from the production line in Abingdon. Derksen drove a Chevrolet. Often you would find them in a continental bar or café consumed by a poker game. Nearly all of them dressed impeccably and, when not in training gear, rarely were seen in garb less impressive than a tailored suit, sometimes bought at the men's boutique that Plattner owned in Zurich. They mercilessly mocked Scherens' old-fashioned frugality. The Belgian had had all his possessions taken from him by the Nazis and, it seemed, had worn only his one remaining suit ever since.

As their success grew, so women became vulnerable to their charms. Often they were beautiful; sometimes they were famous. Gérardin, though married, had an affair with Edith Piaf that gripped the singer more profoundly than any other relationship. 'You have taken me like no other man has ever done, and I have given you what I have never before given, which is to say: myself,' she wrote in one of more than 50 letters to him in a relationship that lasted less than a year. The correspondence suggested that her feelings were not reciprocated.

The British cyclist Cyril Bardsley said Harris was involved with a famous Danish actress called Kate, possibly Kate Mundt, who was 10 years younger than him and had appeared in 20 films. 'She was married and he was with Dorothy,' Bardsley said. 'But he wasn't the kind of chap who stayed with a woman for long.' Bill Brown recalled a Parisian girl whom Harris saw often and who fell for him completely.

Once at Manchester Velodrome, I was told a story about a lavish dinner engagement in the south of France when word was passed to the world champion that Princess Grace wanted to dance with him. Strangely, he refused, explaining coyly that he had not been taught to dance and wished to embarrass neither himself nor royalty. That he might have risked improvisation could not be countenanced, presumably because it might reveal something profound about him that he wished desperately to keep hidden. So instead the social interloper was confined to his table while all around him high society twirled.

Much like the incorrigible sailor of lore, Harris managed to maintain concurrent relationships in many of the cities he visited. One former member of the British team who wished to remain anonymous reckoned Harris squired more than a hundred women.

Alan Nuttall was a friend of Jim Paterson, a cycling mechanic, who travelled with Harris abroad and witnessed many of his libidinous deceits. On a visit to Ghent, Dorothy turned up unannounced when Harris had a woman with him on the track. Nuttall recalled the scene that ensued: 'Quick as a flash, Reg said, "Dorothy, meet Jim's girlfriend." Then off he went to his next race. Jim was red with embarrassment, his big old jowls shaking. This woman spoke Flemish and no English. Dorothy said: "Don't worry, Jim, I know what's going on."'

Trevor Fenwick recalled a story that Harris told him about a night out in Denmark that illustrated his attitude to this other sport. Hugo Koblet and Rik van Steenbergen, two leading road cyclists, were involved. 'They met up with three women and arranged to go back to the hotel, but the riders went in a taxi and the women followed them on their bikes,' Fenwick said. 'Reg thought this hilarious.' Each man was in competition the next day. 'Van Steenbergen complained that Reg had been leading him astray. Reg said to me: "You would think it had been me pulling his pisser." It was all right for Reg, but road men had to look after themselves more.' Fenwick saw little guilt from Harris over his many infidelities. 'When telling me about his adventures, Reg would say, "I am only doing what other businessmen do when they are away."'

Through his relaxed schedule and a reduced road regime Harris was 12 pounds over his racing weight when in March the UCI agreed the most significant rule-change to World Championship sprinting in living memory. In a development that had been proposed and heavily argued by the French delegates who enjoyed a majority within the union, from now on the event would be decided on a three-up format.

This had dramatic implications. In a three-up race, two riders could easily conspire against the third and prevent him winning no matter his talent. This could also occur even if the favourite's opponents did not team up. All that needed to happen was for one to attack early because that presented the favourite with a dilemma that often was impossible to resolve. Either he tracked the lead man and brought the other along in his slipstream or chose not to follow the attack and risked never making up the gap. Harris had fallen victim to just such a scenario in the final of the Grand Prix of Paris the previous year. In a race that had always been three-up and was open to amateurs because profits were donated to charity, Harris lost to a barely proven French mechanic called Maurice Verdeun after the 21-year-old had jumped at the bell and Harris had been reluctant to give Derksen the opportunity to draft him for the best part of a lap.

The French delegates argued that three-up would create a more entertaining spectacle, suggesting that three-up increased the tactical variety in a race and made all contests much less predictable. This was a reasonable claim but nobody else thought that that was their true motive. Instead, as the Australian cyclist Russell Mockridge, then a leading amateur, wrote: 'The popular belief was that this new system was an attempt by the continentals to stop Harris's continued dominance.' Michael Breckon, formerly manager of the Canadian national team, put it differently: 'There wasn't anybody who could beat Reg, so they wanted to screw him out of a world title.'

Harris was furious. He considered this to be punishment for his refusal to ride the winter circuit. He knew also that he could not expect his influence of the circus to extend to the World Championships when only two riders needed to conspire to undermine him successfully there, a great temptation given the increased earning power for any new champion. Typically, though, Harris did not allow the decision to depress him. Instead it sparked him out of his winter's complacency. 'I resolved to fight back and to show them they could not stop me just by changing the formula,' he said. 'I had to make myself the best in the world by an even wider margin.'

With only a month left until the start of the outdoor season, and the rain that for weeks had fallen across northern Europe showing no sign of abating, Harris left for the French Riviera to begin an intensive training regime. Always happiest riding in the heat, he doubled his usual mileage, spending four to five hours each day on the road in the hope that he could fast-track his acquisition of core stamina. He continued with his sprint sessions, too, most often teaming up with Georges Senfftleben, who that season had turned professional. Tall, ruggedly handsome and outgoing, the Parisian was another sporting *bon vivant*. A medallist in three out of four world amateur championships, he was also exceptionally talented and had slipped easily into the inner circle of the elite.

Inevitably, the paucity of Harris's close season told in his initial return to competition at low-profile events, among them defeats at races in Ostend and the Belgian town of Zwartberg, but by the summer he was sharp again. In a race meeting organised by the Mansfield Labour Party, which attracted a 5,000-strong crowd, he beat Van Vliet in three of four races. Returning to France, he won the grands prix of Boulogne and, for the first time, of Paris. In the final event before the renewal of World Championships in Milan, he lowered two track records at Fallowfield, clocking 27.8 seconds for quarter of a mile from a standing start and four minutes 10.2 seconds for four kilometres motor-paced.

Harris recalled how he pooled opinion on the new format in the few days before the competition. Derksen admitted he preferred it because it meant that he might get 'to take Harris unawares'. Scherens said it persuaded him to return from the retirement he had entered after the previous season. 'Now I have a chance again,' the 42-year-old said, his fastest days long since gone. The Australian Syd Patterson, another recent graduate to the paid ranks, took the same view. Champion in the amateur pursuit 12 months earlier, he was not a specialist sprinter but knew that three-up gave him a chance in the blue riband event. Van Vliet was non-committal, but that did not concern Harris. The honesty of their enthusiasm suggested that at least there was no underhand plan to unseat him.

The first rounds took place on Saturday evening beneath a warm, indigo sky. The Vigorelli looked resplendent again, with its boards freshly creosoted and track lines repainted in yellow, red and blue (the first being the inside line that measures the track distance, the second the sprinter's line and the third the line inside which you cannot overtake when motor-paced). In the three-up format, there was only one race per round, so Harris had minimal room to err in his second-round contest against Von Buren and Primo Bergomi, the young Italian who had the support of the capacity crowd. Given that the new format had already inflicted defeat on Van Vliet, Derksen and Plattner after several wild but enthralling races, Bergomi also had good reason to feel that he might cause an upset. 'I have never seen such fast moving, split-second action and reaction in the past 22 years at the championships,' Harry England wrote. 'A piece of cycling history could be lost if one so much as struck a match to light a cigarette'.

Heading into the back straight for the second time, Von Buren led with Harris in second and all three men close to the top of the banking. When Von Buren dived towards the middle of the track, Harris followed him, albeit keeping on the outside of his wheel so as not to get trapped against the apron. To their surprise, Bergomi responded with an attack on the outside, regardless of the extra distance involved. Harris overshot his reaction and collided with the Italian, to much derision from the crowd, even though both men had stayed upright and the incident slowed Harris more than his opponent. Thus Bergomi attacked again, creating a lead that defeated the tiring Von Buren and that Harris could not make up. Harris's punishment was a four-up repêchage of an unusual lustre, featuring Plattner, Ghella and Senfftleben. His compensation was that the winner went through to the final.

Until now Harris had been riding a relatively low 92-inch gear, to maximise his acceleration, but he felt that others had been going quicker than him over the slick surface. Enquiring, he found that Platter was riding a 96-inch and that Patterson was on 100. Though Harris never usually dared to change a part mid-competition, he instructed a mechanic to fit him a new chain ring and sprocket, moving him up to 94.

With none of the men prepared to risk an attack, they were bunched emerging from the final bend. Suddenly they spread out four-abreast in a sprint to the line, helmets touching once or twice, elbows intertwining, frames threatening to bend beneath the pressure applied to them. Usually, Harris prevailed with little difficulty in such circumstances but the new parts did not fit properly and had slowed him fractionally. He could 'hear them grinding'. He was deeply relieved to win after a photo finish.

As if to reassure Harris that his captains would not dare to undermine him, Derksen lent Harris his transmission for the final, in which he faced Patterson and Bellenger, the young Frenchman in his second year as a professional. Each was a very different proposition. While Patterson had attacked early in each of his races and hung on grimly to progress, Bellenger made up for what he lacked in speed with track craft and saved his attacks until as late as possible. Like Patterson, he was seven years younger than Harris, with pale skin pulled tight across his face, making him more resemble a weathered road rider than a typically muscular sprinter. Patterson was built like a bear.

The Australian made his move at the bell, pushing hard on his heavy gear through the top of the banking, but this time was unable to open up a lead. This was because Harris stayed with him, keeping his front wheel just inside Patterson's back tyre, preventing him from turning down the banking to generate extra speed. That allowed Bellenger to take the lead through the inside, but Harris held it until there was no longer enough time for Patterson to wind up his speed but sufficient distance for Harris to close down the gap to Bellenger. The Italians within the crowd had booed Harris for the Bergomi infringement but they fell silent as they watched Harris chase reward for his patience. Almost all that was audible were the distant cheers of the small British contingent, made up partly of men from the Brighton Stanley Wanderers cycling club, who had spent months saving for the trip. Among them was a musician called George

Woodham. He blew hard on his trumpet when Harris passed Bellenger 20 metres from the finish to claim probably his smartest victory yet.

With this triumph Harris began to transcend cycling to become a name that everybody knew, regardless of their interest in it or any sport. Within a few months his waxwork was put on display at Madame Tussauds beside one of his bikes. It had needed half a hundredweight of wax, much more than usual, such was the musculature that it attempted to depict. Twentieth Century Fox soon released a short film that purported to show the life that underpinned his success. At a time when documentaries were rarely made about celebrities of any ilk, it followed Harris at home, in training and in competition. In the autumn, he accepted an invitation to appear as a guest of honour at the El Alamein reunion show at Earls Court, where he took to the stage along-side luminaries including Winston Churchill, General Eisenhower and General Montgomery, the men who had conducted the Allied effort when Harris had been a mere private.

He appeared at the Royal Command Performance with an exclusive clique of sport stars that included Stanley Matthews, Stirling Moss and the motorcyclist Geoff Duke. As the only one able to perform for the audience, Harris was given centre stage, bowing regally for the future Queen and Princess Margaret before performing his rollers routine. Nobody seemed to notice that he was half-cut, having spent the preceding hours drinking in a pub nearby with the comic actors Harry Secombe and Eric Sykes. Photographs of the after-party depict him holding court alongside Frances Day, the actress and singer who scandalised polite society with her bisexual affairs. As Harris's friend, Jimmy Savile, then an aspiring music-hall compère, said: 'He had broken the mould. We didn't have world champions then but he did it again and again and again. What he had done was legendary.' A cycling enthusiast, Savile had competed in the inaugural Tour of Britain that year. In time, Harris would demand that the television and radio shows employed Savile when they wished to interview him because Savile's questions were informed. Harris hated to have his time wasted.

His legend was enhanced with the conclusions that the physician Sir Adolphe Abrahams drew after a physiological study of Harris. The founder of modern sports medicine, Abrahams said that Harris was built like an engine that was capable of producing 'the highest possible horsepower' over a short lapse in time. 'The muscular development of his legs surpassed that of any cyclist I had ever examined,' he wrote, detailing the measurements: the circumference of Harris's thigh just above the kneecap was 21¾ inches, while his calf measured an awesome 15 inches. His leg muscles were perfectly separated, too, with none overlapping as they did on many a lesser mortal. 'He was what we called thin-skinned, so his muscle definition was very prominent.' Geldard said. 'You looked at him and you thought, "Wow, this guy must be good."' He also had the largest chest expansion (four inches) of any athlete that Abrahams encountered, betraying his explosive respiratory power. His back and upper arms had hypertrophied through the force with which he pulled on his handlebars. 'I used to sit on the 200-metre line at a race to watch Reg jump,' Jim Love said. 'When he pressed down with his right foot, the whole side of his body tensed up. Likewise then with his left. You could see every muscle in his back. It looked like a bag of snakes.'

Abrahams even took Harris's admission that he was 'highly strung' as evidence that he was psychologically suited to his profession, given that 'instead of solidity, he must be capable of rapid decisions and of inspired enterprises, of brain and brawn'. Writing for *Cycling*, Abrahams illustrated his findings with a collection of photographs that depicted Harris in only a pair of briefs, muscles clenched in different poses. Though his upper body is hardly impressive compared to a modern athlete – partly because Harris never lifted a weight – one interviewee of mine recalled seeing one such portrait pinned up in his doctor's surgery to illustrate the ideal physique.

Away from the public eye Harris lived a life that reflected such rarefied status. At the time he lived with Dorothy in Frensham

Cottage, a handsome detached property on Handforth Road in Wilmslow, the pleasant Cheshire village. Soon he would pay £27,000 for a much bigger Tudor-style house close to the nearby village of Mottram St Andrew. The average house then cost £1,500, but Harris got much for his money, including a vast cellar that would store his thousands of bottles of wine, several acres of professionally maintained gardens and a lake with two swans. As well as part-time ground staff, he employed a French housekeeper who lived with them. After visiting it, the circus began to refer to him as 'M'Lord'.

'People assumed we called him "M'Lord" because he resembled a well-to-do English aristocrat, but that was only partly true,' Derksen wrote. 'It was also because he always dreamt about owning such an estate.' Taken from his autobiography, this precluded a surreal allegorical passage that you assumed was designed to depict (and perhaps mock) the fierce aspirations Derksen identified in his friend. 'When M'Lord rode a velodrome, often he would imagine that he was on horseback inspecting his land. When dressed in cycling gear inside the track, he would imagine himself in leather boots and peaked cap, surveying an estate that ran to the horizon. On his first trips abroad, he slept overnight in the back of his car, dreaming of a sweeping driveway, open fire and servants attending to him. Many people have such dreams but few are able to realise them.

M'Lord did though, single-handedly, and he needed only ten years.'

Harris did not seem to mind his nickname, even though it was gently satirical. Presumably he liked the power it implied: he wanted, it seemed, to rule not only cycling but also some impossible private fiefdom. He would also have liked the lineage that the title suggested. For, as he trampled over opponents in those heavy boots, he wanted to feel fresh roots holding steady beneath him. Little wonder that the abiding image from Derksen's imagining is that of a man who was essentially alone.

CHAPTER 10
1952

In the early spring of 1952, Harris approached a young cyclist called Cyril Bardsley and suggested they spend a couple of weeks training together on the track. Aged only 20, Bardsley had emerged suddenly over the past 12 months to become the best young amateur sprinter in Britain. A year earlier, he had beaten Alan Bannister to the national title and surprised even his club-mates within the Manchester Wheelers afterwards by reaching the semi-finals of the World Championship. Harris had seen Bardsley at the track but did not know him well. Having heard positive opinions about him, he wanted to find out more about the young pretender for himself.

Their fortnight together went well. Harris found Bardsley powerful but not so much to suggest his status as the country's best might be under threat. The apprentice plumber was reserved and respectful, too, and showed an enthusiasm to learn from Harris. His precocious success had not gone to his head. Harris decided, then, that he would serve as an ideal training partner and demanded that Raleigh draw up their second professional contract. 'They offered me £10 a week,' Bardsley said. This was only a few pounds more than Bardsley earned already – and three times less than Harris – but Harris promised that he would earn much more in appearance fees, as long as he applied himself properly to the challenge. 'Cyril's track education will have to start all over again,' he said. 'He may never rise above professional mediocrity. But it is enough that Britain's most promising young sprinter is getting his chance to make good. As his mentor, I will do everything possible to groom him for cycling stardom. If I were not confident of success, I wouldn't even dream of taking on the job.'

On Harris's suggestion, Bardsley spent his first few months at a track school in Paris. As Harris had been, so Bardsley was invigorated by the Spartan education and returned to Britain hopeful that Harris would continue his fast-tracked education and ensure he could hold his own by the start of the outdoor season. Instead, he found that Harris was actually reluctant to pass on advice and preferred simply to ride. Perhaps he felt Bardsley should learn for himself, just as Harris had done, though the apprentice suspected his supposed mentor did not want him to develop lest that might threaten the status quo. 'I thought Harris might have been able to coach me better,' he said. 'Not just train me but actually give us advice on tactics, but we had to find out for ourselves. He was being protective of it.' As Bardsley began to travel abroad, he encountered similar resistance from the circus. With only so much appearance money available to them, they did not easily welcome a newcomer unless his talent gave them no other option. 'They wanted someone to race against. They couldn't just race against each other all the time, but it was hard to break into [the elite]. They wanted to keep it for themselves. You had to be really exceptional.'

Bardsley's confidence was further undermined because Harris was so competitive in training, even in the most casual ride. Though they trained together every day when both were in the country, Bardsley got the better of his partner only twice, and even then found that Harris refused to accept that he had been surpassed. 'He would never admit to it,' Bardsley said. 'He always let you win, by either slowing up and not competing or, if he did lose, he would let it be known that he wasn't at his best. He would have an excuse.'

Others identified that trait in Harris. An international in the individual pursuit, Neville Tong trained with Harris in his first few road rides after the Scunthorpe cyclist fractured his skull in a crash at Fallowfield. 'He was gentle with me but he was always half-wheeling me,' Tong said. 'He couldn't help it. I'd think that I'd go along with him but then he'd push forward a bit more.

He were a competitive bloke. He had to be to win. That's all that really mattered to him.'

Pete Brotherton was another Lincolnshire pursuit specialist who trained with Harris. In return for a discreet five-pound payment, Brotherton and his tandem partner Eric Thompson would pace Harris at Fallowfield because he struggled to find individuals strong enough to push him as hard as he wanted to go. In cycling, they called such men 'chopping blocks', training partners who were there simply to lay the platform on which a stronger cyclist built his strength. 'We'd come in to train in the morning but if his times weren't good, he'd say, "Let's come back in the afternoon,"' Brotherton said. 'He wouldn't say, "We'll try again tomorrow." He would train until he was good on that day. Only when he got the times, then he'd relax.' Often it seemed as if Harris was competing against himself. 'It's called ego. You're not going to be beaten. You're not going to be put down. Some athletes have that. Reg did.'

Harris's relationship with Bardsley and other leading domestic riders was not helped by his reluctance to fraternise with them. Cycling then was fiercely communal. People were attracted to it partly for that reason, with many of the men who rode together then remaining friends in their dotage. Yet Harris was rarely seen with these riders away from the track. He did not invite them into his home. This may have been partly because he was about a decade older than most of them; only a professional could afford to continue cycling into his thirties. It probably also owed something to him being fiercely private. Almost to a man, however, his training partners on the track now felt Harris considered himself above them. 'I say this very advisedly but you admired Reg as a sprinter, as a bike rider. End of story,' Norman Sheil, a former world amateur pursuit champion, said. 'You never got close to him to know him. This was the point. You didn't socialise with him. Let me put it another way: he didn't socialise with you. He was out of our league financially and every other way.' Don Burgess, another member of the Britain team then, drew a similar conclusion. 'A lot of the English riders in those days were working-class lads who had grabbed a bike from somewhere and did a bit of racing but Harris didn't like to associate with the down-and-out bikies,' he said. 'He was civil. He conducted himself well but he wasn't giving any secrets away. He thought a lot of himself.'

Other cyclists were more cutting in their analysis of him. 'He wasn't nice to a lot of people,' Bardsley said. I asked for an example. 'His mother. It was just the general attitude towards her. She seemed very nice and ordinary. She used to go very early [to the track] because the seats she liked were by the finishing line but he cleared off afterwards and would hardly speak to them [Elsie and

Joe Harris]. He didn't live far away yet he wouldn't even take them to a lunch. They used to have to take their own sandwiches.'*

Even worse was an accusation from the wife of a former Wheeler, who said: 'Reg used to say, "I've slept with every wife in the Wheelers." I'd say, "Well, you haven't slept with me." He'd say, "Well, I haven't caught you yet." I think it was all wind and piss, though. He was showing off. They were all quite respectable girls."'

Such behaviour prompted Cyril Cartwright's reluctance to train with Harris. Alan Bannister held a similarly low opinion of his club-mate. 'Alan summed him up to me: "Reg was a great cycling champion, a thorough professional, but as a man a failure,"' Fenwick said. 'I think I would change that to, as a man a shit, but Alan was a kind chap.'

Brotherton read a little deeper into Harris's dark side. A thoughtful, perceptive man, who went on to train a generation of Australia's best cyclists, Brotherton focused on Harris's perceived arrogance and regarded it as evidence of inner weakness. To his mind, Harris needed to feel above those who were below him in the sporting or social hierarchy. 'He wasn't confident,' he said. 'I was close enough to him to know that. He made

---

* It should be noted that this was Harris's *public* attitude towards his mother and stepfather. In private he doted on Elsie. In photographs you find him hugging her at a time when few men managed such maternal affection. For years he provided the couple with money that he eventually found stuffed down the back of the sofa, which exasperated him: to the socially aspirant, savings represented the worst wastefulness.

himself confident with his performance.' Tentatively, I wondered if this potential self-esteem shortfall was connected to his past. Brotherton agreed, revealing that a handful of cyclists knew about the uncertainty surrounding Harris's father but had never dared to discuss it with him. 'That's a big factor in what we're talking about,' he said. 'He never talked about it. People don't talk about what they're fighting against. But why would you push yourself so much if it wasn't to cover something else up?' Brotherton admitted to psychic pain he was wrought when mercilessly bullied at school. Brotherton suspected the absence of a father troubled Harris. 'Many sportsmen are sportsmen for a reason,' he said. 'Either they had a rough upbringing or they don't feel confident in themselves or in the work they do, and they try to make themselves elite so that they have a better position in life. Reg made himself confident with his performance, with his sports cars, in relationships: with everything he did in life. He had to convince himself he was number one.' If this was true, Harris's first tragedy was that his solution to his weakness only stoked it. His second was that nobody really cared about his background. They judged him only on the consequences of him rejecting it.

In the past year Harris's fondness for competing at the Parc des Princes had grown. With its long straights and tight bends, the layout of the track suited him, while French supporters had always liked him for the polite, gracious way in which he conducted himself. He felt comfortable in the city from having lived there and had picked up enough French to be able to communicate with its inhabitants (even though French riders mocked his command of their tongue behind his back). 'I enjoyed riding there even more than I enjoyed riding at home,' he said. At Fallowfield he found the proximity of the fans to the track could unnerve him. 'This never happened in Paris. I felt completely at ease; Parisians had taken me to their heart.'

It was unusual, then, to see him suddenly lose his cool in an early round of the 1952 World Championship following a contest involving Van Vliet and Bardsley. Much to Harris's disgust, Van Vliet had chopped down on Bardsley while high up the banking, forcing several spokes to fly from the Briton's wheel and effectively forcing him out of the race. On winning the race, the Dutchman had clearly infringed rules to extricate himself from a bad position – he had also tried to barge Bardsley out of position – but the debutant lacked the confidence to lodge a protest against such an experienced opponent. 'Harris put in the protest on my behalf,' he said. Harris picked up Bardsley's bike and held it up before the judges to give them evidence of the collision. 'He did it because we were on the same team, but he would sooner have had me in the final or the semi-final than Van Vliet.'

After a brief conversation, the judges decided that the result should stand, but not before word of Harris's actions had reached Van Vliet and infuriated him. As Woodland wrote, Van Vliet regarded Harris's conduct as an act of great betrayal, and 'a long friendship ended there and then'. Within minutes, Van Vliet had begun seeking partners with whom he might be able to conspire against Harris, regardless that the circus had agreed to ride only as individuals in the event. Harry England was told that Derksen had agreed to sacrifice himself for Van Vliet should the two of them be drawn against the champion. Others reported seeing Van Vliet holding intense conversations with Plattner and Bergomi. As Van Vliet, Harris and Plattner prepared to contest the first semi-final, England said that British reporters among the press corps feared that 'the circus wanted a continental winner'.

With three-quarters of a lap left, and Plattner in the lead ahead of Van Vliet in second, the Dutchman wound down his speed just below the top of the banking, thereby narrowing the gap to Harris behind him. This was a bizarre tactic unless Van Vliet wanted to lose. When Plattner then attacked and Van Vliet failed to respond, Harris realised that not only was this the case but that Van Vliet was concerned specifically with preventing him from winning. 'I was too close to get past,' Harris said. 'I was effectively blocked. I shouted. Arie paid no attention. I was in the right place in a "right race" but there had obviously been collusion and I could do nothing about it.' When eventually Harris got out from behind Van Vliet – it is very difficult to overtake when travelling slowly on bankings – Plattner was 40 metres ahead. Even for Harris that was too much ground to make up.

Similar happened in the repêchage when Van Vliet got his front wheel to overlap Harris's back wheel just as Senfftleben launched his jump on the back straight, thus preventing Harris from following the Frenchman as he surged ahead unassailably on extended cranks and a huge 100.5-inch gear, the perfect equipment for just such a circumstance. The circus had completed their coup, leaving Plattner to win his professional world title, with Senfftleben and Derksen third. 'It was one of the bitterest pills I ever had to swallow,' Harris said.

His response was ruthless. Considering the old rules of the circus void, he went about inflicting on his opponents as many devastating defeats as he could. Within 48 hours he had beaten Plattner and Van Vliet in successive two-up races before 55,000 fans in Amsterdam. In the weeks that followed, Harris scored victories in Zurich, Copenhagen and Paris (twice), smashing a Vel d'Hiver track record that had stood for 39 years. For the first time considering the so-called revenge races to be just what their name implied, he posted four consecutive wins over Van Vliet. 'In his anger, Reg just decided that, "If they're going to do that [conspire against him], I'm going to show them what I can do,"'

Peter Procter, British road race champion in 1951, said. 'It was a matter of pride. I remember Reg telling me that he swore he would never let them beat him again. In about 20 races after the World Championship, he won all of them.'

As hostilities ensued into the following season, races that had once unfolded pleasingly were now increasingly physical, brutish affairs, with every man fighting for himself and giving little thought to the spectacle. In Aarhus, Van Vliet shut down Harris so sharply that he lost control and crashed, prompting rivals to insist unsuccessfully that he lodged a protest: Harris did not care much for the rules any more. In Brussels, Gerardin, Senfftleben and Scherens collided in a four-up race with Van Vliet. In Zurich, Harris suffered what he considered his worst-ever crash, tearing the skin on his right arm from the wrist to elbow, hitting his helmet against the concrete and grazing his knees and back. He cut his hands, too, punishment for refusing ever to wear gloves lest they might fractionally reduce his control of the bike. He claimed that afterwards he fainted four times on the journey back to England. 'It was an enormous bloody war,' he said, in an interview with Woodland. 'Life was getting bloody tough every time we were engaged anywhere. The other riders were saying, "When are you two going to shake hands, Reg?" There was crossfire and the other guys were getting caught in it. But I was determined to win on every possible occasion, regardless that one of us could crack up and that outsiders could come in and take our places.'

By the time of the following year's World Championships at the Oerlikon track in Zurich, the situation had improved only because Harris had been forced to miss much of the season through injury and illness. Even before that second crash in Zurich, he had fallen ill with pneumonia, which in turn led to him contracting bronchitis as his immune system deteriorated. On his return to training, he had suffered another setback with a complaint that was diagnosed as an anal fistula, submitting him to great pain in his lower back. When he claimed also to have caught pleurisy, you wondered whether a few in this long litany of complaints had been exaggerated, though others do at least remember him being very unwell. He was absent from the circuit for several months.

As a result, he arrived at the Oerlikon a week before the event unsure whether he should even compete, particularly as its short 333-metre circumference made three-up even more unpredictable than it was elsewhere, despite its unique 'prickly concrete' – Harris's term – that provided riders with increased grip against the surface. His mood worsened with the discomfort he felt in his hands and back during the first training session (Harris had earlier refused medical advice to have surgery on his spine). 'I was feeling terrible and I was not terribly interested in getting silver or bronze,' he said. 'I needed gold and the accident seemed to have put that beyond my grasp.' MacDonald persuaded Harris to postpone any decision until the end of the week, by which time he clocked close to 11.4 seconds for four sprints. 'Time after time, after crying off, he would return so quickly that he would be considered Superman with his powers of recovery,' Godwin said. 'One of his failings, his way of controlling the sport almost.' Perhaps, but that made his progress through to the final all the more compelling.

There he faced Van Vliet and Enzo Sacchi, the Florentine who had broken into the elite in only his first year as a professional, a mark of the power that had propelled him to win the past two amateur world titles and the kilometre time trial at the previous year's Olympics. As the sun fell behind the venue's one grandstand, positioned along the back straight, there was even talk that Sacchi should be considered favourite to win, though this owed as much to the speculation that the Italian federation had bribed Van Vliet as it did to Sacchi's nascent talent. The rumour reached such a pitch that Van Vliet felt obliged to visit Harris in his cabin shortly before the race. 'He confided to me that such attempts had been made,' Harris said. The Dutchman, however, insisted that he had rejected them, despite the breakdown in their relationship. 'I was puzzled,' Harris said. 'Why should he warn me? Was it a psychological tactic or a fact?'

Concerned that Van Vliet wished only to unsettle him, Harris called Sacchi into his cabin. 'He asked me to believe that he had absolutely no part in these attempts, and moreover assured me that there would be no cooperation from him.' Seconds before they mounted, Van Vliet reiterated his claim. 'I give you my word, Reg,' he said, putting Harris's mind at ease. 'I will go for my chance.'

Harris was encouraged when Sacchi was drawn as lead-out man as this would allow Harris to track the Italian, whom he regarded as more of a threat now than Van Vliet. Within 100 metres, however, Harris had reason to doubt the Dutchman's intentions again when he moved into the lead. This seemed an inexplicable tactic. Even a cyclist of Van Vliet's staying power could not expect to hold a lead against such opponents so far out. 'The situation just did not add up,' Harris said. 'I became certain that Van Vliet was not riding for himself.' With no alternative, Harris moved into second to keep Van Vliet within striking distance, despite that manoeuvre allowing Sacchi to draft him.

Now part of a train around the top of the banking, Harris then made a critical mistake, looking over his shoulder to check Sacchi's position, even though Van Vliet had his eyes fixed on Harris. The Dutchman spotted his chance and attacked instantly, opening up a 50-metre lead that Harris could not make up neither on the Oerlikon's short back straight nor on the bend, leaving him to sit up early, long before the finish line, exhausted, embarrassed, and unconcerned that it allowed Sacchi to take second. For by then Harris realised that Van Vliet had sold him the perfect double bluff. His only compensation was confirmation that his former friend had not betrayed him. 'Arie was world champion fair and square,' he said. 'The least I could do was offer my hand.'

CHAPTER 11
1953

The history of drugs in competitive cycling is almost as old as the sport itself, with stories dating to the nineteenth century about the substances that riders used on the road and track. Had you then visited Celtic Park in Glasgow, say, or the concrete track in Catford, you might have seen the man perhaps most commonly linked with the practice, James 'Choppy' Warburton, a shady Lancastrian who served as a riders' agent and supplied them with bottles of liquid of uncertain content in full view of the crowds, feeding men such as the brilliant Welsh roadman Arthur Linton and his compatriot sprinter Jimmy Michael with what *Sporting Life* magazine – as Les Woodland noted – understood was strychnine, trimethyl and heroin. Both men died young, Michael aged 22, Linton when he was only two years older, and a Sydney anti-doping forum in 2004 cited him as the first cyclist to have died as a result of substance abuse.

The practice grew more widespread at the Six-Day Races that are thought to have started in the now-destroyed Agricultural Hall in Islington before gaining huge popularity in America, most notably in Madison Square Garden, hence the name of the modern incarnation of the race: the Madison. These lasted just as long as their name suggested – albeit with breaks for a nap – with the winner being whoever completed the most laps. Typically, riders there started on black coffee, moved on to peppermint, then had either heroin dropped on to their tongues or strychnine rubbed into their muscles, or both, once they began to lose consciousness. Six-Day Racing was still thriving in Harris's time, with most of his contemporaries competing in them because the money was good. Though given several lucrative offers to join them, he always resisted, probably because he lacked the stamina for the event.

Doping became gradually more prevalent through until the 1930s, but was suddenly widespread after the war once the drugs that had been prescribed for the military flooded the market. By the early 1950s, professional riders were openly consuming phials of substances inside the track or cracking them open in dressing rooms in full view of their opponents. Occasionally you saw a rider having his stomach pumped after a race to get whatever poison had boosted him out of his system. Because it happened mostly among the professional class abroad, the NCU commissioned the team doctor Christopher Woodard to conduct a study of the situation. Having travelled to all the major races, interviewing riders and their support staff, he concluded that 'the drug-taking was not practised by the ordinary run of cyclist. It was exclusively used by some international champions who, apparently, have discovered that their performances are so close to each other that the result can depend upon the taking of artificial stimulants'.

Harris inevitably was asked for his response. 'The habit of taking stimulants prior to important and international events is becoming increasingly prevalent,' he admitted. 'Results, particularly finals, are totally unpredictable simply because stimulants are used. Until the practice is stopped, I feel that it will not be a case of the best man winning.' Asked whether he doped, Harris claimed that he had tried it only twice but on neither occasion found any benefit. In private, he told Fenwick likewise, citing one instance as the final of a Grand Prix of Paris, which he lost to Mockridge after Derksen had delayed the conclusion of the race by balancing still while in the lead for so long that the short-term effects of Harris's dope had passed. 'He said Mockridge pissed on him,' Fenwick said. 'I don't think he ever took drugs again.' Other interviewees of mine felt the same, though two did reveal that Harris took amphetamines to stay awake while driving overnight between meetings abroad.

Yet, in a BBC TV interview years later, he opened up a little more on the subject. 'Yes, I experimented with drugs, in world-record attempts and important races, but never in World

Championships,' he said. 'But I found that my nerve control was harmed by it. It was a failure, although I am not ashamed to admit that, had I found it a success, I would have used it in world-title events.'

It might seem strange, then, that Harris had by 1953 built up such a close relationship with Louis Guerlach, the wily, silver-haired Belgian who was then the most coveted soigneur on the track scene and admired both for his subtle tactical insight and for the pharmaceutical contents of the carefully packed black case that he carried to all events. Harris insisted that he chose always to work with Guerlach at World Championships for his skills as a masseur, as well as his personality, claiming that the lean 63-year-old former road rider 'had a very penetrating knowledge of men and their ways, particularly cyclists and all who surround him'. Given how much time they spent together, this was almost certainly an honest opinion of Guerlach's qualities though it was far from the only reason that Harris insisted Guerlach worked exclusively with him in the fortnight before a World Championship, as well as during them. He also wanted to ensure that none of his rivals profited from Guerlach's substances. 'Guerlach was the big dope soigneur of the time but Reg didn't use him for drugs,' Pete Brotherton said. 'He hired him so nobody else got to him. That was the deal: Guerlach had to stay with Reg.'

*

By the close of the 1953 outdoor season Harris was disillusioned with cycling. Even aged 33, he was still the fastest man in the world but as long as the UCI persisted with the three-up system, he was resigned that only with great luck would he reclaim the world title, a prospect made more depressing when it was the only event that he really valued. After his illnesses through the previous winter, he was also troubled by the thought of spending another three to four months in the cold and damp around Manchester. It was with fortuitous timing, then, that Ted Waterford, an Australian promoter, offered Harris the opportunity to spend the winter competing Down Under.

In theory, Waterford's proposition seemed straightforward enough. In return for a handsome salary and full travelling and accommodation expenses for both him and Dorothy, Harris had to ride at a fixed number of meetings over three months, competing both in handicap races against local riders and exhibition events against Patterson and Stan Daly, the Australian national champion. Only on arriving there, it seemed, did Harris realise that Waterford had arranged for him the most exhausting schedule imaginable, while also cheekily fixing media arrangements that were not part of the initial plan. On a typical week, Harris would race in Melbourne on Tuesday, Geelong on Thursday and Adelaide the following day, before returning to Melbourne to race at the MCG at the weekend, with minimal opportunity to train. Often this would involve flying overnight and travelling directly from the airport to the track. Christmas was perhaps the worst period, with Harris racing in Geelong, Tasmania and Melbourne (twice) in less than a week, covering about 1,000 miles.

To make the experience even more difficult, track riding was consistently as aggressive in Australia as it was in Europe during the height of Harris's row with Van Vliet. Based mostly in Victoria, it had yet to produce a European-style professional class and was contested mostly by amateurs who had been reared on converted horse-trotting tracks that were then found in most small rural towns. Harris even competed on a few of these, with several local clubs having bulldozed clear the surface and relaid it with sand, then sun-hardened asphalt for his arrival. This produced a fast surface for events that, in the case of the handicaps, were chaotic by European standards. Riders were paced up to 200 metres around the track and invariably had conspired with the bookmakers that lined the venue. 'You weren't allowed outside the track because you could talk to people who were betting,' Brotherton, who settled in Australia, said. 'But it was funny. The riders went to the mark with all sorts of signals to the punters, touching their nose, their ears, putting their helmet on and touching their knees.' Away from the politics of the circus, Harris was gradually invigorated, regardless that the tour had involved him in 75 meetings in three months. 'For the first time, I decided to run away from an atmosphere that was unhappy and seek new scenes. The sunshine, the clean atmosphere and hard outdoor racing did all that I hoped. I returned to Europe in good mental and physical condition.'

After a brief holiday in Honolulu to recuperate, his mood improved further soon after his return to England in late March when he discovered that the circus had successfully petitioned the UCI to demand that the World Championships revert to two-up. Though some of the elite might have been glad that Harris's power had been dissipated, they were also frustrated that the three-up format meant that most of them did not even progress as far as they did under the old system. Even Van Vliet had signed the letter sent to the federation. 'In ordinary events, three rides make it easier [to beat Harris] but, in the World Championships, I like to be sure of my chance of winning and that is only possible when you have only one to beat,' he said.

Buoyed by this development, Harris attacked his road training with vigour. Having been able to do hardly anything but compete in Australia, he was badly out of condition and had many lost hours to make up. Initially, he called on his trusted road partners from around Manchester, a small collection of club riders that included young Alan Partington, Harris's old friends Joe Pilling and Bill Brown, and Albert Bagnall, whom he had got to know when both visited Sibbit's shop. Harris had even arranged for Raleigh to give Bagnall a job in their Manchester depot once he was discharged from the military in the late 1940s. In return, Harris could call on Bagnall whenever he was short of a training partner. 'I'd get a call from Reg in the morning, then go in and say, "I'm away at lunchtime,"' he said. Harris's clout within the company was such that Bagnall's boss never complained.

Once reasonably fit, Harris then teamed up with the British road team that Hercules had put together. This pitted him alongside the best long-distance riders in the country, including the national champion Bob Maitland and runner-up Brian Robinson, both of whom rode the Tour de France. Once close to his competitive weight of 11st 4lb, Harris soon found that he could more than hold his own on their shorter rides. 'He was training fanatically,' Norman Sheil said. 'The Hercules team used to hate him going training with them. He would go out with these fellas and be yakking all the way, and then would rip the legs off them after 70 miles. It was brutal.'

Finding it harder now to keep weight off, Harris reverted to a more stoic lifestyle too, cutting out all sugary food and red meat on Woodard's advice. Wistfully he admitted 'the glamour of the early days has gone' though he was still on the red wine and consuming three to four ounces of pipe tobacco a week.

When eventually he returned to competition, he posted results almost as encouraging as any of his best seasons. In his first big race back, he beat Sacchi by inches then defeated Patterson in the final of the Grand Prix of Odense. He claimed the Grand Prix of Amsterdam and scored a spectacular win over Van Vliet in the deciding race of the Grand Prix of Copenhagen. Perhaps his only significant defeat came in the Grand Prix of London, a competition that pitched professionals against amateurs, when he lost to his young compatriot Lloyd Binch. The unspoken dynamics of the circus were uncertain now but that Harris was in peak condition was made clear when he equalled the world record for the final 200 metres of a race with a time of 10.9 seconds in his final contest before the World Championships in Cologne.

Of all cities in the old West Germany, Cologne had the richest track-cycling history. It had produced the country's most celebrated sprinters, Albert Richter and Toni Merkens, both of whom had been among Scherens' closest competitors before the war. Colognians still craved for a successor who might match their achievements: an Olympic gold in Merkens' case, three World Championships finals for Richter. Their best chance of success in these championships was with Walter Lohmann in the motor-paced event on the Monday after the more prestigious races had finished, hence it was the only day that had sold out its tickets.

When Harris turned up on the Saturday morning, however, he found a venue that somehow reflected his new Spartan lifestyle, with scaffolding dominating the track and terracing open only alongside the home straight. The UCI had given Cologne the championship as a gesture of support but the city had yet to recover from the destruction it suffered in the war and they had not completed the reconstruction of the venue in time. With grey skies and unseasonal damp adding to the gloomy intensity of the event, Harris found that his opponents were prepared to resort to unpleasant tactics now that the format made them much less likely to beat him.

Gosselin was the first to try to unsettle him, sharply turning up the banking on the penultimate corner in the second of their first-round races just as Harris had jumped – forcing him to slow up, but still he recovered to win, finishing in 11.6 seconds.

In their quarter-final, Ghella forced Harris on to the apron with a similar switch, a dirty tactic that got the Italian disqualified. In the semi-final, Sacchi dared to try a similar stunt, though this time Harris leant back into the Italian to hold his position on the cement edge. For about 30 yards, the men persisted in that position, like conjoined twins, until eventually Sacchi relented and ceded to Harris a critical lead. In desperation, the younger man shot up his arm in protest down the back straight but it was a forlorn request.

By now the relationship between Harris and Van Vliet had thawed. Quite who had reached out first was unclear but there had been successive gestures designed to build a rapprochement: a shared taxi ride, an offer to cover the other man's bill in a café, Harris calling an end to the brutal defeats that he had inflicted on the Dutchman. Harris, it seemed, realised that ultimately he would suffer just as much by maintaining the impasse. Woodland wrote that 'they became grudging colleagues, if not friends'.

They were still prepared to engage in a few mind games, though. Now aged 38, Van Vliet had claimed in the build-up to Cologne that he might retire after the competition, given that his world-title victory the previous year had finally sated the 'hunger' that had driven him since Harris usurped him in 1949. That seemed an attempt to convey his old insouciance, implying he did not care so much about the result in Cologne. Harris responded with a devastating insult, claiming that Van Vliet's advancing years had left him in 'weakened condition'. Yet still Van Vliet also qualified for the final.

With rain falling through much of Sunday afternoon, the men were not called for their contest until close to midnight, by which time many of the 12,000 spectators were shivering in anticipation of the event. Harris emerged first from his cabin, accompanied by Guerlach, his son Armoury, a 20-year-old amateur on the Belgian team, and Scherens, who had visited Harris before the race. It must have made an intimidating sight: the last great sprinter, the incumbent and the man who carried with him the most effective drugs. Later Harris would tell Harry England that his preceding tactical discussions with Scherens had been 'significant'.

It could have been Scherens that suggested to Harris that he attack midway through the penultimate turn, taking Van Vliet by surprise because Harris could not usually be expected to hold his sprint so far out from the end. By the final bend, the champion had edged ahead of Harris on his outside shoulder and was apparently poised to punish him for his ambition. Harris, however, seemed to know exactly how much power Van Vliet had left – perhaps he was weakened – and held his front wheel in front of Van Vliet's rear spokes, forcing him to stay high on the banking. As the finish line emerged, Harris then kicked through the transition to win by half a wheel.

In the second race, Van Vliet responded with an even more unexpected manoeuvre, shooting through a three-foot gap between Harris and the concrete wall on the outside of the track with three-quarters of a lap to go. Harris kept his position until eventually the men dovetailed, emerging on to the back straight riding, as *The Bicycle* report said, 'out of their saddles, shoulder to shoulder', presumably venting a year's worth of frustration with one another and producing a spectacle as thrilling as any race they had orchestrated.

Harris won by a length, prompting another ruinous barb in the immediate aftermath of his victory. 'I should think I was one of the few pros who was not doped for that sprint,' he said. Forever the classical English gentleman, our Lord insisted that his only stimulant had been a strong mug of tea. 'There was no need to take anything stronger. I knew my form was good.' Within 24 hours, Harris had finished behind the French champion Jacques Bellenger in a revenge meeting in Paris. Before the end of the week the new world champion had lost to Van Vliet before 35,000 spectators. His response was only to say that he was 'not unduly worried', though that hardly surprised. Such defeats revealed nothing more than that the old order had been restored.

Overall the championships were Britain's most successful yet, with the amateur team winning four medals in a competition that comprised only three events, with Cyril Peacock claiming gold in the sprint, Brotherton and Sheil winning silver and bronze in the individual pursuit, and Joe Bunker securing a bronze in the motor-paced event. Brotherton admitted that Harris's unprecedented example had been crucial to their success, regardless of any personal issues they had with him. 'Reg paved the way for all of us,' he said. 'He was the one we looked up to. He gave us confidence to go to Europe and win races – we didn't have that before. He broke the mould.'

A surgical instrument-maker from Fulham, who had learnt about self-discipline during his recent national service, Peacock was talked about as a potential successor to Harris as professional world sprint champion. He certainly had strong credentials, having also won the past three national championships, as well as that year's Empire Games. Aged 25, he was approaching his physical peak, too, while his confidence and blue-eyed, blond good looks made him more marketable than some counterparts. Few were surprised, then, when Raleigh rewarded his feat in Germany with a professional contract. 'I aim to make a career out of cycling,' Peacock said. 'It will be tough. There is a limit to one's welcome in a "school" where the bread and butter is limited and shared, but my ambition has always been to emulate Reg Harris, thus my first objective is the professional sprint title. If one Englishman can do it, so can another.'

Such a declaration was a terrible mistake. You did not publicly plan to trump the circus without first having served an apprenticeship, not least when its most powerful figure was your compatriot and thus had most to lose through your potential success. 'If Cyril's ambition was to displace me, it was my job to resist and beat that challenge,' Harris said, with no hint of sympathy. 'I gave him countless beatings.' He also ensured that Peacock struggled for contracts and gained little traction with the other members of the elite. After an unsuccessful first season the effort was beginning to tell on Peacock. 'It's a new type of racing,' he said. 'As an amateur I was able to win easily. As a professional, I've got to race as hard as I can just to get there at all.'

Over the following winter, he tried to compensate for his limitations by training even more fanatically than perhaps even Harris ever did, covering thousands of miles in the saddle while also bulking up his slim physique in the gym. This marginally improved his results the following season as he reached the semi-final of the Grand Prix of Paris and the last eight at the World Championships, but the latter performance proved to be his best as a professional. He retired in acrimony and frustration the following year after refusing to re-run an early round of the World Championships that he felt that he had legitimately won. 'I feel that at many stages of Cyril's career, I could have supplied one or two of the keys that open the multi-locked door, if only I'd been allowed to,' Harris said. Brotherton, a close friend of Peacock's, recalled the difficulties between the two men differently. 'Reg didn't want another Englishman on the pedestal,' he said. 'Cyril was a good sprinter. He had the speed and strength. I was very close to him and he didn't get the opportunities. Reg made sure of that.'

CHAPTER 12
1955

In July 1955, the Pedal Club gathered in a small room above The
Horseshoe pub on Tottenham Court Road with the members
unusually excited about their after-dinner speakers. The first to
address an audience of cycling journalists and influential members
of the trade would be Charles Marshall, a celebrated road cyclist
before the Second World War, who now ran the Raleigh division
that built bespoke frames for their sponsored cyclists. The second
was Sidney Buxton, Raleigh's assistant works manager, thus one
of its senior employees. Together they had agreed to reveal hith-
erto secret details about Harris's bike and, most enticingly, to
discuss the near-mythical stories about the lengths they had to
go to, to ensure the frame could withstand his jump.

Stories abounded then – and persist to this day – that Raleigh
often would give Harris a new track bike only for him to force
out the bottom bracket with one powerful kick, a feat that is
almost incomprehensible for the typical amateur cyclist.

As it turned out, Buxton did most of the talking, revealing – as the cycling historian Tony Hadland noted – that the champion insisted on components drawn from suppliers based all over the continent, including Philippe handlebars and Christophe toe-straps from France, Italian Binda pedal straps, and several British parts: Williams cranks and Airlite hubs, as well as the sponsored components from Dunlop, Brooks, and Sturmey-Archer, who paid to supply his gears. Turning to Harris's preferred frame – Buxton had even brought one with him – he revealed the measurements that Harris had settled on shortly after turning professional, while adding that he had since reduced his forkset: the distance between the steering axis and the centre of the front wheel offset, again to give him increased control. Finally, Buxton discussed the measures they had to take to increase the strength of the frame. On all of Harris's bikes, he explained, the chainstay, down tube and seat tube were filled and a lower lug was reinforced, overall making the frame 17 per cent more resistant to what Buxton called 'bottom bracket displacement'. The handlebar stem was made from 'special steel', because Harris had, it transpired, bent and broken plenty of frames merely in practice, a fact confirmed by Bardsley (who by then had joined the army). So, though modern sprint cyclists ride the lightest possible frames, at 5lbs Harris's was actually 20 per cent heavier than the frames on which countless club riders struggled in his wake.

To the untrained eye, Raleigh's replica version looked much the same as Harris's bike, with similar geometry, tubes built with the same carbon-based compound, red enamel finish and RHH initials engraved on the seat tube. With Harris's help they sold millions, not only in Britain and on the continent but also world-wide, helped in large part by the efforts to which he went to promote it. For already, Harris had visited, among other countries, Colombia, Venezuela and Guyana as Raleigh opened franchises there. Jim Hoyte, formerly club secretary at the Guyanese national cycling club (and father-in-law to the football manager Chris Hughton), recalled the showmanship that Harris employed. 'He let every man pass him until there was about 200 metres to go,' he said. 'We thought, "This man cannot ride. Why have they brought him over?" Then suddenly, oh gosh, he flew, taking over everybody, including the last man right before the line.'

Harris toured French-occupied Tunisia with Van Vliet, too, and later would head to Nigeria and Ghana to coincide with the latter's independence-day celebrations. Raleigh arranged for him a demanding schedule, including rollers demonstrations in bike shops and a stint commentating on the country's national track championships. To his astonishment, Accra's biggest cycling club had agreed to form a guard of honour for him at the city's airport, with each man dressed in Raleigh gear to ensure the photo opportunity was not lost. In Lagos, Raleigh arranged for a city club to escort him on a public ride along Marina Highway into the city centre. Like Rocky acquiring disciples on his run through Philadelphia, so many cyclists joined Harris's train that a police escort had to be called. A friend of mine who grew up in Lagos two decades later recalled a history lesson that was devoted to Harris. She had imagined him as a kind of cycling evangelist seeking to spread the sport's popularity abroad.

At much the same time as Harris's association with them, Raleigh had been enjoying a stunning global expansion. From 1946 to 1952 alone, they increased their output by 250 per cent, which meant that they were producing more than a million bicycles a year, employing 80,000 staff at a Nottingham headquarters that now covered 60 acres and was expanded around the same period to the tune of £2,000,000 – almost £50,000,000 in modern currency. The company had become the biggest exporter of bicycles to the United States and had continued to build into the Far East, as well as many of the countries Harris visited. His role in this growth cannot be overstated. As Geoffrey Houston Bowden – great grandson to Sir Frank Bowden, the founder of Raleigh – wrote in his history of the company, Harris's 'outstanding achievements increased the demand for Raleigh bicycles even beyond the level to which the post-war boom had brought them and meant those were years of considerable expansion'.

By 1955, Harris had begun to discuss with Raleigh his future with the company once he had retired from competition and had been promised that they would want to keep him on. However, Harris's ambitions stretched much further than what he assumed would be some form of ambassadorial work and, in the spring of that year, he gave several interviews to the cycling press in which he effectively volunteered himself as national coach, even laying out his vision for the squad.

To his mind, the NCU would only continue to build on its recent international successes by abandoning the committee-based structure that had previously governed the national squad in favour of an all-powerful figure, who would be given a wage to allow him to devote his energies to the job and a four-year contract that would allow him to work within the Olympic cycle. He was willing to take on the task. 'Democracy is all right in its proper way but can be a distinct liability in sporting matters,' he said. 'Several continental countries employ a commissaire technique. We need an individual with decisive ideas on policy, not unwieldy committees.' Though this proposed taking much power away from the union, the NCU secretary, Harry Anderson, said that he was impressed by his plan and claimed that he would be delighted to employ Harris in it if only they could afford him. The role was, and would remain, voluntary. 'We have never had the money to provide the kind of wage that a high-quality candidate would demand,' he said.

Possibly in response, Harris spotted an opportunity to make money from coaching through another avenue when the Manchester Athletic Club put the lease for Fallowfield up for sale, having struggled to turn profit in recent years as attendances to cycling and athletic events had begun slowly to decline. When Harris discovered that they had rejected bids from the city council and Manchester City football club, of £13,500 and £18,000 respectively, because neither could guarantee that the venue would be retained for its two traditional sports, he formed a limited company called RH (Manchester) and, in June, had his undisclosed offer accepted.

Harris's proposal for the venue had been typically grand. He had promised to build a new stand, with improved press facilities and a new 100 by 20 foot dressing-room area, with showers, massage facilities and more than a hundred new lockers. He would get the turnstiles painted, the grass strip relaid between the cycling and running track, and had erected new iron bike hooks against the stadium wall; he hated the clutter that gathered around the track. He indulged in a little egoism by renaming the venue Harris Stadium, though nobody seemed to mind. He had earned that privilege by salvaging the regional cycling community's facility.

His name bestowed glamour on the place anyway, adding lustre to the advertisements that he placed on buses and billboards around the city for future events. Giving the venue its first full-time promoter, Norman Grattage, and groundsman, Len Myatt, Harris also increased the number of billboards and gave companies the opportunity to sponsor tickets. Determined to reverse the decline in attendances – and to prove wrong the several affluent Wheelers who had refused to invest with him – he told Grattage to start subletting the venue to newly fashionable sports such as show-jumping and stock-car racing, too.

Ultimately, he wanted to create the kind of elite track school previously found only abroad, believing the presence of him and other leading professionals would persuade national federations to pay for their best young riders to learn there. This began promisingly, with Derksen, the Germans Werner Potzernheim and Claus Henson, and Marino Morettini, of Italy – the latter three had won medals at the 1952 Olympics – all agreeing to spend time at Harris Stadium over the winter. That, in turn, prompted the German federation to spend £400 on sending its amateur squad to Manchester as part of their preparations for the 1956 Olympics.

Claiming that the project cost him £25,000, Harris then began to use the media – Granada television recorded a film on the stadium's overhaul – to call for the cycling trade to help fund training schemes for the best young British talent at his school, too. 'Our amateurs have always suffered because of poor facilities,' he said. 'Like any school, we produce showmen but we teach track skills too and training is always serious.' That plea fell on deaf ears. Instead Harris's elitist approach soon began to divide opinion. One club rider told me how upset he was to find that now he had to pay an entrance fee to train on a facility that he had previously been able to use for free whenever he wished. Harris offered free admission only on Thursdays, mostly to encourage schoolchildren to take up the sport.

In retrospect, you realise that cycling's ruling body needed another four decades to realise the good sense in what Harris had proposed here and in his vision for the national coach. For only in the 1990s, when British cycling destroyed its old structure, employed a technical director and focused on finding Olympic success with an elite talent group based at Manchester Velodrome did its international status improve. National Lottery funding made that possible but, as Brian Cookson, then the body's president, said, 'Reg was way ahead of his time in that regard.'

A few weeks afterwards Harris had his offer for Fallowfield accepted, he was out riding with his fellow Wheeler Alan

Partington when a dog darted out from beneath a bush by the side of the road and forced both men to swerve and crash. Spotting them in the ditch, the driver of a passing car drew suddenly to a halt to check on them. As they recovered from the shock and got out from beneath their bikes, Partington found that he had grazed a knee while Harris had cut the side of his face. Neither had suffered serious injury, so Partington found it strange that Harris should tell the driver to wait while he examined his face in a wing mirror. 'I thought he was being a bit particular,' he said, by which he meant fussy. 'In those days, Fallowfield, being cement, there were quite a few accidents. They used to keep two ambulances parked up ready to take people to hospital.'

Though 12 years younger than Harris, Partington knew him well. He had first met him aged 14, when Harris was world champion and Partington had slip-streamed him while out on the road. Amused by such impudence, Harris had engaged his young fan in conversation and gave him some advice about his bike, before regretfully saying that he needed to leave him behind. Inspired by the encounter, Partington took up competitive sprinting as soon as he was old enough, aged 16, and quickly became one of the Wheelers' quickest men. Being a young man, he had also the time during the day to accompany Harris on his daily runs. But he still knew better than to question Harris's vanity beside the ditch. 'The following day we were out again, doing our road training,' he said. 'Reg said, "You may have thought I was being a bit particular. I couldn't tell you why because I had to keep it a secret. But what you didn't know was that I was getting married that afternoon."'

Harris was able to wed Dorothy now because Florence had finally agreed to a divorce, but he did not want anybody to know about the ceremony lest the press found out. Dorothy, it transpired, had carried his name until then because she had changed hers by deed poll. 'He said that she dragged him to the registry office,' Partington added.

The added responsibilities that the stadium brought forced Harris to scale back his competitive schedule that summer, so that he arranged to travel abroad only for grands prix and the World Championships. Yet while still able to train hard in Manchester – once the plan for the venue was in place, he left much of the administrative work to Grattage – and being restored to his old role within the elite, he was still able to score impressive victories in Brussels, London and St Etienne. In July, he travelled to Ordrup for the Grand Prix of Copenhagen hoping that it would serve as a good preparation for the worlds in Milan. His professional interests were expanding but he was no less ambitious on the bike, not least because the emergence of a new generation of rider over about the past year had for the first time in a decade threatened to upset the status quo, with men such as the quickly improving Sacchi, his brilliant compatriot Antonio Maspes and the Frenchman Roger Gaignard now all producing performances as impressive as almost anything from the old guard.

Instead, Harris suffered a rare crash in Denmark, smashing his shoulder so hard against the concrete that it shifted an inch out of place. (I know this particular injury to be true because Shelagh Dennis recalled how Harris popped his shoulder for her entertainment in the weeks afterwards.) Initially, he showed his old defiance of medical advice and insisted that he would defend his title in Milan regardless but his body no longer recovered as swiftly as it did in his youth and he found instead that he was unable to race again that year. In his absence, Maspes blew Van Vliet away in the semi-final at the Vigorelli and defeated Plattner in the showpiece.

Harris had first encountered Maspes in the winter of 1949 when he was 17. The Milano's coach, Guido Costa, had asked Harris if he would spend a few weeks training with his rider at Vel d'Hiver. Harris had remarked how well the shy, swarthy teenager was able to stick to his wheel even during sessions that reached 'speeds that normally should not be possible for a boy of his age'. Maspes was a wily apprentice, too, being careful always to finish behind Harris regardless of his condition.

In the immediate years afterward, he had enjoyed steady progress on the international circuit, winning four Italian titles and a bronze medal on the tandem at the 1952 Olympics. Turning professional afterwards, he had needed time to get established within the circus and up until 1954 posted his most impressive result with a third place at the Grand Prix of Paris. Since then, however, he had suddenly blossomed, showing both acceleration and staying power that his teenage performances had hinted at. He was unusually detailed in his approach, too – he insisted on boiling his ballbearings in British oil, perhaps in deference to Harris – and rarely showed emotion on the track. George Pearson described him as 'Mephistophelean-countenanced' even in the white heat of his breakthrough win at the Vigorelli.

Harris beat him in Manchester at the start of the following season but probably more revealing was the subsequent victories that the new champion scored over his predecessor in Paris (by three lengths) and Milan (four). That was followed by two successive defeats for Harris against Plattner, who, aged 33, was two years younger than Harris. However, as if to confirm that one world-title victory in Harris's absence would not dethrone him, he recovered from that to win the grands prix of Amsterdam, Copenhagen, Belgium and Odense. Yet, as he headed into the World Championships at Ordrup, he was still troubled by not having had the opportunity to reverse those four critical losses.

'Reg couldn't bury defeats,' Brotherton said. 'He carried them with him.'

Harris's relationship with Plattner had always been fractious. They fraternised away from competition but often would go weeks barely speaking to each other after another especially fraught confrontation on the track. Usually this was sparked because Plattner would go to more lengths than most professionals to try to find a way to make up for his speed-deficit to Harris. 'Against Reg and Arie, I ride close, stall, do long and short sprints, anything to gain a psychological or tactical edge,' he said. 'The public, the people who pay me, want skill as well as speed.' He could also ride fractionally slower than Harris on a banking, which made it easier for Plattner to give up the lead. A tall, robust man, with full lips and dark eyes, who could have been a model for one of his clothes lines, he applied physical intimidation as far as the rules would allow (and sometimes beyond). 'I do not like rough riding but neither does it frighten me,' he said. When he was drawn against Harris in the semi-finals in Copenhagen, he 'decided to use everything that I had learned'. That entailed him drawing to a standstill seconds after he had led Harris out at the start of their first race.

In track cycling today, sprinters are not allowed to remain stationary on their bikes at all on the first lap and cannot do so for more than three minutes of the second circuit, lest they delay for too long with a tactic that is designed to force an opponent into the lead. In 1956, there were no restrictions, which meant that nobody in the crowd knew how long Harris and his opponent would remain in position at the transition into the first bend, shifting back and forth to stay balanced, eyes fixed on each other to spot the first sign of movement: if the other man broke the impasse, you had to respond quickly to ensure you caught their slipstream. Mockridge recalled how it felt to be involved in this singular battle of wits. 'The crowd would fall silent, loving every second of the strain on our faces, wondering how long our taut muscles could keep up the balancing act,' he wrote. 'We looked like cats preparatory to a fight.'

Harris and Platter stayed in position for 31 minutes, eventually defying slow hand-claps, whistles and shouts – fans put up with only so much of nothing happening – to break the world record for the longest ever stand-off. Only with the landmark reached did the judges call them back to the start line, aware that neither was going to crack. 'It was not so much physically as emotionally exhausting,' Bardsley, who watched from the stand, said. 'But you were never going to intimidate Reg in that situation.'

Like a pool-hall hustler showing off his tricks, in the re-run Plattner attacked from the start only to stop and abruptly restart twice on the back straight, eventually forcing Harris into the front. From there, Plattner then tailed Harris before dipping beneath him on the final bend. Harris held his line, accelerating through the middle of the banking along the back straight. The two men ran parallel, holding the spectators breathless, but still Harris was too strong. He won by a length.

In the next race, Plattner happily sat in Harris's pocket until three-quarters of a lap remained, then attacked from a height with such fluidity that he opened a critical five-length lead. By the turn, Harris had closed the gap but not without hitting his maximum speed. Trying to maintain as narrow a line as possible outside Plattner around the bend, Harris went so close to him that their shoulders collided. To most neutrals he seemed at fault – Plattner had held his line – but when Harris was left trailing he shot up his arm in protest, claiming Plattner elbowed him. If he did, it happened in a flash, yet the judges agreed, with a vote of four to two. Years later Plattner still claimed that 'two of the judges who sided with Harris did not see the incident' – and he rarely complained about physical riding. His resentment festered because Harris won the re-run by riding hard from the front, ensuring he did not fall prey to Swiss cunning again.

The delay left Harris with only half an hour to recover for the final against Maspes. As Harris told a Sunday newspaper the following December, that was time enough for men from the

Italian federation to offer him a bribe to throw the race. 'I never thought twice about accepting the offer,' he said. Apparently he understood that guilt was corrosive. 'Acquiescing in a transaction of that nature would have started an inward deterioration that could have had only one end.'

Instead he put his chastening 2–0 defeat – the first by eight lengths, slowing up; the second, half a wheel – down to approaching middle age. 'I was tired,' he said. 'I gave all I had. I wish I were ten years younger.'

Even to this day rumours persist that he threw the race. People still struggled to believe that Harris could lose a two-up race legitimately when close to his prime, regardless that Maspes underlined his talent by winning five more world titles. Whatever the truth, Harris's response to the defeat was telling. The title had passed from him but still he was unwilling to give up his unofficial crown. 'Maspes hardly won another race for a year. Maspes pleaded with him but Reg wouldn't budge,' Geoff Cooke said. 'This was from Reg's mouth: he said to Maspes, "You've got your World Championship, you've got your contract. You don't need to win races now." That was the sort of guy Reg was. He was ruthless. He was the boss.'

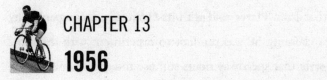

CHAPTER 13
1956

In his first months at Auty & Lees, Harris would sneak into the workshop when the mechanics had gone home for the night, slip behind the wheel of a car jacked up off the ground and run through the gears, imagining he was emerging from the grid at a professional track. As Auty learnt to trust him, Harris was allowed to manoeuvre the vehicles around the forecourt, too, and to run them over to the workshop on the other side of The Rock. Often, Harris would take a detour and learn to drive properly, dropping down a gear up Belmont Hill, then accelerating into the premises a fraction too fast. It made him feel adult. 'I got a great sensation of pride,' he said.

He liked motorcycles, too, and occasionally learnt to ride them with Harold 'Ginger' Lees, Auty's business partner. Lees was not around the shop much, but had still inspired in Harris his first thoughts of being capable of sporting competition. Lees was a national speedway champion at a time when that was a mainstream sport. Red-haired, square-jawed, he appeared on the cards that John Player sold with its cigarettes, accompanied by profiles claiming he was the first to experiment with the foot-down style that speedway riders still use today. For a while, the young Harris considered following him into competitive motor sport. In 1952, he had been invited to do so when *Motor Cycling* magazine challenged him to a race at Silverstone against the world motorcycling champion Geoff Duke – another Lancastrian – in which both men would drive Austin A40s. By then Harris's passion for pushing fast cars to their limit was legend.

Duke was a competitive driver and had represented Aston Martin on the sports car circuit, but Harris beat him by a length in a three-lap race, jokingly claiming that it was revenge for Duke having beaten Harris into second place in the recent Sportsman of the Year award – Harris had retained the award in 1951. Soon similar motoring opportunities began to flood in. When cycling commitments allowed, Harris raced at the best circuits in Britain: Silverstone and Oulton Park, Brands Hatch and Crystal Palace, often competing against the best British motor-racing drivers, such as Stirling Moss, Mike Hawthorn and Tony Brooks, all moonlighting from Formula One. Often Harris competed in a borrowed D-type Jaguar, a factory-built race car with ground-breaking disc brakes and an innovative 'monocoque' chassis in which the frame of the car helped to support its load, much like an aeroplane. It was difficult to handle but Harris was not prepared to compete in a machine that might have been second best.

Other times, leading manufacturers lent him a car. As Peter Procter, who gave up cycling for a long career as a motor-racing professional, said: 'It was good publicity for the factories. In the 1940s and '50s, quite a lot of television people got drives. The fact that a world champion cyclist like Reg would drive for them would generate a lot of interest.' Procter understood why both sports might appeal to Harris. 'Bombing around the banking at 45mph would get Reg excited. It's you and the machine: totally physical,' he said. 'But the adrenalin rush was even greater in a car.'

Dorothy drove a convertible MG for her daily errands, while Harris turned up to race tracks in his Jaguar. One associate of Harris's said that he admitted in private that his wife was more adept behind a wheel. Both of them competed in the Monte Carlo Rally, though inclement weather prevented them from completing the journey from Paris to the south coast. In that race Dorothy used her domestic car while Harris drove an Austin A90 that had once been owned by Ken Wharton, another F1 driver from Britain. That was only the latest in a long list of expensive marques that Harris had by now housed in his garage. To name only those that I could confirm, they included two MGs, a Triumph, Mark IV and Mark V Jaguars, an Allard, a Ford V Pilot, the six-cylinder Rover that he took to Europe and the Wolseley that he crashed in 1948. One friend said that Harris light-heartedly admitted that he might have had a problem with this acquisitive streak. 'To Reg, they were a bit like shoes are to a woman,' the friend said.

In 1956 Harris claimed that he received offers from Vanwall and Aston Martin to drive for them permanently, a rare privilege at a time when only the select few were offered professional contracts. Given his age, and that his physical powers would soon be in decline, the approaches seemed perfectly timed. Then, a motor-racing driver could expect to last several more years than a sprint cyclist. 'I had a fundamental decision: to give up cycling completely and devote the rest of my life to motor racing, or else to drop the sport completely,' he wrote in his autobiography. Quite why he felt the second alternative necessary was unclear. He said that he turned down both opportunities anyway. 'I may have turned out to be less of a driver than I thought I was [and] motor sport was a young man's game with no future that I could see after my retirement from it.' That made sense, though it contradicted the explanation that he gave to *MG Enthusiast* magazine for eventually leaving motor sport behind. Then he said it was down to 'not having a brilliant navigator, not having the right car and not being dedicated'.

Procter suggested neither account was true. 'Reg didn't make the grade,' he said. 'He did get a few drives but the sponsors soon realised that he didn't have what it takes. It was publicity for them: the fact that a world champion cyclist would drive their cars – and it did generate a lot of interest – but he didn't do very well at it.' Procter recalled starting a minute behind him in a Rally of Britain, a race that Harris entered twice. Unable to negotiate his car through the snow that had settled on the Lake District, Harris had repeatedly to ask Procter to get out and push him. 'Whenever we came to a hill, Reg would get stuck on it,' he said, laughing. 'We would have to keep stopping to move him on. I pulled his leg about it in later years.'

From the back seat of the helicopter en route from the airport, Harris could see directly into the track at Rocourt. Through driving rain – it always seemed to rain in Liège – he could see that only small pockets of supporters were scattered through the two stands, even though the preliminary rounds of the other events were due to begin. Asking the pilot to hover for a moment, he could make out the crude advertisements that had been painted on the track. They seemed unfinished but that was a trick of the distance. In fact, they were half-covered in moss. The place was underprepared.

Rarely could Harris recall feeling more nervous for a World Championship. Rationally he knew that he should have been confident about winning back his title. Only a few weeks earlier he had banished doubts about his declining powers by reclaiming the kilometre world record from his friend Fritz Pfenninger, the young Swiss. Over the summer he had posted his usual collection of victories, too, putting the new world amateur champion, the Australian John Tressider, in his place at the Grand Prix of London and reminding a pair of young Italians, Guiseppe Ogna and Marino Morettini, that they had much to learn with a devastating win on the Isle of Man.

But his decision to announce that he would retire at the end of the season had left him carrying a great burden of expectation. Ending months of speculation about his future – rumours that had arisen perennially since his world title win in 1954 – Harris had announced his decision at another gathering of the Pedal Club. 'At 37, I know that I am as fit as I was at 17,' he said. 'I am still the fastest sprinter. I can win a race from the front and the back, but I have promised my sponsors that I will retire while I am still at the top.' Harris never understood the British instinct for self-deprecation.

However, such bravado was as familiar to his audience as the subsequent self-doubt was to Harris. Privately he had grown exhausted by the mental toil of having repeatedly to excel, and more so after his defeat by Maspes the previous year. As Norman Grattage said in the weeks before accompanying Harris to

Rocourt, for an athlete meeting expectations never tastes as sweet as upsetting them. 'A terrific strain comes with trying to stay at the top of the tree for so long, with everybody gnawing at you, trying to topple you,' he wrote. 'Physically, Reg said he was as fast as he had ever been. It is mentally that he has suffered most with the passing of the years.' That strain was written over his face when he sat alone in the dressing room after a first-round victory over Nakai, the technically gifted rider from Japan. 'I just wish the title could be run now, with no waiting of any kind,' he told the *Daily Mail*, like a well-behaved child impatient for his sugar reward.

In the next race he beat Tino Oriani, a well-built Italian, but still his mood showed no sign of softening. Benny Foster, the British team manager, said in his autobiography that he could not recall ever seeing Harris so pent up. With Guerlach retired, Harris had employed a new soigneur, known to most as Van Cautier. He had begged Harris to reveal what was troubling him. He refused, probably because that would involve admitting to weakness.

Later Harris revealed the reason for his concern: the identity of his quarter-final opponent. When thinking clearly, Harris should not have worried about Gaignard. He was almost unbeatable over 150 metres but easily beaten if you launched your attack earlier, yet Harris seemed spooked by him. 'I could not understand it,' Foster wrote. 'Normally Reg didn't bother whom he met.'

Probably it owed to him knowing that his opponent had any kind of advantage over him, regardless that it was easily neutered. Possibly also Harris was troubled by the possibility of losing to a man whom he had publicly admonished. The son of an acrobat, and once a circus assistant to his father, Gaignard celebrated a triumph by flipping somersaults on the track, a practice that Harris considered disrespectful to Gaignard's opponent. To Harris's mind, track showmanship in victory meant accepting it with gentlemanly good grace.

He was, then, in complaining mood. He demanded that the moss be removed from the concrete. On Saturday afternoon he was among several riders who demanded that the advertisements be scrubbed from the track surface because they were slippery when wet. That was a 12-hour job that required ground staff to work through Saturday night, by which time rain had forced the contest with Gaignard to be put back until the following morning. That ensured Harris another near-sleepless night.

The decline of track cycling's popularity had quickened over the past 12 months. Even with the emergence of Maspes, Gaignard and a few others, fans had finally become tired of watching mostly the same men win the same races over and over again. In Holland attendances for the biggest meetings were down about

50 per cent. In France the fall was similarly steep. Herne Hill now struggled to sell out. 'In Belgium, land of 1,000 professionals, summer track racing has virtually disappeared,' Wadley wrote, making the choice of Liége as host city difficult to fathom.

Barely 4,000 supporters went home disappointed on Saturday. Almost the same number had returned by the time Harris and Gaignard took up position for the race early on Sunday afternoon. Bottling his tension, Harris attacked just at the perfect moment in his opening race, leaving Gaignard trailing him shortly after the bell and sustaining a speed that triumphantly exposed the Frenchman's stamina shortfall.

Quite what happened in the second race is unclear. Harris claimed that Gaignard crossed the sprinter's line and slowed Harris just as he was about to overtake him. Others suggested Harris was punished for leaving his attack too late. Whatever the truth, the judges decided that the Frenchman had won by a hundredth of a second after consulting the photo finish.

Most agreed on how Harris should avoid losing the deciding contest. 'He had to have the lead three-quarters of the way down the back straight on the first lap and he had to hold it until the 200 metres on the second and last lap,' Alan Peters wrote.

Harris managed the first task but inexplicably hesitated with a half a lap to go, allowing Gaignard to close the deficit and cut inside for a three-length lead. Within 100 yards, Harris had drawn level with a rocket-like attack down the incline. But Gaignard now was travelling just as fast, with his back steeply arched, his square head jutting from side to side, and his tiny body – no more than a spit over five feet long – forming a perfect comma over the frame. Within seconds of the judges revealing their interpretation of another photo finish, Gaignard was sharpening the sting of the defeat with what Harris disdainfully called 'a series of front rolls'.

'Harris only wins when he is confident,' George Pearson wrote. 'It is mental conditioning he needs more than physical. Today he was fit but nervous.' Harris admitted that tension had gripped him at a critical point of the race but he was certain also that Gaignard had needed chemical assistance to produce a finishing sprint of 11.2 seconds when usually he struggled to dip below 12. 'I don't believe that,' he told trackside reporters, adding that Maspes had expressed his suspicions about the Frenchman's performance, too. 'It's quite ridiculous. Gaignard isn't the man for that.' Certainly Gaignard did not produce that kind of performance in losing his semi-final to Derksen – who had surprisingly toppled Maspes – allowing the quiet Dutchman to go on to win the professional title for the first time since his one other such victory in 1946.

Unburdened by expectation, Harris closed his career with a succession of victories as stirring as any in his pomp, beating Van Vliet and Derksen in Amsterdam revenge races, defeating Derksen and Maspes in a kilometre time trial at Harris Stadium, and prevailing against the Italian again in Paris. As if to rule out suspicions that he was winning only because of his status, he equalled the world record for the fastest recorded finishing sprint, too, clocking 10.9 seconds in Copenhagen – a landmark he shared now with Van Vliet. Before this run of races began, the Dutchman announced that he too would make this his final month of competition. In explanation he pointed to the difficulty he had recovering from races now but most felt he had been inspired by Harris's decision to say farewell, too. Both were diminished without the other to race against.

They concluded their rivalry with a two-centre farewell, first at Amsterdam, then Herne Hill, racing alone to ensure everything went to plan. For the first time in months, the London venue sold out, regardless of a biting September wind. They began with two one-lap sprints, winning a race apiece, and followed that with each attempting to break Harris's world record for a quarter mile from a standing start. As if overcompensating lest he struck the wrong note, Van Vliet crossed a full second outside the mark. By finishing in 24.2 seconds, Harris missed it by only a tenth of a second; though he could still manage the results of races, he could not quite get time to bend to his will. They concluded the day's programme with a classical two-lap, two-up match. After swapping the lead several times, they broke with tradition and produced a clear four-length winner. You could probably guess who had his arm raised in a victory salute before crossing the line.

By way of tribute, the cycling world was quick to offer insights into Harris's career in the weeks that followed. Now the NCU president, Dick Taylor took the familial angle: 'Having been born within 200 yards of Reg, I know that the role his mother played in his success should not be forgotten. She made great sacrifices for him. She went out and scraped enough for them to get by, and was willing to do anything for him as he tried to get to the top.' Louis Jacques, a Parisian frame-builder, highlighted a personal quality: 'Many great names frequented my workshop as young men, whether in search of a vital part, food, or a room for the night. All the great ones forget me but Reg, with his Christmas cards, letters, and occasional visits, remained the most faithful.' George Pearson underlined his consistency: 'Others have had and still have their days on the track but the past decade has been the Harris story.' Only Alan Holby, chairman of the Sports Journalists' Association, was prepared to pinpoint the quality that set Harris apart: 'Reg once told me that a champion must be a killer. He must forget friendship or that the other man is a sportsman. He must be absolutely ruthless until the contest is won. Many people disagreed with his outlook, but "lone wolf" Harris didn't worry. He went his way and made a fortune.'

CHAPTER 14
1958

Initially Harris improved the fortunes at Harris Stadium, increasing the average attendance from 6,000 to 8,000, mostly by continuing to attract the best talent from abroad. Most often people turned up to watch the proprietor race against his friends from the circus, but they were also attracted by the amateurs who continued to pitch up in Manchester for the first few years of his ownership. After the Germans, an Italian team turned up the following winter at the behest of Costa, still the national team coach. That meant that spectators got to witness the best young national squad in Europe – comprising of Olympic champions such as Sante Gaiardoni, Valentino Gasperella and Leandro Faggin – and that the venue retained an international complexion. Harris undercut the benefits of that progress, however, with a series of decisions regarding the business that continued to ostracise the club rider.

In an act that was practical in its motivation but devastating in its symbolism, he built a fence around the stadium to deter the teenagers who were sneaking onto the track when nobody else was around. To improve the spectacle of meetings, he cut back severely on the many preliminary rounds that extended the length of the programme, regardless that this wiped out the age-old domestic tradition that allowed amateurs the slim chance of riding against the best in the world. He cared not that the format had once fuelled his dreams as a young man. 'A promoter must scrub out the scrubbers,' he said, with an increasingly typical disregard for the sensitivities of his constituency. Warming to this theme, he castigated British amateurs for failing to match the professional qualities that Costa had enshrined in his men. 'The young Italians would rather miss a meal than ride in a torn or dirty jersey. If they have a pain in the stomach, a headache or a grudge against a rival, they will still take to the arena smiling, perfectly turned out and apparently full of confidence.' He could have been talking about himself. 'Yet British riders go out of their way to avoid becoming showmen. The very thought of develop-ing and putting over a personality – of becoming their own public relations officers – appears to frighten them.'

Apparently failing to realise that he needed to apply the same pragmatic duplicity to his new profession that he had done as a showman competitor, Harris showed no compunction in upset-ting the emerging women's track scene either, regardless that it was about the only aspect of the sport growing in popularity. His friend John Lewis's wife, Joan, née Weatherer, was among the best riders in Manchester. She recalled how Harris actually tried to prevent women from competing on his track. He was not alone among middle-aged men in thinking women unsuited to competitive cycling then but his outspokenness was still striking. 'It is one sport for which women are entirely unsuited, physically and temperamentally,' he said, laying out the hurdles a woman had to overcome to succeed as a sprint cyclist. 'To make sharp decisions, and to act on them for good or bad, the first thing she must do is lay aside her feminine indecision and natural "backwardness at coming forward". And her sense of "sportsmanship", which engenders a rather delicate approach to the game, especially to close and rough riding, must, I'm afraid, be replaced by something of the "killer" outlook.'

Harris's brutal honesty – or tactlessness, depending on one's perspective – was only one contributor to his struggle in trying to turn a profit at Fallowfield after a first season full of such promise. He was also set back by the failure to attract any sustained television interest and by the gradual decline in sponsorship. Several of the grand new advertisement hoardings went unfulfilled and no business was interested in putting their name to his ticket stubs (why be associated with something that was quickly torn up and scattered over the ground?) He also suffered terrible luck with the weather and was forced to cancel several of the track's most prestigious meetings owing to rain. Perhaps most damagingly of all, however, he soon found that he had taken charge of the stadium ahead of the most precipitous downturn in cycling's popularity.

'The big demise of cycling: you can actually pin it down to one year,' Roger St Pierre said. In 1959, the British Motor Corporation produced its first Mini, while Ford trebled the production of its Anglia and played the leading role in transforming young people's attitude towards personal transport. Previously they could afford only a bike, but now, through the coincidence of an improved economy providing them with disposable income and the availability of relatively cheap small cars, they could afford something much more convenient, fashionable and, for men, attractive to the opposite sex. 'Growing up, you had a pair of roller skates, then a bike, then a cheap motorbike and then a car, but all of a sudden that middle chunk was taken away,' St Pierre said. 'Everybody used to go to work by bike. In pictures of the '50s you see a flood of bikes emerging from factories. By the '60s it was, "Why are you riding a bike? Can't you afford a car?" It became a reverse status symbol. It was a symbol of no status. If you rode a bike, you were a pleb.'

All aspects of the bike business suffered. Phillips Cycles, previously Britain's second biggest manufacturer, closed its factory in Birmingham. British Cycle Corporation and Raleigh, the market-leaders, merged and outsourced work to Japan, dispensing with

WORLD *SPORTS*
THE INTERNATIONAL SPORTS MAGAZINE

REG. HARRIS
Britain's Sportsman of the Year

MARCH 1950 PRICE 1/6

With superstardom beckoning, Harris graces the front page of *World Sports* magazine. He had recently been named as Britain's Sportsman of the Year.

ABOVE: Hilary Marquand, the minister of health, awards Harris the highly coveted Sportsman of the Year for a second time in 1951.

LEFT: Giving his speech after receiving the award; Harris was known for being outspoken in his speeches, once criticising the government's lack of support for elite sport, which was considered highly rebellious at the time.

ABOVE: Harris wins his third world title in 1950. Harris's soigneur Louis Guerlach is on his right and Tom MacDonald, the Manchester Wheelers president, his left.

BELOW: Harris leads a demo ride at a Dunlop meeting in 1951 with (l-r) Arie van Vliet, Ray Pauwels, Jan Derksen and Sid Patterson. The ride only lasted 100 yards before the back wheel gave way under the weight of 14-stone Patterson.

By the early 1950s, Harris's fame and popularity meant that brands from cigarettes to sporting goods manufacturers were desperate to be associated with him.

REG HARRIS

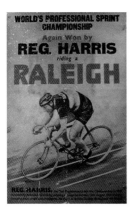

Raleigh, Harris's sponsor and later employer, made him one of the first and most high-profile sporting ambassadors for a brand. Raleigh understood Harris's status as a self-made hero and how that resonated with the public.

The local hero: Harris is watched by a road sweeper while on his regular training run in 1951. He went on to win his fourth world title that year in Milan.

63 H7

CYCLING
and Mopeds

February 26, 1958

Every Wednesday 6ᴰ

THIS ISSUE FEATURES

THE WINNING *CYCLING* GIRL FOR FEBRUARY

Reg Harris on His Greatest Rival
Traffic Dodging on the Devon Coast
Home of Mopeds—The Mosquito

Harris and Van Vliet on the cover of *Cycling and Mopeds*. Inside there is a double-page spread written by Harris about his relationship with his long-standing friend and sporting rival.

Harris, aged 51, races a 25-year-old Reg Barnett ahead of the 1971 National Championship. In spite of the huge age difference and Barnett's apparently huge effort, Harris shocked everyone when he defeated the young star. Four years later, Harris appears on the cover of *Cycling* magazine with rising star Maurice Burton, which features 'the young ones' – the new generation of professional cyclists.

thousands of jobs. At the grass roots, clubs began to close and independent bike shops fell away. St Pierre outlined the impact around his home in Essex. 'In 1959 there were a dozen clubs in and around Romford,' he said. 'In 1959 there were 27 races held on the Little Waltham circuit round Braintree. There were at least nine good light-weight bicycle shops within a six-mile radius of Romford. By 1960 there were four races on the circuit, three cycling clubs and two bike shops.'

As Harris discovered, its decline as a spectator sport suddenly quickened too, with Fallowfield rarely attracting more than three to four thousand fans, and Herne Hill even fewer. Shortly afterwards, the Morris Minor – that other ubiquitous economy car – had become the first British car to sell 100,000 models.

To his credit, Harris saw beyond the gloom into which cycling had descended and predicted that it would recover in a new form as a healthy lifestyle choice. With suburban Britain rapidly expanding into the countryside, he even imagined that one day people would recover from the consumerism that had blighted cycling and want it incorporated into the landscape's infrastructure. Several decades before the National Cycling Network was instituted in the countryside and long before urban planners considered bike lanes essential, Harris said: 'In planning of new suburbs we will see carefree shopping and recreation areas where everyone will cycle. In time, I imagine that we shall see more quiet country clubs, perhaps reached by car but where movement on tracks within the park will be on foot or cycle only. There could well be more cycling for exercise in the urban parks. Certainly I feel that we have to be prepared for a change in cycling habits.' He was not the first with such a vision – the CTC had tried and failed to institute cycle lanes in the 1930s, and there were already a few, sparsely used paths in new towns such as Harlow and Stevenage – but such optimism ran contrary to popular opinion of the sport. For all his visionary instincts and still-great ambition, he was just less suited to managing the finer details of turning around a small business rapidly acquiring debt.

His money-spinning ideas soon took on an increasingly desperate hue. Struggling to pay the salaries for his two full-time employees, he unsuccessfully demanded that the council contributed financially to the running of the stadium, with Harris claiming now that it was a community amenity. He set up something called the Reg Harris Testimonial Fund to which he hoped 'cyclists up and down the country' would subscribe through a desire to keep the track in operation. He rented out the facility to footballers on Sundays even though that broke the law, prompting the Lord's Day Observance Society to take him to court. As punishment, he was forced to pay a £5 fine and guarantee that he would not repeat the crime. Shortly afterwards, he found himself before a magistrate again after the engines at a

Fallowfield go-karting event produced an unacceptable racket. This time, his fine was doubled and he was forced to pledge a similar promise not to repeat the crime. Somehow these episodes captured his swift personal decline. On the day that it worshipped some other idol, a community that had once feted Harris now regarded his struggles as too much white noise.

Few were surprised, then, when he accepted an offer for the ground's lease from Manchester University in June 1960. 'Track racing has been deep in the doldrums for some seasons,' the editorial in *Sporting Cyclist* magazine said. 'But this is sad, even disturbing. The sport will never be made a paying proposition in Britain again until we have a small, indoor track near the centre of a major city.' This was perfectly true, though that track was not built until Manchester Velodrome opened 34 years later.

Raleigh always tried to keep retired cyclists within the family. It added kudos to the company and lifted morale. There was not much for which they were qualified but still they found them a position as, say, a tester or salesman or another low-skilled role. For Harris, however, they had much grander plans. They wanted him to represent the company at home and overseas, serving as an ambassador who would front campaigns, travel to emerging markets and advise on new product lines. They also offered him a seat on the board. 'The qualities that have made Harris Britain's most successful ambassador will now be employed in promotional work at home and abroad,' Sir Harold Bowden, Raleigh's chairman, said. 'His prestige and popularity will be of great value in helping to sell British cycling.'

Harris was enthused by the task. After years as the ageing hero whose powers were slowly beginning to wane, suddenly he had a new project to which he could apply himself and to which he seemed perfectly suited: at 37, he was old enough to earn the respect of company leaders but fit and hungry enough to work formidably hard. Within months, he had already hatched a plan for a new project that he felt would exploit a gap in the market and help Raleigh to address the declining demand for track bikes. They needed, he felt, to produce a line of bespoke road bikes for the discerning bike man who Raleigh would never lose to consumer fashion but who wanted more from his machine than the casual cyclist. Raleigh liked the idea. They decided they would call the new division Reg Harris Bicycles and asked Harris to oversee its direction. In return they offered him a salary increase that brought his earnings close to £12,000, the figure he had earned from them before retirement. 'I was very happy about this,' he said. 'I had grown used to a certain standard of living.'

Very quickly the scheme began to fall into place. Harris handpicked his friend Gerard O'Donovan as the lead framebuilder for the operation. As the co-founder of Carlton Cyclists,

O'Donovan produced some of the best road and track bikes in Britain, and had several commissioned by Harris. Now his factory in Ilkeston, Derbyshire, would become Raleigh's 'special unit' and Carlton would continue to operate but as part of the Raleigh brand. On 10 February 1960, *The Times* noted that Harris had been appointed in a 'sales and consultative capacity' to the Carlton board, but really his role had far greater reach than that. He began to source suppliers abroad, travelling to suppliers around Britain and overseas, arranging to buy componentry for what he was confident would become a product to outstrip any back home.

He began to meet with the owners of leading bike shops, too, while sending out personally signed letters to smaller franchises notifying them of the new range, and adding that he looked forward to them engaging in business. Scarcely anybody in the industry could believe it, then, when, before the year was out, Raleigh announced that Harris had been sacked. 'Everybody thought he would have a job for life with Raleigh, Reg included,' John Lewis said. In his brief explanation, Harris suggested that the growing enthusiasm for the project had prompted 'resentment in some circles', implying that Raleigh's most powerful employees had come to feel threatened by him. Given that the company's owner had given him licence to implement the line, to most that hardly seemed credible. Within weeks, the true reason for his dismissal began to leak out. 'It was well documented,' Procter said, by which he meant it became widely known, a suggestion confirmed by Fenwick and Brown. Godwin also said Harris told him why he left: 'It was because of an underhand arrangement with Campagnolo. He had arranged a deal with them to supply Raleigh with their components but, in the tie-up, Reg had a deal which brought him a percentage of all sales.'

Suddenly without an income, Harris began desperately to talk to his contacts in the hope of finding somebody who would pick up the project, eventually striking gold with a neighbour called Arthur Whatmough. The head of a family engineering business that supplied parts for Sturmey-Archer gears, Whatmough initially offered Harris space in his Blackpool factory before they eventually decided that its coastal location was poorly suited to nationwide distribution and located the workshop instead in vacant premises on Beech Lane in Macclesfield. This also had a shop out front in which Harris arranged to set up a flagship store. The factory at Reg Harris (Cycles) Ltd began business on 1 February 1961, with the shop due to open shortly afterwards.

Harris used his advertisements to make some grand claims. He said in them that he had been careful throughout his career to discuss the ideal specifications on a road bike with the sport's leading practitioners and applied their suggestions to his design.

Apparently, he discussed parts in details with the renowned Frenchmen André Darrigade and Roger Rivière, both former world champions. He proudly mentioned the time that Fausto Coppi lent him his road bike before he died. However, he did not feel obliged to admit that he had asked Manchester's best-known frame-builder to produce his first orders because the workshop was not ready. 'They came out with Reg's name on them but they were made by Johnny Berry,' Brown said.

Perhaps it was no surprise then that his first range, entitled the 'International', did not quite live up to his billing. Writing in *Cycling*, the journalist using the by-line 'Nimrod' said that at £25 Harris's bike represented 'a good buy but was not quite worthy of his reputation'. Harris effectively agreed with that assessment in a speech given to the Pedal Club, revealing that he had received 'long letters' from bike-shop owners complaining about the bike's shortcomings and suggesting improvements. Harris promised to take them on board, while also insisting vaguely that he would 'show more patience in the solid task of establishing a factory' over the next 12 months.

Though none of his audience realised it, Harris had drawn up an unfeasible business plan in which he could break even only by producing a number of bikes that was beyond the work-shop capacity. Joe Pilling was given an idea of these erroneous economies of scale over a dinner conversation with Whatmough.

'I don't know the exact figures but, say, he needed to produce 150 frames a week to break even, his capacity was 120,' he said, chuckling at Harris's typically wild ambition. 'It was a dead duck from the off.'

The next 12 months, then, only made a bad situation worse, as Harris fell behind on payments due to his three major suppliers, Ron Kitching, Gerry Burgess – both of whom Harris had known since they were competitive cyclists – and Walter Flory, a London-based businessman who provided Harris with parts from Switzerland. The situation reached crisis point at a bike show in Earls Court when Harris took the three men aside and demanded more time on his repayments. He had, it seemed, spent anything earned in his cycling career on his lifestyle or on Fallowfield. 'We were each owed about £10,000, which was a lot in those days,' Kitching wrote. 'Reg told us the only way he could possibly survive would be if each of us doubled his credit to £20,000.'

Clear-sighted, unsentimental and hugely successful in business, Kitching refused the request, having by now realised Harris's shortcomings in his new career. So too did Burgess, regardless of their friendship. Only Flory agreed, a disastrous decision given that Harris was forced to wind up the business within months, owing thousands to the bank. 'All his stock went out the back door dirt cheap,' Kitching added, clearly disgusted with Harris for trying to make a quick buck even in the desperate final hours of the business. 'Dealers were getting it all, and Reg probably didn't do so badly out of it himself.' Kitching was never paid. Michael Breckon, his biographer, recalled how he had to rewrite the parts devoted to Harris after Kitching decided to tone down his criticism. 'Reg played naughty games businesswise and Ron was saddened by that,' he said. 'They were two of a kind, aggressive and tough, and they wanted to be big and successful, but Ron was a lot more successful financially. That might have stuck in Reg's craw a bit.'

Suddenly Harris was bereft. After his fall-out with Raleigh, no employer was likely to trust him. Given the circumstances of his failure in business, no right-thinking investor was going to get behind him. He was broke, unskilled, and losing contacts. In September 1962, he took the only option that he could see available to him when he applied for an amateur cyclist's licence, a requirement for anybody who wished to take up coaching seriously. 'We do not have any active pros to help our amateurs,' he said. 'Perhaps I could do something at Fallowfield, along the lines of a sprinters' school.'

The British Cycling Federation, the recently established successor to the NCU, needed less than a month to refuse his application. In explanation, Peter Itter, the chairman of the Racing Committee, invoked the rule that prevented a professional from ever returning to amateur status. 'However, Reg can certainly have an independent's licence,' Itter added. 'This will enable him to race against top-class amateurs if he wishes to emulate Gerardin and Van Vliet as a coach.' Swallowing his pride, Harris submitted a request for an independent's licence the following month. This time, the Racing Committee did not even bother to accompany their rejection of it with an explanation.

With Harris having repeatedly put forward his case to be national coach, most assumed that the ruling body did not want to allow him the opportunity to get set on that career path. Partly this was through the resentment that still existed between him and the federation but perhaps more so because they knew he was unsuited to the task. 'At one time, there was talk of him being national coach but that would have been a disaster,' St Pierre said. 'He would have used every resource. He would have had the best tyres, the pick of the clothing and all the rest of it, but he would have butt against reporting to a committee. If he'd had to have given a weekly report, he would have lasted five minutes. They would have had to have given him full responsibility and said report back in a year. But they were never going to do that, not when they were probably operating at a loss.'

Amid this turmoil in his professional life, Harris's marriage was unravelling, too. For while Dorothy had known about his philandering and put up with it for years, by the autumn of 1962 she could take no more and filed for divorce. The short news article published in the *Daily Mirror* in October reported how Dorothy had named Shirley Furey, of Altrincham Road, Wilmslow, as his mistress in court. It did not mention that Furey was more than two decades younger than Harris and claimed that he had made her pregnant. Harris, born illegitimate, had conferred the same status on his child.

 **CHAPTER 15**
1966

Jennifer Oliver could not recall exactly what attracted her to Harris when she first encountered him at a dinner party in 1966. Certainly it was not his fame. Then aged 21, she was not a cycling fan and only vaguely knew of him. Nor on first appearances did he seem her usual type. She was tall, slim and unusually attractive, with perfect teeth and wide, dark eyes. Though fit for his age, Harris was 46, balding and well past his prime. It was not his charm that drew her to him either, for they did not get to talk that evening, yet still they locked eyes long enough for both to know the other was interested. 'You know when people say they look across a room and see somebody and there's something between you?' Oliver, then called Brazendale, said. 'There was something between us right from the first meeting.'

When they were invited to a similar soirée about a year later, Harris did not let the opportunity pass and before the end of the evening had arranged for them to go on a date. In his classically charming mode, he soon set up another evening out then several more, buying her flowers, taking her to his favourite restaurants and generally treating her in a way to which she was not accustomed from men about her own age. 'He was the same age as my parents but he seemed a lot younger in his ways,' Oliver said. 'I didn't feel an age difference with him from the word go.' She recalled his clothes to illustrate the point. 'He didn't look like a typical Englishman of that era. When I looked at the way my father was dressing, Reg was more with it. He'd have little suede boots, blue cotton trousers that looked like jeans, shirts with the cuffs turned back. In the '60s, that seemed quite continental.'

They had much in common, including a love of the countryside and fine food, as well as a shared sense of humour. Harris was not the type to tell jokes but he was careful with his words in a way that Oliver liked. 'I used to grow vegetables. We were having mangetout one night for dinner because they were cropping. I remember him saying, "You know, darling, I could quite easily tire of mange tout, but I would never tire of peas." I thought, hmm, I've got the message now, he doesn't want any more. Somebody else would say, "Oh, we're not having these," but he wouldn't put it like that. This is how he would talk. Rather than upset you, he would have a little way round. His glass was always half full. That's how his life was.' Their differences only brought them closer together, with Harris's confidence complementing Oliver's youthful reserve. 'When I met Reg, I went bright red if anybody spoke to me. I learnt my confidence from him.'

Within a year, Oliver had moved into Harris's rented home in Rainow, a village near Macclesfield, having been told much about his past life. She knew about his marriages and about his recent difficulties, which had led to him taking out a huge loan from the financial company Lombard simply to survive. He told Oliver that the bike business had folded because Dorothy had taken advantage of her status as a leading shareholder by with-drawing all the money from their accounts in response to a relationship 'bad patch'. 'A lot of people probably thought, "she came along and [saw] he had a nice lifestyle", but Reg didn't have a roof over his head when I met him,' she said.

At about the same time, Harris managed to land a position as a sales agent with a flourishing Yorkshire-based company called Gannex. Set up by a Jewish Lithuanian called Joseph Kagan who had fled his homeland during the war, Gannex manufactured a waterproof fabric of the same name and had grown successful once the Prime Minister, Harold Wilson, had decided to wear a Gannex raincoat on what seemed to be nearly all of his public engagements. Soon other world leaders favoured the unusually lightweight material, too, among them the American president Lyndon Johnson, his Soviet counterpart Nikita Khrushchev and even Chairman Mao. With that kind of reach, Harris did not need to work hard to promote the brand. Instead, new customers came often to him while he spent most of his time keeping existing clients onside. As he became more powerful within his department, the only difficulty Harris faced was that he could not bear his boss. 'Reg liked to run things his way and Joe ran a business his way, so they didn't always meet eye to eye,' Alan Rushton, a cycling promoter who worked for Gannex then, said. 'Most people fell out with Joe Kagan in the end.'

A year into the job, Harris did not need to think twice, then, when his friend John Webb offered him a similar position with Kay-Metzeler, a company that produced polyurethane foam. He moved again shortly after that when Webb joined a rival firm called Draka. Here he enjoyed great success in what was not a difficult task, given foam's rapidly increasing popularity and the few companies selling it then. Such were his commissions that Harris was soon appointed to the head of the sales division and given licence to work from home. There he would manage the two travelling sales agents employed elsewhere in the country, while earning a cut of all commissions. Webb did not mind that Harris held most meetings with them in his house and gave up most mornings to ride his bike, while spending evenings talking to the agents or meeting clients. His role was simply to serve as a celebrity face of the company whose sheer presence alone would impress potential customers. 'He had an ideal job,' Peter Jackson, one of the agents who worked for Harris, said. 'He just seemed to have the right influence with John Webb. Certainly subsequent people who did his job didn't have the same arrangement. He would go out for an hour or two in the morning and argue that he made up the time later on. It wasn't what I would call a full working week, though I wouldn't like to have tried to convince him of that.' That Harris was not actually a skilled salesman made the set-up even more fortunate. 'I learnt next to nothing from him. I quite admired him but the only sales skill he had was that he was fairly personable.'

Ian Thompson was the other agent. He at least learnt from Harris the importance of personal appearance. 'I remember the first time I met Reg,' he said. 'He looks at you from top to bottom and he looks at your shoes to make sure they're clean. It was the same if he was meeting a customer. He would even clean his shoes underneath. He had his own rules. He could bend them from time to time, but he didn't like other people to.' Harris liked to preserve the part of his shoe between the sole and the heel. Such fastidiousness must have been exhausting. You wondered if he was trying desperately to scrub away the dirt of his childhood, the irritant specks that had lodged in his psyche and spun him so many pearls.

Both Jackson and Thompson said that Harris seemed to think boasting about his achievements would impress. 'Some customers liked it but, after a period of time, some would say, "oh no, not again",' Thompson recalled. It seemed Harris liked to highlight his more recent successes, too. 'A few times he would remind me, or even mention it to customers, that he reckoned he was earning more than the Prime Minister.'*

With that money, Harris was able eventually to pay off his debt and buy a cottage on the outskirts of Leek, the Staffordshire town. A two-up, two-down property on a one-and-a-half-acre plot, this was a modest purchase compared to the home he had owned at his athletic peak, but the couple threw themselves into its renovation, carefully making pretty the unkempt garden, decorating throughout with the help of Oliver's father, Jim – she recalled fondly the trompe l'oeil wallpaper – and eventually commissioning an extension. By that time, they were married, too, having made their vows at the register office on the King's Road, Chelsea. It was a small affair, with Harris's friend and former cyclist Jack Tighe serving as his best man and celebrations

---

* Harris was once asked in interview about his perceived arrogance. His answer was opaque: 'I would have thought that I was a person full of self-assurance, who knew how good he was and, hopefully, never reacted or thought in a way that he was better than what he was, who had a capacity of tackling something that showed a better than 50–50 chance of success, because the man who picks a fight on the wrong occasion is generally going to lose. The downside of that is that there is a time and a place when you have a good chance of winning. This sort of thinking might give the impression that I could be big-headed. Who am I to judge? I don't agree with it.'

spent at Harris's favourite Italian restaurant, Ponte Vecchio, which he quite often frequented.

From having lost everything, then, Harris had recovered and re-established a life similar to his old one. He could afford hand-made shirts from Hilditch and Key on Jermyn Street. He bought bespoke shoes from Wildsmiths, also near Piccadilly. With Oliver he travelled abroad, most often visiting old acquaintances in Italy or the south of France. Senfftleben's restaurant on the French Riviera was a favourite haunt. 'We had some good times,' Jennifer said. 'I had a lovely life with him.' Through his celebrity, they were still often invited to functions. They hosted and attended dinner parties among what some might have snootily called Cheshire's nouveau riche. Though not part of that social group, John Lewis knew Harris well then and recalled how much effort went into an evening at his house. 'If you went round to dinner at Reg's it was something worthwhile,' he said. Often Oliver had cooked a recipe that Harris had acquired from the chef in a restaurant. 'Jennifer was a wonderful cook. The whole presenta-tion was superb. The right sort of furniture, the right sort of cutlery. That's what Reg expected.' Oliver did not mind that Harris had high expectations of her. She regarded him as her 'soulmate'. 'According to Jennifer, he had a very strict manner,' James Butler, the sculptor who produced the Manchester Velo-drome statue, said. 'He lived by a code. He always came back at the same time. He wanted his dinner at the same time, that sort of thing. He was a very methodical man.'

Perhaps just as satisfying was that his new lifestyle allowed him to ride his bike again, competing in local time trials – though rarely winning – as well as going on his morning rides. He tried to explain his continued attachment to the bike: 'The Italian road man [Fiorenzo] Magni once said to me: I'm getting old, Reg, and perhaps I'm getting past it, but I enjoy being on the road: always something to see, plenty of air to breathe, a good bike under you. I feel the same when I'm out on the Cheshire lanes.'

That may have been true, but it could not replace the rush he had felt in competition in his prime.

Benny Foster first began to turn a profit from cycling by promoting rural meetings in the East Midlands as a young man in the 1930s, a sideline that helped him to supplement the money he made as a musician in a show band. Short and often overweight, prematurely bald other than a few wild strands of hair, he was a reasonably successful cyclist but his unceasing enthusiasm for the sport helped him to rise through the administrative levels so that he had become coach of the national team in the 1950s, leading them to their unprecedented success in 1954. An innovative, tempestuous personality, he could lose his temper with a rider one moment yet willingly give up a meal for them the next. He was involved in a cycle accessory firm but he spent as much time travelling the country to fulfil his voluntarily responsibilities as Britain's coach, leaving home on Monday morning with a box of sandwiches that would last him the week. 'There weren't many like him,' Norman Sheil said. 'Everything he did was for the team.'

Through the force of his personality, and sheer resourcefulness, Foster had in later years wangled a weekly radio show on regional BBC radio in which he discussed the latest sports news with co-presenter David Coleman. In 1968, he persuaded the same employer to allow him to commentate on hockey – as well as cycling – at the Mexico City Olympics, even though he had no background in the sport. At about the same time, he had pulled off his greatest trick when he successfully led a bid to bring the 1970 World Track Championships to his home town of Leicester. He had then pooled the support of the Duke of Edinburgh, the minister of sport Denis Howell and Walter Winterbottom, formerly manager of the England football team but then working for the government, to ensure that the event earned the funding required. Most assumed that nobody else within the sport could have managed such a feat. 'British cycling has never really replaced him,' Mick Bennett, an international track cyclist then, said. 'He was a Dickensian character, the man of many blazers, a red-faced showman and loud as a set of bellows.' Yet for all Foster's entrepreneurial cunning even he struggled to make money in a sport that had, for years, been in gradual decline.

In Britain there were still committed cycling fans who retained an interest in the road game thanks mostly to the continued success of the Tour de France – and the compelling rides of the brilliant Eddy Merckx – but the track version of the sport had become a minority concern to the point where it scarcely existed. Venues such as Fallowfield and Herne Hill would struggle to attract a few hundred people to meetings. The journalist Noel Henderson wrote that, despite Foster's tireless efforts to promote the World Championships, the Saffron Lane Stadium had been 'almost empty' during it. In previous years, Foster had encountered a similar problem when hosting the National Championships there. Had Brietling not agreed to sponsor the event, he would have repeatedly finished in the red. 'The great days of track racing in Britain, when Herne Hill used to pack in thousands for duels between professional sprinters when they were really professionals – Harris, Van Vliet, Plattner and the like – had become a thing of the past,' Henderson wrote.

This was only partially true. Those men were long retired but Foster insisted that Harris could still hold his own against Britain's best, if only as a desperate measure through which to attract crowds back to the sport. As Oliver said in 1971, 'it was Benny's idea that Reg should come out of retirement'.

He proposed that Harris compete against British professionals at a time when they concentrated on road competitions because that represented their principal source of income. They received appearance fees at the National Track Championships and a few other meetings, but that was not nearly sufficient to justify training for such events. That had helped to further diminish the status of the championships, ensuring scant press coverage, but Foster felt the return of the sport's most famous son could resolve that problem and even attract the holy grail of television interest. The only problem facing Harris was limited preparation time, with the championships taking place in July, only a few months' away. Though in good shape for a 51-year-old, Harris knew he would not get race-sharp by then, which left him with one obvious means by which to succeed.

'I don't want to get involved in all that again,' Reg Barnett said, over the phone, much to my surprise. At the time, I did not know his relationship with Harris. I knew only that he had raced against him in 1971.

I repeated the interview request, promising that I would not press him to talk about anything with which he was uncomfortable. After a moment's thought, he said: 'Okay, fuck it, I like the sound of your voice. But if we're going to talk about it, we're going to talk about all of it.' He insisted that I met him in person.

By 1971, Barnett had won a national sprint title three years in succession, first as an amateur, twice as a professional. By then concentrating on the road as the sprint specialist with the Falcon-Tighe team, he was commonly regarded as Britain's fastest cyclist. 'I don't mean that as disrespect to the super riders who were there, but it was all so easy,' he said. 'Not until Sid Barras got his act together could anyone beat me. He was a better road sprinter but, still on the track, he couldn't do it.' Three years younger than Barnett, Barras was a formidably tough rider from the north-east who was only beginning to emerge on the professional scene.

We met at a hotel near London's Victoria Station. Barnett was polite, and quick to crack a joke, but still he had an intensity that is common among many professional cyclists, his eyes twinkling beneath long lashes as he recalled his adventures back then. Some involved women he encountered, others the profound friendships he made. His good humour darkened a little, though, when he recalled the phone call he received from Harris in the spring of 1971. 'It came out of the blue,' he said. 'I knew who he was but didn't really know him. I was in the process of buying a new house with the money I'd made. He said: "We need to get together, Reg. I've got a project I'm going to do."' With Barnett based in south London, Harris suggested that they met at Ponte Vecchio, then a celebrity haunt. Having grown up in a tough neighbourhood in Penge, and often found in a pub along the

Old Kent Road, Barnett thought an establishment such as Ponte Vecchio to be the height of pretension. His opinion of his host worsened when Harris tried to ingratiate himself with Barnett. 'He said, "I can get you a job, Reg. You can work for me. You can do all the leg work for me." I'm sitting there, looking at him, thinking, "Why would I want that? What are you trying to tell me?"' Barnett had erected steel before entering professional cycling. 'I could probably earn more than he was earning then.'

Rebuffed, Harris switched to a favourite topic. 'He was: "Could you fetch a few birds for us?" It was as much as I could do to stop laughing. He was mad for women. He was trying to act like he was back in the '50s. This old man trying to relive his youth.'

Eventually, Barnett told Harris to cut to the chase. 'I was under no illusions,' he said. 'I had an idea about what was going on.' Barnett knew how the sprinters' circus had worked. 'He didn't know it but I had learnt about him on the continent.'

What Barnett did not expect was that Harris might actually want to compete in a fixed race. 'I said: "Don't be ridiculous." But then he started talking about money and I got very interested. Makes the world go round.'

Though Harris almost certainly did not realise it, he could not have chosen a more suitable ally in his covert plan. For after three years as a professional cyclist, and several more as an amateur, Barnett had become completely disillusioned with sport. Mostly he was disgusted with the drug-taking that he had discovered once he had begun to compete abroad, a practice that he had initially resisted but like so many others he had eventually freely indulged, buying most of his dope from an infamous chemist in the Italian town of Bol de Guerra. 'The designer drug then combined mephedrone with ephedrine, one for the lungs, one to drive the heart.'

He had also discovered race-fixing to be endemic among professionals, even in the most prestigious events. 'You could buy and sell a World Road Championship or a World Sprint Championship,' he said. 'I've seen it happen. A dear friend of mine, he said, "I couldn't beat him anyway, Reg, I might as well have a big suitcase of money." The whole sport was entrenched in filth, but I was too far into it then to get out.'

By comparison, Harris's proposition was small fry. He wanted to organise a series of exhibition races around the country between the two of them for each of which he would pay Barnett £400 to lose. The plan would climax at the National Championships at Salford Park in Birmingham. 'He said: "I'd like it all to culminate with you and me in the final." I replied: "What about the other riders? Trevor Bull could beat you with one leg." He said: "I'll finance it, you speak to them."' Barnett was earning only £125 a week. 'I said I'd do my best.'

Staged in London, Birmingham and Manchester, the races followed a carefully choreographed pattern. After a first lap when both riders pretended that they wished to gain an edge, Harris would attack at the bell, prompting Barnett to feign struggle before closing the gap either at the final turn or on the home straight. As they approached the finish line, he would edge up to Harris's shoulder but just fail to pass him. The crowds were thrilled. The other cyclists smelled a rat. 'They said, "Ah, did you let him have it, Reg?" I said, "No, he's quite fit for an old man and anyway I concentrate on the road now. I haven't got the speed."' He dismissed the possibility that Harris might have beaten him anyway. 'You could see that some of that old power was there, but he was dying with a hundred metres to go. If I'd have taken off at 300, they'd have been calling A&E because my road stamina would have kicked in.'

The results soon troubled the management at Falcon. They did not like to see their brand undermined by the spectacle of a middle-aged man defeating their star sprinter. Knowing that Barnett was throwing the races, the team's co-owner Ernie Clements told him that he was in breach of his contract. Barnett cared little for the small print. 'I told Ernie, "Yeah, but they're only exhibition races. He's Reg Harris. He's more of a marketing thing. Anyway, you've got other problems. He's offered me a lot of money to lose the final of the sprint championship."' Clements promised Barnett a 'win bonus' of £1,000 if he refused to give up his title.

Barnett accepted the money, knowing that it would not matter to Harris because there was a flaw in his plan. While Barnett might have been able to arrange for the other British professionals to lose to the returning hero, he was not going to be able to similarly persuade Gordon Johnson, the Australian world champion. Harris had not realised that Johnson had accepted an invitation to compete as an overseas entrant. Johnson beat him in the semi-finals before doing likewise to Barnett in the deciding duel. 'Gordon Johnson would never have taken a bribe from Harris to allow him to win,' Brotherton, who knew Johnson well from the cycling scene in Australia, said.

Despite the defeat, Harris and Foster departed the tournament encouraged by how close the former had gone to winning the title. Even if only by foul means, they knew now that Harris could still beat his compatriots. No surprise, then, that Foster was soon lobbying British Cycling to prevent foreign talent from competing in the National Championships again.

CHAPTER 16
1973

Initially, Harris was reluctant when Foster approached him in 1973 about competing again for the national title. 'He said, "Look, Benny, I've proved my point,"' Oliver recalled. 'But Benny insisted.' His argument was typically persuasive, too. In the two years since Harris's failed comeback, the authorities had agreed to Foster's demand that only Britons should compete in the event. Foster had also given Harris much more time to prepare, approaching him in the autumn with a view to Harris training over the winter, a prospect that his flexible working arrangement with Draka would allow. After an evening's discussion, Harris eventually agreed.

This time, the only problem facing him was the paucity of potential training partners. As a middle-aged man, he no longer knew of young men in their twenties with days to spare. Given track cycling's decline, there were much fewer of them around who were interested anyway. There were one or two suitable amateurs but they would be too quick for either Harris or them to gain any benefit from training together. His best alternative, then, was to team up with the teenage son of an old friend, Roy Swinnerton, who had once competed alongside Harris but was running a bike-shop business in Stoke-on-Trent, while also serving as mechanic to the national team. 'I was 15 at the time,' Paul Swinnerton said. 'Reg had taken me to be the level that he needed to be to start with.'

Even for his age, Swinnerton was far from exceptional, having finished third in the school district championships that year. But he was ambitious and knew that he had been given a rare opportunity when Harris suggested that they should work together. 'He was hard, firm. You got a feeling that when you were with Reg, you didn't mess about. Everything had to be done right. Everything had to be on time. He was so efficient, even down to the way he presented himself. He was immaculate. He was a cyclist but you never saw him with dirty hands.'

Harris would pick up Swinnerton in his BMW and drive to a patch of road that he had chosen as suitable to undergo the sprint training that he had been taught as a teenager by Jimmy Battersby. Very soon the sessions were just as tough. 'His training was very intense. You had to give every last ounce. Eventually we became friends but it was an agreement. I helped him and he helped me.' During their rest periods, Swinnerton would ask him about his career, about the cyclists he had raced and the different tactics employed. He told Swinnerton that, with his light build, he should turn to pursuit riding, but by then it was too late. Having always fancied being a sprinter, spending so much time with the discipline's greatest practitioner sealed Swinnerton's fate. Within two years, he was competing at a national level. He went on to become British champion. As if touched by Harris's magic, Swinnerton even smashed his mentor's rollers record, putting his name in the *Guinness Book of Records* with a speed of 107mph. 'He helped me in that he taught me a lot of tactics and a different way of training, much shorter, sharper than other cyclists. That affected my career.' When we spoke, Swinnerton was training his son, Barney. 'We incorporated Reg's regime. We still ride out to the stretch of road, do three sprints.' In September 2011, Barney claimed a national title.

For his stamina work over the winter, Harris rode both the rollers in his house and on the road, teaming up with Les West, then a leading Briton in distance races. Here Harris's attitude was far more relaxed. 'He would greet me at the gateway to his house, waiting with a silver service tray,' West said. 'I would be, "Reg, I thought we were going out training." He'd say, "We will but there's time for coffee in the garden first." So, we'd sit there chatting, and I'm thinking, "I need to be getting the miles in."' You wondered if Harris was strict with Swinnerton because he knew that was the treatment an aspirational young cyclist needed.

By the start of the summer, Harris was happy enough with his physical condition to announce his comeback, adding that he expected to win. Swinnerton felt the confidence was justified. 'He was very fit by then, very strong. He still had quads the size of which I've never seen anywhere else. He knew exactly what he needed to do and how he needed to do it.'

Harris followed his news by approaching Raleigh with a request for them to lend him his old track bike, then stored in the company museum. With so much time having passed since his dismissal, he was certain that they would accede to such a simple request, not least when it would provide them with free advertising. Instead they refused, claiming that they did not want to be associated with his unlikely project and that they were focused now only on promoting their professional road team. When Harris subsequently defeated Raleigh's best rider, Trevor Bull, in an exhibition race in the week before the championships, however, the company swiftly changed their mind.

That left Harris with less than 48 hours to get the neglected bike into competitive condition. Swinnerton recalled how he and his dad worked on it long into the night. 'We had to rebuild all his wheels,' he said, referring both to those on the bike and his spares. 'They were 36-spoke wheels. We had to try and solder the joins on the spokes where they cross over to make it much stiffer. Even then Reg still had a very, very strong kick.' They fitted Campagnolo parts on to the bottom bracket and the head-set because the originals were lost. Having since inherited the shop, Swinnerton keeps that transmission carefully locked away, like jewels from ancient royalty. 'The bike had the geometry that he'd been used to but he needed to get his old stuff back on it. He wanted to get that feeling again.'

People who turned up to the Saffron Lane Stadium to watch Harris in 1974 seem to suffer from a little selective amnesia. They recall packed stands and endless cheers. They marvel at how Harris was able to attract supporters of all ages, both old-timers who had left the sport about the time he retired and young fans who had heard endless stories about him. Swinnerton was typical when he said: 'Everybody went there to watch Reg race. We all went there to see it happen. It was exciting stuff.' The truth was that the main stand along the home straight was not much more than half full. (Foster never released the official figures but suffice to say even that would have represented a good crowd for track cycling then.)

The track itself was similar to those abroad on which Harris had excelled in his youth, with a fast wooden surface, steeped bankings and a relatively short circumference for an outdoor velodrome at 330 metres in length. In 1971, Harris had grown thick sideburns and dyed his hair – possibly brown, though it came out ginger – but this time did not attempt any such cosmetic tweaks. With only a few wisps of hair left over his crown and the strands touching his ears turned grey, facially he did not look like the star attraction at a major sporting competition. Physique-wise, while once as willowy as an old-fashioned rugby winger, he now resembled more a 1980s prop forward, stout and carrying more weight than was ideal. Only his formidably sized thighs recalled the build of his youth. Draka Foam had agreed to sponsor him, providing him with a dark blue and red strip that was emblazoned with the company's name.

The sprint championship was seeded, with Harris considered to be among the favourites. That meant he was pitched in the three-up first round against two long shots for the title, Dave Linehan and Bob Jones. Previously a cyclo-cross specialist, Linehan had taken up track cycling only that season and had never previously competed on a track as steeply banked as Saffron Lane. Part of a decent Holdsworth-Bantel road team, Jones was a tougher proposition, but still lacked the explosive power of a true sprinter.

Harris began by indulging in gamesmanship, first delaying his arrival at the start line so that his opponents had to loiter, then spending a few moments examining different parts of his bike. You could assume both were done as much for the crowd's benefit as his.

In a three-lap race, Linehan attacked from the start, little wonder given that he lacked finishing speed and the technical skills that would have helped him to survive a more tactically involved race. Harris stayed on his wheel apparently without much exertion, with Jones laying off him by a couple of lengths. Propelled by shouts from a crowd desperate to see his legendary kick, Harris did not disappoint when he eventually attacked emerging from the final turn, narrowly holding off Jones in second, while leaving Linehan to appear to be travelling backwards. Not that he seemed embarrassed. 'I started cycling the year Reg retired,' he said. 'I never dreamed I'd be riding against him.'

In an event with a small field, that put Harris through to a semi-final against Nigel Dean, a senior figure in the Holdsworth-Bantel team and a step up in class of opponent. In the past few weeks alone, he had posted several good results on the road, including second place in the tightly contested Tom Simpson Memorial race and fifth in a Chilterns grand prix. He had only just recovered from a lung infection but was comfortable on the track, too, and had spent much of the winter competing in Six-Day Races on a tour of Canada.

Harris was drawn to lead out in their first race, and was in first place when Dean attacked at the bell. Again Harris had the legs to stay with his junior rival, and dipped inside him on the home straight to win. In the next, he jumped on the final banking and again with Dean unable to stay with him. In both, Harris covered the final 200 metres in 12.6 seconds, which was fairly fast but well down on what he managed easily in his pomp. Most assumed he would need to go quicker to beat Bull in the final.

A tall, powerfully built cyclist, Bull was among the best British riders of his generation and in the form of his life. In that year alone, he won seven road races in Britain. As an amateur, he had won bronze in the 20-kilometre scratch race at the Commonwealth Games. Unusually committed in practice, he had deep reserves of stamina but had finishing speed, too. He would not have touched Harris 20 years earlier, and was not as quick as Reg Barnett (by now temporarily retired), but he was certain to provide a sterner examination of Harris's capabilities than his previous opponents. 'Trevor trained extremely hard but had a turn of speed when it came to pure sprinting too,' Mick Bennett, a close friend, said. 'He had actually always wanted to be a pure sprinter.'

Their first race followed a plotline as compelling as some of the best races in which Harris had been involved. Drawn as lead-out man, Bull tracked a slow course around the top of the banking until he returned to the start line, at which point he drew to a standstill, prompting Harris to do likewise. The impasse lasted five minutes, with Bull a few yards ahead of

Harris, directly below the spectators and, it might be worth noting, beside a Breitling advertisement hoarding – several interviewees of mine suggested that often happened for the benefit of television viewers.

Harris's control of his bike was still immaculate. He shuffled back and forth with the ease of an insouciant teenager on a skateboard, faintly smiling, all the time his eyes fixed on Bull until eventually the young man acquiesced to the crowd's shouted suggestions that he restart the race. Harris stuck to his wheel for another lap then attacked from halfway up the banking. However, rather than dart for the inside lane, he swept up and forced Bull to check his pace. A strict official might have disqualified Harris for snaking but the judges were benevolent towards the star attraction that afternoon. With a three-length lead, Harris then denied Bull's late surge for the line.

In the second race, Harris dictated a slow pace at the top of the banking for the best part of the first two laps, his eyes locked on Bull behind him nearly the whole time. When Bull jumped with 300 metres left, Harris initially appeared to struggle as he tried to stay with him, but the gap closed at the end of the back straight and the men were level as they emerged from the final turn. Now the crowd were on their feet, urging Harris to summon his mythical second jump. It took a little longer for him to unleash it than it once would have done but eventually, only yards from the finish line, Harris hit that imaginary gear and won by half a wheel.

The *Observer* ran the story of his victory on its front page the next day, publishing a longer paean to Harris's unlikely achievement inside the paper in which he was hailed for 'being cycling's matinee idol again'. 'There was an uneasy feeling that after the build-up, he might be humiliated by the younger men,' Geoffrey Nicholson wrote. 'When he held off Bull in the final sprint, the relief and sentiment was comparable to Drobný's Wimbledon.' Jaroslav Drobný was the popular Czech who had won that tennis tournament while exiled in Britain.

The Times paid similar tribute to Harris, praising him not only for his age-defying athleticism but also for reviving the lost art of showmanship. The writer was impressed with the confidence with which Harris first bowed to, then addressed the crowd, and how he had regally presented Jennifer with his victory bouquet close to the finish line. The article complimented him also on the professionalism with which he had conducted his promotional work. 'The new champion measured his success by the seven broadcasts, three television networks and countless press conferences,' it said. A few days later, the *Daily Mirror* claimed that Harris had sparked a 'cycle revolution' among famous men of his generation, publishing a photograph of the actor Richard Burton, 48, on his bike in Winchester, while adding that news of the victory had travelled to the south of France and prompted 58-year-old Gregory Peck to spend his holiday in the saddle.

Elsewhere, Denis Howell said that the victory should help the BCF to earn a crucial grant from the Sports Council that they had previously been denied, while experts tried to explain Harris's victory. Nicholson said such an upset was inevitable given the sport's decline, adding that Harris had helped the sport by dramatising 'the great height from which present standards have fallen'. Harris offered a similar explanation, albeit more diplomatically, saying that the 'standard of sprinting is not what it used to be'.

Ken Evans, the editor of *Cycling*, suggested that Harris's confidence and reputation had intimidated his opponents in the first rounds into defeat. He said Bull was beaten through tactical inferiority. 'He might have had the legs of a champion but he didn't have the head,' Evans wrote. Bull effectively agreed, pointing out that 'match sprinting is a lot different from winning bunch sprints' on the road, adding that he lacked the killer instinct required on the track. 'You need a particular type of mind and I haven't got it,' he said. Offended by all the criticism, Linehan wrote a letter to *Cycling* in which he suggested that the result might have been different had the younger men been able to tailor their preparations as Harris had done. 'But our sponsors pay us to produce the goods in our speciality,' he said.

All of that sounded plausible but, given what Barnett revealed about Harris's first comeback, you could not help but wonder if underhand tactics had been involved as well. To try to find out, I began by contacting Nigel Dean, who has settled in Zimbabwe. A modest, genial man running an IT business, he initially denied that he might have let Harris beat him but then corrected himself. 'Put it this way, I didn't try as hard as I might have done,' he said. 'I rang my manager just before the race and asked for a win bonus. He said he wasn't interested. So, then it just seemed wrong to win. The occasion was all about Reg. All these people had come to see him. The television cameras were there. I didn't gain anything from winning.' He denied that money was exchanged between them and could not comment on whether Bull had been bought off. Finally, I asked him how he and Bull responded to their defeats. 'I think we probably laughed.'

Bull died in April 2009, shortly after contracting an aggressive strain of leukaemia. A quiet, popular man, his passing was widely mourned within the sport even though he had been retired for 28 years. Bennett was probably his best friend in cycling, having run a bike shop with him in Birmingham when both were young men. In later years, Bull married the sister of Bennett's late fiancée (who died tragically young in a car crash). At the time of writing, he was the long-established race director of the Tour of Britain. I asked him if it was arranged for Harris to beat Bull. 'I need to be guarded about what I say, but you're putting it very politely,' he said. 'Put it this way: Trevor was happy with the result and I'm sure Reg was delighted with the result.' Though respectful to his friend's memory, Bennett did not mind implicating Harris in anything untoward. 'I think it was a big ego trip for Reg. He was very aloof. He put himself on this pedestal.'

The photograph of Harris and Bull approaching the finish line would appear to support what Bennett suggested. In a superbly evocative shot, their shoulders are aligned, their muscles tensed and faces twisted in apparently similar pain, yet the scene beneath them tells a different tale. To the left of the picture, Harris's chain is taut, confirming he is driving himself to the limit. Bull has allowed his to fall limp, suggesting he has stopped applying pressure to his pedal in the most crucial stage of the race.

What, then, did other people who were there think, the casual fan aside? 'Everybody knew it was fixed,' St Pierre said – and he was a great admirer of Harris. 'What are you going to do? You're a young lad. It's of no great importance. Here's this bloke with a fair bit of money to splash around who was prepared to buy you off.'

The more I talked to people, the more I discovered that this was the general view both from those involved in the sport then and those who had heard about Harris's comeback second-hand. Usually, the conversation followed a curious pattern. The interviewee would begin by asking if I knew about Harris's victory and remark how it underlined the breadth of his talent. When I suggested that it was fixed, they admitted they had heard likewise, saying something similar to what Bob Barber, then a cycling promoter, said: 'I think there was show business involved.' It seemed people were more interested in stoking Harris's legend than in questioning the legitimacy of his win. Just as he needed their adoration, it seemed they needed to exalt him. Perhaps that is not unusual in cheating's long history. Maybe we are often complicit in demanding of our sporting heroes feats that are narrowly beyond them.

You might even argue that these fans were justified in colouring the truth. For here was a great story in a sport that by then had seen countless fabricated results. As St Pierre implied, by comparison, this was an event of limited consequence. The cycling writer Tim Hilton even called it all 'a bit of a laugh'. The ethics of it are not important, for this book at least. Far more interesting is that Harris carried it all off with such implacable chutzpah. Never once did he show a trace of nervousness or guilt in the 'countless' press interviews. In his autobiography he devoted a chapter to his comeback without any suggestion that any of the results might have been staged. Some years later, he invited BBC television into his home and smiled modestly when the presenter, Barry Davies, addressed perhaps his most unlikely win. 'I'm not quite sure how it started and who it was to please,' Harris said, sitting in his garden, aged 64, top two shirt buttons undone to reveal a tanned chest. 'Perhaps it was some old friends or people who say the young ones aren't like the old ones, or whether somebody had made a misguided remark to my wife and said, "It was a pity you never saw him race, he wasn't at all bad, you know." I think that might have helped lead me into a demonstration.'

Perhaps such deception came easily to Harris because he had so often tinkered with the truth: from the implausible reason for the failed mechanic's apprenticeship, to the myriad exaggerated injuries, to the desperate need to explain away any defeat. He changed his accent, fudged his background and, as many of the quotes in this book should demonstrate, was unnecessarily formal with his speech. Like James Gatz became Jay Gatsby, he even improved his name: Reginald Hargreaves Harris, double-barrelled yet patently not aristocratic. Hargreaves derives from the word for thicket and is thought once to have referred to a homeless inhabitant of the land; Harris means son of Henry, formerly England's king. Ultimately Harris fell between two classes, the one he left behind and that which he craved to join. Little wonder he was so impassioned whenever the image that he strived so hard to project was threatened: the crushing of Cyril Peacock, the way that he scorned his mother in public – nothing more brutally revealed his background than modest Elsie.

Perhaps it was fitting then that his final misdeed in middle age should have been squalid and small-time in a way that most who remember it have chosen to forget. 'Most people didn't give a damn,' St Pierre said. 'There weren't more than a few hundred spectators there. It meant nothing. Professional sprinting in Britain had virtually died.'

A year later Harris agreed to defend his title, yet he seemed not to have realised that opinion had since begun to turn against him. Geoff Cooke, the winner of the amateur sprint title in 1975, said that Harris had 'devalued my championships immensely' by drawing attention away from him even though his times were quicker than Harris's. Travelling to the World Championships in Italy, Cooke recalled how the British team were mocked mercilessly for allowing a middle-aged man to become the national champion. 'The Aussies were taking the rip out of us: "A 54-year-old guy can do that to you?"' he said. Brotherton, then coaching Australian cyclists, said Bull suffered so much embarrassment that he came to regret being involved in the race. 'He couldn't live it down,' Brotherton said. 'Trevor said: "I never should have done that."' He beat Harris in two successive races in the following year's final. 'He wouldn't be bought off again,' Brotherton said.

Harris was humble in defeat. 'Trevor was a great deal stronger and faster,' he said. 'He's a bit younger, too. He is a worthy champion and I wish him all the luck in the world. I don't intend riding any more races. I've had a fairly long innings, and I hope there's not been too much nostalgia in it today. I haven't ridden to please myself, but to please other people.'

You wondered if that final statement was true. He had sympathised with Foster's financial predicament when the promoter had successfully pleaded with him to return for a third time, but others suggested that Harris's motives were not entirely altruistic. John Lewis said: 'Reg enjoyed being well known. He enjoyed the kudos that came with being in the lime-light. I think he always wanted to do something which would put him back in the limelight.'

Barnett drew a similar conclusion, adding that 'it was almost like he was trying to be Peter Pan'. However, he also insisted that Harris had another motivation. Though Harris had been awarded on OBE in 1958, it seemed he now wanted an upgrade. 'At the bottom of it was a knighthood,' Barnett said. 'That's what he was really after. Harris was on speaking terms with Harold Wilson through Gannex. If he was still alive, I'd say the same thing because he knows what I'm telling you is fact.' Why say it now? 'To this dying day, Reg still owes me some money. He never paid the full balance for the exhibition races. I was so cross because we're all part of the same filthy hypocrisy. If it costs one pound, a hundred pounds or a thousand pounds, it's irrelevant. A deal is a deal. Races are bought and sold all the time. I couldn't count how many times I've been asked to lose.'

In 1975, perhaps because politicians had yet to realise quite how well sporting success could reflect back on them, it was more difficult for sportsmen to earn knighthoods than it is now. Only three English cricketers had been knighted since Harris's retirement. Sir Geoff Hurst and Sir Bobby Charlton, World Cup winners in 1966, did not earn their prefixes until the 1990s. Stirling Moss, Harris's near-contemporary, was knighted in 1999.

However, Harris was closer to Wilson than Barnett suggested and believed that their relationship could help him to succeed where other athletes had failed. He had become acquainted with Wilson while working for Joseph Kagan, who donated such large sums of money to the Labour leader's office that he was made a knight of the realm (though he was later stripped of it after evading tax, while MI5 posthumously discredited him further by revealing that he had regular contact with the KGB while courting Wilson).

Since leaving Gannex, Harris had been careful to cultivate his relationship with Wilson, telling Barnett that they bonded because of shared northern roots: Wilson, hailed from Huddersfield, only 22 miles from Bury. Two weeks after Harris's defeat by Bull in the 1975 final, he took lunch with Wilson and Joop den Uyl, then Prime Minister of Holland. What they discussed was not revealed, though Harris did not appear in the New Year's Honours List. And within four months of its announcement, Wilson had resigned.

 **CHAPTER 17**
1976

In the spring of 1976 Harris received an unusual request from a Draka client, a senior executive whose furniture company used Harris's foam. He wanted Harris to meet a junior employee called Brenda Atkinson, who was working part-time while trying to pursue a career as a cyclist. Over lunch the client asked Harris if he could help Atkinson. In response, Harris suggested that she left her Yorkshire home and move in with his parents-in-law so he could coach her full-time voluntarily.

Though aged only 20, Atkinson had already had minor success, finishing third in the sprint at the national championship a year earlier. But that was not quite good enough to earn her a place in the national team and the time she needed with their coaches to progress. Muscled and durable, she had the raw physical power but sorely lacked track craft. As a fall-back plan, the opportunity to learn from Harris was more than adequate, particularly as he promised to turn her into a champion.

Even almost four decades later Atkinson was unsure exactly why Harris offered to give up so much of his time. 'He certainly had nothing to gain financially from it,' she said. She did not know that the BCF had previously blocked his attempts to remain within cycling as a coach. Nor did she realise that his split with Raleigh effectively ended his relationship with the business side of the sport, too. Given that he had also failed as a promoter, she represented the only means by which he could remain involved in competitive cycling. She might even help him to show the ruling body why they were wrong to overlook his potential as a coach. 'I knew I had a once-in-a-lifetime opportunity and I gave it everything I could,' she said.

His first task was to travel down to Gerald O'Donovan's factory at Ilkeston and persuade him to open up the cage in which he stored the Raleigh team's professional equipment in return for a crate of vintage wine. Known to like a drink, O'Donovan happily complied and allowed Harris to pick the best of his frames and a boot's worth of Campagnolo parts. 'I got two track bikes and a road bike,' Atkinson said. 'Ger was still a great friend of Reg's. That was how they did things then.'

Then the hard work began. On Harris's insistence, Atkinson trained every day. Naturally disciplined, she spent hours out on the road alone, joined Roy Swinnerton's Stoke team at weekends and occasionally did bit and bit with Harris when he was in the mood. For their sprint work, they travelled down to a tarmac track in Stoke where Harris asked her to train with a professional jockey friend of his who wanted to keep fit. Often they did his old sprint routine on the road, too, albeit this time with Harris leading her out in his Mercedes.

In the evening she joined him and Jennifer for dinner, turning her wine glass upside down once Harris had uncorked the second or third bottle of red. 'He was good at making you relax,' she said, laughing. It was at these times that Harris schooled her in the psychology of the sport. 'It was about mystique, about being one-up on somebody,' she said. 'Sometimes that would be without them knowing. So you wouldn't tell somebody if you had changed your gear for a race. Other times you would let them know. Turn up with a good pair of wheels that nobody had seen before or get your handler to say something that might unsettle them.' She recalled his lesson in how to trick an opponent into false confidence. 'Let them think they'd beaten you: let them go, so you could track them and beat them. There were all these little psychological tricks. Nothing malicious, it's just the way sprinters are.' Inevitably, he demanded that she looked the part, too. 'He'd be reminiscing about his early days and say you can always turn up neat and tidy. Soap and water doesn't cost anything.' She got a sense that he did not have much as a child. 'He didn't like to see wastage, dripping taps, leaving the lights on. He hated anything like that.' She remembered him as fiercely unsentimental. 'He told me he'd given the dogs his rainbow jerseys for their bed.'

By the following summer, he was satisfied that she was ready for the major races on the domestic circuit and offered to serve as her escort, strapping her bikes to his Mercedes, then showing less concern for excessive energy usage as he smashed speed limits while transporting her to races around the country. 'Oh crikey, we'd be hurtling along a country lane doing 70 miles per hour. He'd just flash his headlights at everybody to get out of the way.' Success came quickly, both in sprint races and long-distance events. Harris would rather Atkinson specialised but understood that this was not possible with fewer races available to women then. At some point, it seemed, he had learnt the folly of his initial opposition to women's potential to excel in his sport. 'We seemed to have a connection, a rapport,' Atkinson said. 'I knew what he expected from me and he knew that I could deliver what he wanted.'

By the summer of 1978, his stardust had helped her to become the first British woman to win each event at the National Championships: the sprint, the pursuit and even the road race. Like many an autodidact – he was, after all, his own coach for most of his career – Harris had proven to be an exceptional teacher. 'My ability would probably have come through eventually but, without Reg, it wouldn't have been easy and it would have taken a lot longer. He opened my eyes to a different way of doing things.' She knew that he divided opinion but found no reason to criticise him. 'His way of doing things wasn't everybody's cup of tea. Some people didn't like him at all, but I found him to be a gentleman, a one-off and a complete individual. He went about his life as Reg Harris, doing what he wanted and not what somebody else would expect him to do.'

Their partnership was his last contribution to elite sport.

In 1982 Harris was taken aback by a small entry in a cycling trade journal. An old acquaintance, John Lewis, had fallen ill with a devastating illness called cauda equina syndrome. Put simply, it attacks the nerve endings at the base of the spine, causes great pain and at worst leaves its victims paralysed. Harris had known Lewis through the Centenary Club, an exclusive social institution for senior executives of the cycling trade. Harris was invited to their rides by Gerry Burgess. Lewis had worked in cycling most of his career, learning the trade with Johnny Berry in Manchester, while later turning around the fortunes of the ailing Holdsworth company. Among the few active cyclists at the club's events, Harris and Lewis had struck up a bond through riding together ahead of the field.

That they had not seen each other for a while did not matter to Harris when he discovered Lewis's plight. He found out where Lewis was hospitalised and was at his bedside within days. 'You couldn't have wished for anybody who was more caring,' Lewis said, who by then was in a serious condition.

He had been paralysed within hours of the illness taking hold and remained so for a long time even once discharged. Previously as fit as almost any 50-year-old and successful in his work – he was featured on the front page of the *Sunday Times* business section for his success with Holdsworth – he was soon jobless, partially mobile and his money was running out. Harris never abandoned him. 'He and his wife lived in Cheshire near Knutsford. Joan and I were in Preston. I was on my uppers, having lost everything. We were in a parlous state financially. But he would turn up in his Mercedes and off we'd go.' Harris would bring the couple back home for a lavish dinner or take them to his favourite restaurants. When slowly Lewis began to recover some movement, he would reciprocate Harris's goodwill by servicing the Italian bikes that Harris kept in his outhouse. 'He was competent on bicycles but he didn't have that finesse with which he could, say, true the wheels.' Eventually, Lewis became solvent again and dependence turned to balanced friendship. 'He took a lot of getting to know but when he became a friend, nobody could ever have had a better friend.'

Others reported this fiercely loyal streak in Harris. When negotiating the sale of Fallowfield, he demanded that Manchester

University retain Norman Grattage and Len Myatt in its employment. Neville Tong still marvels that Harris insisted he convalesced in his home after fracturing his skull at Harris Stadium. He spent six weeks there as his guest, with Harris even running him to the hospital for treatment. His only payment was that he helped Harris to move house. 'I only ever rode in one meeting with him,' Tong said. 'I think he felt responsible because it was his ground.'

Bill Brown first met Harris when both were adolescents riding alone along the East Lancashire Road. They fell in line heading out to Liverpool and talked about riding together again. Friendships were forged that way among cyclists then.

As their life took different routes, so Brown found he occasionally needed Harris's help. Usually he did not need to ask. When Brown fell seriously ill with a kidney condition, Harris was the only cyclist from their club to visit him in hospital. When Brown's kitchenware shop fell into the red, Harris stumped up the £400 needed to keep him afloat. In return Brown put his friend's name above the shop, allowing local restaurants to boast about having bought their sinks and cookers from a world champion athlete. Shortly before Harris's first World Championship as a professional, Brown made a cheeky request. 'We were out on the bikes and I said, "When you win next week, Reg, there's just one thing that I want. I want me vest."' Brown's intention was to encourage Harris by assuming the rainbow jersey would soon be his. Brown was surprised to discover the historical contents of the parcel waiting for him on his doorstep within a fortnight. 'I asked him, "Don't you want the first one?" He was: "What for? I'll get another one."'

I have seen pictures of Brown as a young man in the Harris family photo album. With his pinched face and bulldog build, he stood out among the professionally taken portraits of famous cyclists from abroad. In one he is posing alone at Fallowfield, suggesting Harris was behind the lens. They were no other photographs of club riders in the collection that I could recall. 'He was always good to me: right from the start,' Brown said. 'He either liked people or disliked them.' If he disliked them, he did not hide it. 'Reg could be very nasty with some people. Some people could borrow his bike. Other people, he wouldn't even lend them a farthing or even a tube for a punctured tyre. The better he became, when he became world champion, he was worse. Then everyone wanted to know him, wanted to shake his hand, everyone wanted to say: "I know Reg Harris." He didn't like that.' Others resented his success. 'People stuck their nose up at him.'

Albert Bagnall reprised his youthful friendship with Harris during the 1980s, riding with him often in retirement. He was similarly equivocal about his friend. 'He was very, very complicated,' he said. 'Looking back on it, after all these years, I remember the things he would say to me: well, I wouldn't [have] put them that way. "He's only a bloody postman, he can't have any brains", that type of thing.'

He recalled how quick Harris was to emphasise the privileges of his lifestyle, noting that he had instructed Jennifer to have an aperitif prepared for him on his return from a ride or that the couple liked to dress smartly for dinner. Those who actually dined with them said this was untrue, though it is interesting that Harris should wish to create such an impression. 'He had that charisma so he could carry if off, and people accepted it, but it was all bloody swag to me,' Bagnall said. 'I let it go over my head.' He sensed in Harris an internal conflict. 'Somewhere he had completely shut himself away from his working-class background.'

Lewis hinted at this, too. 'He gave the impression of being this very wealthy country gentleman,' he said. 'He dressed and acted the part, but he didn't really have the wherewithal. He was quite prepared to spend money he hadn't got. I don't really want to say any more. That would be disloyal.'

This aspect to his character might explain the aloofness that many identified in Harris. Brown, for example, felt Harris's need to feel superior even corrupted his sense of humour. 'I never heard Reg tell a joke, not a simple joke,' he said. 'When anyone else told it, he would walk away. Or he would listen but it wouldn't be going in. I think he thought only common people did that, and he wasn't a common person.'

Roger Law's parents owned a second-hand shop on Rake Street in Bury that included Harris's mother among their customers. On delivering a piece of furniture, Law recalled how once Elsie pointed to a huge photograph of her son winning at a World Championships that she had positioned at the top of her stairs. 'Do you know our Reg?' she asked. Not only did Law know him but he had listened to people gossip about his background. Like Frank Jefferson, the Bury grocer, Law was told that Harris's biological father was Henry Hargreaves, an engineer who sold bikes among other metal products in his shop in the town. His company is extant today as an industrial technology manufacturer. 'Henry Hargreaves hurried past me once and a friend said: "That's Reg Harris's dad." He was the absolute spit of him, too,' Law said.

Brown heard such gossip as well. Presumably Harris knew about it, too. I asked Brown if Harris ever brought up the subject of his father. 'At certain times he did. He would say: "You don't know this about me, Bill. Well, I'll tell you," but he'd add: "I wouldn't like anyone else to know about it, just for the moment."' 'This' was the identity of Harris's dad. Brown refused to disclose it, loyal to the end. 'I don't want to answer that. I will not talk to anyone about his past life. I wouldn't say anything about it when he was alive, and I won't say anything now either.'

*

On the morning of Saturday, 20 June 1992, Harris promised Jennifer that he would cut short his ride to about an hour so that they could head out for lunch. As he picked out his favourite Pinarello from its rack in his outhouse, and unhooked his cycling shoes from the wall, he decided he would make up the shortfall by riding much quicker than usual. He knew the landscape so well he could almost have travelled it blind, cutting north towards Knutsford from his home in Withington Green, winding up his speed through Stocks Lane then maintaining his tempo through the sleepy village of Over Peover, impressing a few locals with his septuagenarian speed.

In his youth, the bicycle had compressed time and distance by enabling people to travel more easily than they had ever done, connecting town-dwellers to their countryside and creating the cult of the commute. Harris had extended this process by travelling further on his bike than any Briton had before him, using it to cross national borders and myriad seas. Now, as he did still almost every day, he was riding into that past, accelerating like a young man almost exactly across the course of his first time trial and towards the street where his first watch chain was exchanged – how appropriate that, ahead of a career spent battling with time, he should have given up a prize that might have attached him to it – until finally he emerged from his last bend at the top of Clay Lane and careered sharply across the road. Age had caught up with him. He had suffered a stroke.

Within moments, Celia Elliot had pulled up in her car to find Harris sitting up on a grass verge, disorientated, with the few people who lived nearby chatting worriedly among themselves about the best response. 'He was just sitting there alone,' she said. Though from a cycling family, she did not recognise him. 'I sat down with him. He kept talking about what had happened. He said that he just wanted the pain to go away.'

Harris's health had first shown signs of deterioration seven years earlier when he returned from a wind-whipped ride along the Spanish south coast. That evening, he slurred words and struggled to understand what his friends said to him at a Costa del Sol golf club. Later he alarmed Jennifer while struggling to keep their car straight on the journey home. He had, it transpired, suffered a transient ischaemic attack in which blood congeals within an artery and temporarily cuts the supply to the brain. He was put on a daily aspirin but suffered a few more similar episodes over the years, prompting a medicinal upgrade to Warfarin and regular blood tests. That same weakness had returned a few days before his stroke when he asked Jennifer to drive to a dinner engagement – he did not usually ask her to drive – and needed help to climb the restaurant stairs.

Sitting by the road, he managed to relay his phone number. 'I jumped in the car and went over there,' Jennifer said. 'Rang my parents – they came and took the bike. Then we took him into hospital. He looked all right. He could understand me but he couldn't really talk back to you. His voice had slurred.' That night he suffered a second, much stronger stroke at Macclesfield Infirmary and slipped into a coma. At best the doctors said that he would suffer permanent physical damage. He was dead by the small hours of Monday morning. 'It was a dreadful shock but I don't think he could have coped with being in a wheelchair and not being in control of his faculties,' Jennifer said. 'It was a blessing in disguise that he didn't recover. Everybody remembers him as he was, rather than half a person.'

Jennifer postponed her grief in preparing for the funeral, arranging for it to take place at St John the Evangelist's Church in the village of Chelford. A pretty eighteenth-century building, with seating room for only about 150, it cannot have ever seen such a large congregation when Harris's coffin was delivered on the following Tuesday. Police were called to direct the traffic into an overflow car park. The tightly boxed pews were full. Mourners flowed up the stairs to the balcony. Many more were forced to listen to the service through speakers set up on the stone drive outside. There were friends and acquaintances there from each chapter of his life. Fans turned up on bikes.

A vicar from Bury, Reverend Reg Smith, delivered the homily. Harris had never attended church but he knew him from the dinner circuit. People recalled the sensitivity with which he said his piece. At one point, he turned to Jennifer in the front row and suggested that Reg had moved on to a sunny cycling idyll, with the wind on his back and a soft gradient that went forever downhill.

Afterwards, the mourners formed a short procession to the graveyard behind the church and watched as Harris was laid beneath a white tombstone on a plot chosen for its uninterrupted view of the hills that were his second home. The local newspaper took a photograph of the scene. It shows Jennifer at the head of the congregation, trying hard to remain composed. Beside her is her mother, Anne, a petite, elegant lady, and father Jim. Just beyond them is a blond lady who looked a little like Harris. A few moments later she would leave quietly with her husband while all those who knew Harris went to a reception in his home. 'It was rather odd,' Shelagh Dennis said. 'She didn't talk to anybody, just came and left. Nobody knew who she was.'

CHAPTER 18
2011–

Early in the afternoon of the final Saturday of August 2011, I visited Manchester Velodrome just as it was being prepared for a day devoted to Harris's life. A large video screen had been dropped from the ceiling and had started to play on a loop extended clips of Harris competing at his peak. Amid a cycle jumble sale that included at least a few traders who knew Harris, a red Raleigh on which he won a World Championship had been put on display. Towards the opposite end of the track, Paul Critchley had rolled his freshly polished MG into position with its logbook opened to signal its provenance. His was the vehicle in which Harris tackled a Tour of Britain.

At about midday, the guests of honour began to arrive and filed upstairs for a modest opening ceremony. Standing beside the statue of her husband, Jennifer delivered a short speech expressing her gratitude. She noted how Reg would have loved to have seen the resurgence in his sport. A short message from Sir Chris Hoy was read out. Peter King, the chief executive of

British Cycling, said a few words: 'In my era, cycling and Reg were synonymous. At school, his name was the one that we all knew. It had an aura about it.'

Similar marks of respect were made by the small group of cycling champions who gathered downstairs to reminisce and narrate over decades-old footage of Fallowfield. They included Tommy Godwin, Les West and Valerie Rushworth, the former British champion who competed at Harris Stadium. Julio César León was there, too, talking about cycling's last golden era with all the wisdom of an old sage. Yet still, though well intentioned, the day lacked something. There was none of the glamour or excitement befitting the man who had inspired it. Possibly races would have helped in that regard. Perhaps inevitably, while people were happy to pay homage to Harris the legend, few would open up about the man. Two men who knew Harris and discussed him at length refused to go on record (they changed their mind at a later date). As Bob Barber, the track manager, said: 'There are as many stories about Reg that you can't tell as those that you can.'

But these were not the only reasons the day did not quite live up to its potential. For perhaps the person who would be prepared to reveal most about Harris was not invited, despite living only a few miles away, and had been left instead to turn up anonymously. She announced herself only to Ray Pascoe, the cycling film-maker, who was selling videos of Harris on his stall. 'That's my dad,' Marilyn Hughes said.

You would struggle to find trace of Marilyn in the evidence of Harris's life. She is not mentioned in his autobiography. She very rarely crops up in his interviews, less so in profiles of him. She is not friendly with anybody who knew him. She had to be persuaded to go to the velodrome. 'I decided on the morning that I just couldn't do it,' she said. 'But my daughter said I should just go.' Shortly afterwards, I turned up on her Bury doorstep unannounced – I could not get a phone number – and concerned about how I would be received.

I need not have worried. Within minutes of my arrival, she had produced the photo-album that she had carefully compiled, combining photographs passed on by her grandmother, Elsie, her mother, Florence, and her father. Soon her husband, David, suggested a nearby Italian restaurant where we chatted late into the evening. The conversations continued for months afterwards. Partly she was being helpful, Marilyn is like that. But I also got the impression that she actually wanted to talk.

Marilyn Vanda Hargreaves Harris was born on 2 April 1946. She was not told the reason for her unusual second name, but she suspected that it was inspired by Van Vliet. Photographs show Harris doting on his pretty baby daughter but in Marilyn's earliest memories her parents had already separated. She recalled visiting Fallowfield where he reserved her seat by the finish line, ensuring he never lost when she was present. He returned home from abroad with mementos for her from his trips: chocolates, say, or an item of clothing. Once he turned up at her school unannounced and demanded that the teacher excuse her from class. He was rebuked and sent home. 'He was shocked,' Marilyn said. 'He was so used to getting what he wanted that he just presumed he could turn up and take me away.'

She lived with Florence and her grandparents in The Stanley Arms but visited Harris and Dorothy often in their lavish home. It led to a confusing kind of double life. 'I would go from this posh house with a lake and swans and horses back to the pub where I would polish the doorstep to help out and be rewarded with a sixpence, and where my mum would be bagging nuts to sell them to customers,' she said.

When Marilyn was nine, Florence fell in love again, with Geoffrey McConnell, a former diver in the Royal Navy who was seven years her junior. She granted Harris the divorce because she wanted to marry him. Harris agreed to give her a small house as part of the settlement. 'He came in the Stanley,' Marilyn said. 'When he told her he was getting married, she said, "So am I." He was livid. He felt he'd been made a complete fool of. I think he saw it that he'd spent money and time buying this house and making it right for my mum, and another bloke was going to move in.' At one point, they went to court over maintenance payments. After a dispute over how much Harris should contribute, Florence's solicitor produced a bill for the meat that Harris bought for his two dogs. 'It was as much as he was being asked to pay for me,' Hughes said. The case was settled. I asked if she found that memory difficult. She supposed that she did.

Even though McConnell brought her up like his own, Marilyn continued to see her father. He invited her to Australia, but she wanted 'Mummy' to go with them. He bought her first bike and insisted that she learnt to ride it properly at Fallowfield – then Harris Stadium – before she brought it home. She recalled lapping the track for hours after school on the handsome Italian frame, trying to get used to its gearing while proper cyclists flashed past. Dad was in the office trying to balance the books. 'They thought I was fair game. I was just this girl who wanted to bring her bike home.' Eventually, Harris taught her how to ride in a Bury park and over the Cheshire lanes instead. 'But he would go too fast. Then he'd give up, push me uphill and everybody used to wave.'

Florence was forever bitter about how Harris had treated her and eventually began to tell Marilyn the truth about his philandering. As Marilyn grew up, she began to discover this for herself. As a trainee hairdresser, she found gossips in Bury would relate how they had seen her father's car parked in unusual places. Women encountered him. A friend of Marilyn's was chatted up by Harris in the street on the day before her 21st birthday. She played along, invited him to the party, then enjoyed the shock on his face when she said, 'You'll like it, Marilyn will be there.' Initially, Marilyn tried to dismiss this trait as human weakness but her patience snapped when she read in the newspaper that he had got a young woman pregnant. 'I just couldn't see him after that,' she said.

Shortly afterwards she married David and moved to Kenya, where he had found work teaching Geography and Maths. They stayed for the best part of a decade though still she could not quite escape the long tendrils of her father's love life. 'Once this man came up to me and said, "We're related." I thought, "Here we go."' The man insisted Harris had married his aunt in Nottingham. 'I said, "I don't think so. I know who he has married and who he hasn't married." He wouldn't have it, but it made sense that something happened because Raleigh were based there.' Somebody had exaggerated the fling's significance. 'She was just another one, of many probably. He couldn't help himself.'

On her return from Kenya, Marilyn was walking through Bury when she caught sight of a television in a shop window showing Harris competing on his comeback. Startled, she stood and watched him claim his unlikely victory. (When told that most within the cycling community understood it to be fixed, she said: 'No. I know money talks, but my father would never have done that.' Jennifer insisted likewise.) The footage stirred emotion in Marilyn. She decided that she wanted to see her father again.

They had not talked for nine years, but she had children now, Amanda and Richard, whom she wanted to connect with their grandfather. She passed word to a family member. Now owner of her own salon in Bury, she soon found her father pulling up in a car outside. 'I remember it like it was yesterday. I heard this voice "Marilyn",' she said. Naturally, Harris had been saddened by his daughter's disappearance from his life. Jennifer recalled him reading about her wedding in the *Manchester Evening News*. Marilyn said 'he had been thinking about trying to contact me, too'.

They quickly became close again. Marilyn had not exactly forgiven Harris, more learnt to accept his weaknesses, partly because he was contrite and admitted that his behaviour had been wrong. 'He was more relaxed by then,' she said. 'He didn't have the same intensity about him. He couldn't do what he did when he was younger, and he had met Jennifer.' The marriage worked. 'I think it was because she was so much younger. She devoted all her time and attention to him.'

Slowly their relationship was rebuilt. As couples they went out for meals, and they visited each other's homes. Marilyn and

David accepted an invitation to stay with Harris and Jennifer in the Italian town of Grimaldi, close to the Alps, where they ate at Senfttleben's restaurant. Harris left a sports car there for the owner of the villa in return for free accommodation.

Marilyn recalled this as the best period of their relationship. For the first time she could lean on her father. 'I felt when anything happened, I could ring him.' She highlighted two instances. 'I was playing tennis and I tore the muscle in the back of me leg. I passed out.' Eventually she came round. 'I said I'd ring me dad and he'll know what to do. Within no time at all, I was seeing this doctor who was a soft tissue specialist. He didn't charge me and me dad sent him a case of wine.' On another occasion the Royal Bank of Scotland were refusing to accept an offer that David and Marilyn had put down on a house that the bank owned. Harris, being friendly with an RBS senior executive, made a phone call and negotiations were suddenly smoothed. The deal went through. 'He was able to fix things. He knew so many people. When you saw him with men, they used to look at him with this idolisation.'

Life had prepared him less well for grandchildren. Amanda recalled their first meeting when we met in a London hotel. 'It was like he didn't know how to behave with children,' she said. 'I just remember him as a bit of a show-off. He was, "Come into my study and I'll show you my trophies."' It hardly helped that

Florence had told her granddaughter the truth about him. 'She hated him. He was always on to a losing thing with me because I knew how much he had hurt her.' Possibly their only shared characteristic worsened the relationship. 'We were both stubborn. That was the problem. Neither of us would give way.'*

When asked by her mother about her renewed relationship with her father, Marilyn initially tried to underplay it, while swapping photographs on the mantelpiece depending on which parent was about to visit. 'My dad was visiting often. Jennifer came with him too. It was really nice, but I just thought I can't live like that.' Florence found the situation difficult. 'She was very upset. She couldn't cope with it. Her health wasn't good. She'd had cancer and had three-fifths of her lung removed. She said, "Your stepdad would be devastated."' As Florence's health worsened, Marilyn felt compelled to cut her father from her life again, just as he had become as prodigious with his paternal impulses as he had with many other aspects of his life. They did not speak again until she rang him to inform him that Florence had died. 'In the end, it just became too much. My dad was calling all the time. It was all or nothing with him. But my stepdad had to come and live with us. While I wanted to

---

* Harris invoked lasting bitterness in more than one woman. Through intermediaries I requested interviews with a few others who had been involved with him. All of them turned me down, usually with a derogatory comment about him.

keep contact with my dad – it was lovely – I felt my duty was to look after my stepdad.'

Once Florence had passed away, Marilyn did not attempt to renew her relationship with her father for a second time, partly because McConnell struggled terribly without his wife and needed Marilyn's near-constant help. 'You have to remember, my mum married my stepfather when I was nine. He had been my father. He brought me up. He was the children's grand-father. So I stopped contacting my dad. I tried to explain, perhaps I did it badly.'

That was 1989. 'Maybe I did hurt him,' she admitted. 'It was at a time in his life, when he was retiring, and a new thing had come into his life and added another dimension: grandchildren, things like that. He just got into it and was being kind and nice and I don't think that had ever happened to him before.' They did not speak again. The next Marilyn heard about him was when Jennifer called to say that he had died. Marilyn was not invited to the funeral. 'We just went. We had to find out the details,' she said. 'Jennifer didn't speak to me, acknowledge me, anything. As we were walking out of the church, her dad came and took hold of my hand. But that was it. I didn't go to the reception. The whole thing was surreal.' It became even more difficult when Marilyn received a tap on her shoulder from a young woman that she struggled to recognise. 'You're Marilyn,' the woman said.

This was the daughter of the girl who claimed Harris had got her pregnant. Years earlier, Florence had seen a photograph of Harris's alleged daughter when the local newspaper discovered that she had taken up cycling and ran a story on it. Florence decided that she could not have been related to Harris because she looked nothing like him. Jennifer had seen the girl, too, and told Marilyn that she was of the same opinion. Now Marilyn had reason to think otherwise. 'I can't remember what she said. I just remember thinking how similar she looked to my Richard. I just said, "I'm sorry, I've got to go now." I turned and walked away. It's a shame. She must have thought, "What a horrible woman." If she had written to me, or had it been before the funeral, it might have had a different outcome. But I was shattered and I had been very upset.' Marilyn did not meet her (probable) half-sister again.

When I met Hughes she had been researching her family history. Through hours spent trawling records, she could trace her ancestors back through the nineteenth century. She helped to provide much of the information that informed this book. But she, too, was unable to solve the riddle about her father's father. Until she called up Harris's birth certificate, she had always understood that Ezbon Holding was her grandfather. Having studied the oil painting of his uncle, Sir Edward Holden, she still believes she

might be related to him. (There is a resemblance between
Holden and Harris.) Yet other snippets from her life did not quite
support that. She recalled how Elsie always insisted that Joe
Harris was her son's father even though the family knew that was
not true. It was as if she felt that was a more palatable truth.
An in-law of her father's told Marilyn that 'there was always
something muted about my grandmother and the son of a mill-
owner'. In the end this essential truth about her father remained
elusive to Marilyn, too.

To this day, she says that she misses him. David does, too.
'He was very affable, easy to get on with,' he said. For years the
circumstances in which they lost contact bothered Marilyn. Judg-
ing by Jennifer's attitude at the funeral, she guessed that there
had been more bad blood than even she thought at the time. As
a result, when she saw Jennifer at Manchester Velodrome in the
afternoon before we first met, she asked if they could meet for
lunch, hopefully to talk through what happened. They had not
spoken in 20 years.

Jennifer travels a lot, but several months later, she set up a
lunch date that began shortly after midday and ran for six hours.
Towards the end of what Marilyn described as a 'heart to heart'
she asked if Jennifer had forgiven her for cutting contact several
decades earlier. That was as close she could get to earning her
father's forgiveness. Jennifer hugged her. 'I didn't think I ever

would,' she said. 'But I have. I understand the position you were in now.'

Marilyn was relieved, but worried also that perhaps she had revealed too much in the interviews for this book. She did not want to damage her only remaining connection to her father again. 'Promise me that you will write a sympathetic portrait,' she said.

Should those close to him read the book, I expect they might find aspects of it difficult. I hope that they do not judge it to be opportunist, inspired by its conflicts and criticisms. I set out hoping to write the life of a hero whose story had not been properly told. Only researching it did I discover him to be more intriguing than I could have imagined.

I promised Marilyn that I would try.

 **EPILOGUE**

When Sir Chris Hoy began to win his track races in the mid-1990s, he met a familiar refrain. 'It especially happened at the big tracks,' he said. 'Whenever we went down to race at Herne Hill, you'd do your sprint and one of the older members of the cycling community, maybe a commissaire, would say, it wasn't actually that good and that Reg had done quicker, or that Reg did that but he did it on bamboo runs and his bike was six times heavier than yours.'

Harris used bamboo-cane rims in the 1930s when many considered them the best type for track bikes, being light and firm. He probably was not going faster than Hoy, yet the comparison was so frequent Hoy grew sick of it. Contemporaries such as Craig MacLean and Jason Queally did, too. 'The feeling towards him was resentment because he was so fast,' Hoy said, amused. 'No matter what you did, it wasn't enough to impress the old guard. You were made to feel pretty small. It became almost a running joke.'

The cycling community nurtured the Harris myth because no Briton since had emulated him. There had been several comparable talents in the individual pursuit, world champions such as Hugh Porter, Graeme Obree and Chris Boardman, who briefly switched the nation on to the sport again when he won gold at the 1992 Games. But that discipline did not capture the imagination like the sprint, nor did it produce champions who could lay claim to being the fastest cyclist.

As a result, in a sport with a strong oral history, stories about Harris were forever passed down. With little footage by which to judge the descriptions, it was easy to embellish them, too. 'Literally almost as soon as you got involved in the sport, you heard stories about this legend,' Hoy said. 'Traditionally in the UK, we've been on outdoor tracks, at which you're prey to the bad weather. So you'd be sitting around in the stand, waiting for the rain to dry, and people would be telling stories about the old days. We still do it now, in between training when waiting for your next effort. You regale the young lads with the stories of old.'

As a young cyclist, Hoy discovered that not much had changed at the elite end of the sport since Harris's time, with British Cycling still unable to afford young talents such as Hoy and Queally the support they needed to fulfil their potential. They did not have a coach, for a start. They were loaned kit and equipment for a week around a World Championship, where they competed with little success on their own bike. It was steel, just like Harris's. 'You would speak to athletes from other countries and try to work out what they were doing,' Hoy said. 'It was a guessing game, trial and error. We thought we were doing the right stuff but a lot of it was detrimental. We were taking two steps forward, one back.'

Only when British Cycling was given the first annual Lottery grant in 1997 did the situation improve. Then suddenly Hoy and others' talent was unleashed, with world titles being secured so frequently it became almost difficult to comprehend. By 2008, the men's team alone had claimed a rainbow jersey 18 times, with Hoy and Queally joined by a new generation that included talents such as Bradley Wiggins and Mark Cavendish. Hoy dominated in the keirin and one-kilometre time trial. Wiggins was triumphant in the pursuit. Cavendish won world titles in the Madison and points race before he switched triumphantly to the road.

However, while Victoria Pendleton had won the world sprint title, too, it had eluded the men. Craig MacLean had gone close, claiming silver in 2006, but that was an anomaly – it was MacLean's only World Championship medal in the discipline. 'In events like the pursuit or the kilo, we were able to do it almost through the science of the sport, whereas the sprint almost has a mystique around it,' Hoy said. 'There's a lot more to sprint than just physical power. It has a lot of skill, a lot of tactics, which make it difficult to win. You have to be competent in several different areas.' Having no past champions to learn from amplified that challenge. 'In something like the pursuit, you would have had Hugh Porter, Chris Boardman, Rob Hayles, guys who passed on success,' Hoy said. 'But it was very difficult for us as young sprinters coming into the sport because we didn't have any role models. Reg was in the past by that point. It's important to have guys you look up to, who you watch train, who watch you race, and who you can have as your benchmark. But in Britain there wasn't the depth of talent or knowledge.'

In his preparations for the 2008 Olympics, Hoy was forced to take up the sprint more seriously when the kilometre time trial – his specialism – was dropped from the Games programme. He had competed in the sprint at World Cups and the Revolution meetings in Manchester but never at a World Championship or an Olympics. As a result, in the 2008 World Championships, he was considered as only a contender for gold in the sprint – he was usually favourite for his event. That status slipped to an outside bet when he qualified fourth fastest in the 200-metre time trial that served as the qualifying round, especially as his brilliant French rival Kévin Sireau had dipped below the magical 10-second barrier with a time of 9.992 seconds.

Hoy posted 10.032 seconds, assigning him the formidable task of having to face the Dutchman Theo Bos, who was unbeaten in match sprinting since 2005. However, that record meant little to a Manchester crowd that had turned raucous in its support for

Hoy and was desperate for him to finally slay Harris's ghost. 'In cycling terms, it was like being Andy Murray and trying to step up to win Wimbledon, with the legend of Fred Perry always there, with people talking about how long it's been and how we've not had a winner for so many years,' Hoy said.

In his first contest, he whipped up the atmosphere further by reversing a deficit to beat Bos 2–1. In the second, he dispatched the Italian veteran Roberto Chiappa. In the final, he faced Sireau, only 20, who had beaten Hoy 2–0 in a recent World Cup. The Scotsman avenged that defeat with a symmetrical result – as the cycling journalist Richard Moore put it – to end 54 years of hurt. Moore described how the British squad's technical director, Dave Brailsford, addressed his staff later in their hotel. 'Anyone who's 54, stick up your hands,' he said. Two did. 'What was done tonight has never been done in any of our lifetimes – apart from you two old fellas.' Later Brailsford described the impact: 'It brought it home. We've been winning so many medals it gets a bit diluted, but no one had won that title since Reg Harris.'

Hoy said the victory gave him the confidence he needed to go on and win the event again at the subsequent Olympics in Beijing, when he became the first Briton in 100 years to win three golds in a Games. That made him the first cyclist to be given a knighthood and ensured him immortality. In a slightly more modest ceremony than that which involved the Queen, it also earned him the gift of a portrait of Harris from The Reg Harris Memorial Fund, which was set up to raise money for his statue.

Drawn by the sculptor, these handsome framed sketchings have been on display above Hoy's mantelpiece ever since. They serve to remind him of the privileges he has had spearheading the second golden generation for British Cycling, with its coaches and scientists and nutritionists and psychiatrists and myriad other world-leading experts who have given him and others the support they needed to excel. That Harris had none of them is not lost on Hoy. 'It must have been really difficult,' Hoy said. 'I got a taste of the old-school way of doing things and I know it was tough. The young guys now don't believe me when I tell them what it was like. And even I wasn't on my own. I had teammates when I travelled over to Europe to race. For Reg to have done all that by himself … he was the last great sprinter in Britain.'

British Cycling used the occasion of the Reg Harris Day to induct him into its hall of fame. Previously it had covered only the 50 years leading up to 2008 – it was created to coincide with British Cycling's fiftieth anniversary – but the ruling body subsequently decided to extend its remit. Harris was the natural first addition. Without him, the collection of plaques on the wall beside his statue would have seemed incomplete, for his achievements outstrip almost all the entrants on that list. Had it not been for the war, the dramatic rule change in 1951, and had he been allowed to compete in more than one Olympics, he would have achieved even more.

Doubtless Harris would have prevailed today, too, although you suspect he would have enjoyed success very differently to that which he was accustomed given that his complexities and misdeeds – had he dared to repeat them – would have invited scrutiny that great sportsmen of his era were spared. Instead his legend has been closely considered only occasionally, such as in the autumn of 2011 when the ruling body edged close enough to see the smudge against the glass. 'Reg is a huge figure,' Brian Cookson, the president of British Cycling, said. 'He deserves his iconic status. But we tend to romanticise our sporting heroes and, the more that you find out about the way that he operated as a man and as an athlete, the more you find out that there were nuances to him, a pragmatic side where he was determined to make the most of his circumstances financially, and every other way.' Cookson had heard the stories about his comeback. 'I've no proof but it has the ring of truth. I don't think it would happen today but, in that era when things were a bit less scrutinised, perhaps they were more likely to happen. Certainly I think that's what happened on this occasion.'

I asked whether such stories complicated the celebration of his legacy. 'Reg's comeback is inconsequential in terms of what he achieved but, from speaking to others, it was maybe not an entirely isolated incident, so that does kind of make you wonder a bit. He was an amazingly exceptional athlete, but he had a businesslike, ruthless approach to his sport. Ultimately, he realised: "This is my one chance of achieving greatness."'

ACKNOWLEDGEMENTS

With relatively few books published on British cycling's first golden age, I was delighted to discover the detail in which *The Bicycle* and *Cycling* – latterly *Cycling and Mopeds*, now *Cycling Weekly* – covered the sport in the 1940s and 1950s. I am indebted to their excellent race reports, occasional interviews and to the insight provided by their expert analyses. I also drew on material published in *Coureur* – later *Sporting Cyclist* – the magazine edited by Jock Wadley, the doyen of cycling journalists then.

I spent many hours reading the national newspaper archives at the British Library, too, in particular its collections of the *Manchester Guardian* (and the *Guardian*), the *Observer*, *The Times*, *Daily Telegraph*, *Daily Mirror*, *Daily Express*, *Evening Standard* and *Manchester Evening News*. The *Bury Times* provided a valuable window into life in Harris's hometown in the 1920s and 1930s.

I used Harris's autobiography (*Two Wheels To The Top*, WH Allen) to plot a path through his life and used race details provided in biographies written by George Pearson and Roger St Pierre (*Reg Harris: An authoritative biography*, Temple Press; *The Story of Reg Harris*, Kennedy Brothers). I also benefited from the following books: *A Bike Ride Through My Life*, by Frank Clements, Trafford Publishing; *British Sport: A Social History*, Dennis Brailsford, Lutterworth Press; *Bury in the 1920s*, Fred Campbell; *Bury Memories*, Bill Byrom; *By A Wheel*, Jan Derksen, with Bert Bakker, Stork; *Cycling Year Book*, N.G. Henderson, Pelham Books; *Heroes, Villains & Velodromes; Chris Hoy & Britain's Cycling Revolution*, Richard Moore, HarperCollins; *It's All About the Bike: One More Kilometre and We're in the Showers*, Tim Hilton, Harper Perennial; *The Pursuit of Happiness on Two Wheels*, Robert Penn, Penguin; *It Wasn't That Easy; Scientific Training for Cycling*, C.R. Woodard, Temple Press; *Raleigh: Past and Presence of an Iconic Bicycle Brand*, Tony Hadland, Van Der Plas Publications; *The Austerity Games*, Janie Hampton, Aurum; *The Tommy Godwin Story*, Tommy Godwin, John Pinkerton Memorial Publishing Fund; *The Benny Foster Story*, Benny Foster, Kennedy Brothers; *A Wheel in Two Worlds; The Ron Kitching Story*, Ron Kitching; *This Island Race*, Mousehold Press, *The Crooked Path to Victory; Drugs and Cheating in Professional Bicycle Racing*, Cycle Publishing, both Les Woodland; *The Penguin Book of the Bicycle*, Penguin. I would recommend Godwin's book to anyone who would like more detail about cycling in his era. Everyone who loves their bike should read Hilton and Penn.

Pathé's archived footage of Harris in action was also invaluable, as was Ray Pascoe's film *Maestro: The Reg Harris Story*.

I would like to thank everybody who agreed to be interviewed. There are too many to name them all here but suffice to say they were all more than generous with their time. A great camaraderie exists within the long-standing cycling community and I have been its beneficiary. I am particularly grateful to Ann Sturgess and Michael Breckon, both of whom went far out of their way in helping to source material and to make contact with old friends and acquaintances of theirs.

I leant on a few people for advice and encouragement, in particular, Sisanda Ntanga, Matt Potter and my agent Humfrey Hunter. And I owe a huge thank-you to everybody at Ebury, especially Susan Pegg and my publisher Andrew Goodfellow, whose suggestions improved the book immeasurably and who was kind enough to hold his patience whenever I threatened to miss deadlines.

Finally, I would like to say thank-you to Marilyn Hughes for her courage, time and honesty. Without her help, I am not sure I could have written the book.

Robert Dineen

London, May 2012

INDEX